Debating Enzensberger
Great Migration and *Civil War*

Studien zur deutschsprachigen Gegenwartsliteratur
Studies in Contemporary German Literature

Band / Volume 5

Herausgegeben von / edited by

Paul Michael Lützeler

Direktor, Zentrum für deutschsprachige Gegenwartsliteratur
Director, Center for Contemporary German Literature
Washington University, St. Louis, Missouri, USA

Gerhard Fischer (ed.)

Debating Enzensberger

Great Migration and *Civil War*

STAUFFENBURG
VERLAG

Die Deutsche Bibliothek – CIP-Einheitsaufnahme

Debating Enzensberger : great migration and civil war /
Gerhard Fischer (ed.). – Tübingen : Stauffenburg-Verl., 1996
(Studien zur deutschsprachigen Gegenwartsliteratur ; Bd. 5)
ISBN 3-86057-205-9
NE: Fischer, Gerhard [Hrsg.]; GT

Gedruckt mit finanzieller Unterstützung des Goethe-Instituts Sydney.

Gedruckt auf säurefreiem und alterungsbeständigem Werkdruckpapier.

Druck: Müller + Bass, Tübingen
Verarbeitung: Braun + Lamparter, Reutlingen
Printed in Germany

ISSN 0946-7459
ISBN 3-86057-205-9

Table of Contents

Preface

The publication of Hans Magnus Enzensberger's essays *Die Große Wanderung* and *Aussichten auf den Bürgerkrieg*, in 1992 and 1993, respectively, created a great deal of public interest, if not controversy, in the media of the Federal Republic of Germany and in Europe. Ever since the pre-publication in *Der Spiegel* of parts of *Civil War*, in particular, some of its more flamboyant and challenging metaphorical abbreviations, such as 'Every carriage on the underground a Bosnia *en miniature*' or 'Our priority is not Somalia, but Hoyerswerda', have made the circuit of cultural talkshow conversations and *feuilleton* debates where they became often-quoted and hotly contested slogans, part of the epigrammatic vernacular of contemporary German political and literary discourse. That the essays received such public attention has of course much to do with the topics they address, but it is equally no coincidence that it was Enzensberger who made these topics his concern and, by doing so, re-established himself as a most perceptive social analyst and literary commentator on current issues affecting society towards the end of the twentieth century. There are few authors indeed who have such a decisive grasp of the central questions of contemporary politics and who are able to present their socio-cultural analyses in a similarly challenging, entertaining and at the same time rhetorically polished literary form.

The two essays, written with Enzensberger's customary elegance, the sharp wit and stylistic economy that is characteristic of his essayistic work, present an argumentative chain that appears on the one hand enticingly persuasive and on the other altogether disturbing, as if meant to invite sharp rebuttal and denial. Enzensberger has a special skill of developing metaphors, parables and analogies that present striking images of complex socio-cultural and historical phenomena in provocative simplicity, turning familiar concepts upside down and forcing the reader to question and to re-evaluate accepted ideas and beliefs. But the global-anthropological perspective adopted in the two essays, a distinct departure from Enzensberger's previous concern with European and German questions, can also result in unsubstantiated generalisations, in details of images which are not so sharply focused or blurred exposures in need of higher resolution and greater selectivity.

The present volume gathers critical essays which, for the most part, are developed from papers delivered at the 1995 Sydney German Studies Symposium devoted to the topic *Debating Enzensberger: 'Great Migration' and 'Civil War'*. Other chapters were specially commissioned for this volume. That a symposium on Enzensberger is held in Australia needs no particular explanation. His work has been critically received and discussed in academic circles in this country since the 1960s; in particular, Enzensberger's essays on the media, on the culture and consciousness industries, can be found in the curricula of cultural studies courses of Australian universities. The two recent essays, published in English translation together in one paperback volume (*Civil War*, trans. Piers Spence and Martin Chalmers, London, Granta/Penguin, 1994; quoted as *CW* followed by page number throughout this volume), have put Enzensberger's work again at the centre of critical attention.

The two essays have been met with a particular interest in Australia. Migration is a very important feature of Australian history and society, and so is violence: the genocidal 'civil war' waged by the European settlers against the indigenous owners of this continent is a continuing feature of the historical landscape as well as of the contemporary political and cultural agenda of Australia. In a sense, it provides a similar legacy as the coming to terms with the historical burden of genocide in Enzensberger's Germany. To some extent and with some reservations, both countries also share a recent history of enjoying the privileges of a comparatively peaceful, civil society. It is before this background that the emergence of new forms of violence and war, which Enzensberger tries to describe and to explain, offers the same challenges of analysis, in Sydney as much as in Munich. The Australian experience of embracing multicultural diversity, finally, may prove a useful and constructive point of departure for a critical discussion of Enzensberger. It is hoped that the peculiar juxtaposition and meeting of a diversity of German/European, American and Australian experiences and perceptions in this volume will make for a lively and multi-faceted, stimulating and challenging debate.

As editor, my thanks are due to all the contributors for their co-operation and to David Roberts, in particular, whose critical suggestions have helped to develop the concept and the final shape of this book from its inception. Moreover, he has kindly agreed to write an introduction to the volume. A special word of thanks is owed to Wolfgang Meissner, director of the *Goethe-Institut* in Sydney where the Symposium was held. I am grateful to the series editor, Paul Michael Lützeler, and the publisher, Brigitte Narr, for their continuing interest and support.

Gerhard Fischer
Sydney, February 1996

Introduction

Debating Enzensberger

David Roberts

I Enzensberger's Intellectual Journey

For 40 years Enzensberger has been the engaged observer, commentator and critic of his age in the diverse modes of poetry, documentary literature, essays, proclamations and polemical glosses. His continuing presence is due not least to his sensitivity to the *Zeitgeist* and a corresponding capacity to rethink and revise positions. It is this which makes him the engaged and never the impartial observer, for revisionism is just as much a mode of engagement as unchanging commitment. Enzensberger refuses to allow himself to be pinned down, identified and classified. The essay has for this reason become his preferred form of intervention. The provocative perspectivism, which the open and fragmentary character of the essay permits, is an ideal instrument for questioning received opinions in the light of historical change. Enzensberger's whole work could thus be thought of as work in progress, as a medium of learning processes and a catalyst of debate. In this sense Enzensberger is both the subject and the point of departure of the present volume, the subject, in that his intellectual trajectory since the 1960s forms the focus of the first section; the point of departure, in that the issues raised in the two essays, *Civil War* and *Great Migration*, are examined in a widening circle of political, historical and sociological frames in the second and third sections.

The chapters of the opening section can perhaps best be described as approaches to *Civil War* and *Great Migration*. They pose from a variety of perspectives the question of continuities and discontinuities in Enzensberger's work since the 1960s. Where continuity is stressed, as in the contributions of Gert Mattenklott and Markus Joch, it is seen to lie in what we might call a meta-principle of form. Where discontinuity is stressed, as in the papers of David Roberts, Horst Domdey and Gerhard Fischer, the focus is directed to the changing contents of Enzensberger's analyses of contemporary history and society and his self-understanding as an intellectual.

Taking Michel Butor's concept of 'iterology' as his cue, Mattenklott proposes that we read Enzensberger's work as a paradigm of travel literature. Writing is a form of time and space travel, an expedition into unknown territory, be it the city as phantasmagoric labyrinth, as in so much modern literature, or the lure of the exotic, from which is arising a new conception of world literature. What

Mattenklott calls the 'relentless extroversion' of Enzensberger's oeuvre – he is thinking particularly of his many translations and adaptations from world literature – charts a journey of self-discovery which must negotiate a delicate balance between the foreign and the familiar. If Enzensberger's critique of the narcissism of German literary culture pulls him in the direction of a romantic aesthetic opposition, this in turn is counteracted by a commitment to the democratic universalism of the Enlightenment. This affinity to contrary political cultures has made the essay the 'thought form' of Enzensberger's growing scepticism, which has retreated from his earlier utopianism into a position of ironic melancholy.

Joch traces the stages of Enzensberger's work in the light of the author's search for profile in the field of competing intellectual discourses. Behind the unexpected twists and turns of position, Joch discerns a strategy for gaining distinction and accumulating symbolic capital (Bourdieu). If the highest prestige is accorded to distinctive difference, Enzensberger's progress can be seen as motivated not only by a number of self-critical U-turns, which respond to objective shifts in the cultural climate, but equally to the desire to outflank rivals, ranging from the radical social critique of the 1960s to the subsequent settling of scores with the Left. Here Enzensberger's praise of normality, which has made the oppositional intellectual redundant, enables him to occupy a distinctive anti-intellectual position. While this motif recedes after 1989, *Civil War* is also distinguished by the strategy of self-assertion and delimitation, directed against a disoriented Left and the discourse of universalism.

What Joch calls Enzensberger's self-assertion is as much an aesthetic as an intellectual programme. As Gert Mattenklott observes, Enzensberger oscillates between literary and intellectual cultures. This oscillation reflects a distinctive conception of the intellectual, which Roberts contrasts with that of Jürgen Habermas, and opens up at the same time Enzensberger's trajectory to a double reading in a somewhat similar fashion to that of Joch. Roberts compares Habermas' normative understanding of the role of the intellectual with Enzensberger's account of the process of normalization in the Federal Republic which has allowed society to emancipate itself from the tutelage of intellectuals. This paradoxical celebration of self-disappearance, which we might call the ultimate form of distinction, can be read in two opposed ways, Roberts suggests: on the one hand, as the odyssey of a self-critical enlightenment which arrives at an ironic reconciliation with normality, on the other hand, as an ironic game of masks with affinities to Diderot's paradoxes on the actor and to Carl Schmitt's romantic occasionalism.

Civil War and *Great Migration* come into closer focus in the contributions by Horst Domdey and Gerhard Fischer. For Domdey the essays of the 1990s represent a new stage in Enzensberger's answers over the years to the question whether the Republic can be lived in. Taking 1968, 1978 and 1988 as representative moments of revolution, disillusionment and reconciliation respectively, Domdey shows how Enzensberger's relation to the Federal Republic moves from a conception of the centre as masked fascism to the centre as the middle way, which has made the possibility of civil war unimaginable, a position which then collapsed in the 1990s. Fischer also plots the crisis and abandonment of Enzensberger's espousal of the middle way in a fundamental shift of perspectives which replaces the primacy of socially integrative processes stressed in the 1980s with the disintegrating forces of the eternal civil war of the struggle for recognition between masters and slaves, the haves and the have-nots. Enzensberger's vision of the 'twilight of social democracy' is fed by a newfound anthropological pessimism which doubts that recognition can ever be achieved. Fischer argues that Enzensberger's treatment of recognition as absolute struggle leaves no room for an understanding of recognition as political process, that is, a politics of recognition, whether in its communitarian form (Taylor) or in the form of a combined theory of political and cultural rights (Habermas), a theme which is also taken up by Stephan Castles in relation to *The Great Migration*.

II *Civil War* and the Politics of War and Violence

Enzensberger has always possessed a keen sense of the disorder of the social order and a corresponding anarchic counter-order. In the late 1960s the apparently irreconcilable opposition between political immobilism and revolutionary renewal left according to Enzensberger no room for the path of democratic reform. By the 1980s, however, the tension between system and the irrepressible vitality of the lifeworld had found its resolution in the idea of self-organizing society. Civil society, it seemed, generated its own self-sustaining autonomy out of the fruitful interplay of anarchy and order. This vision collapsed in the 1990s. The real utopia of civil society disintegrated into the dystopia of civil war and the anarchic counter-image of violence. With the end of the Cold War and its stabilizing constraints long repressed local conflicts erupted. The Hobbesian war of all against all returned as the spectre haunting Europe and the world. If Enzensberger fails to acknowledge that the Cold War spawned its own proxy civil wars from Indo-China and Central America to Africa, it is because the thrust of his essay, *Civil War*, lies in the evocation of the return of the repressed beneath and beyond politics, which confounds not only the hopes of a new world order but also the comfortable assumption of peaceful change in Europe after the fall of the Iron Curtain.

That the disturbing message of *Civil War* provoked unease in readers is amply testified by the present contributors. One theme which recurs in different articulations is the charge that Enzensberger evades rather than faces the dilemmas and challenges he seeks to lay bare. If the pessimistic anthropology of the essay forces us to confront the violence which is denied and projected as the other of civil society, this strategy is in danger of producing self-blocking paradoxes. Against this it could well be argued that paradox has the function of destroying binary oppositions, that the return of the repressed undoes the protective mechanism of distinctions. The concept and the reality of civil war cuts across the divide between war and peace, disorder and order, combatants and civilians. Thus Pam Stavropoulos, in setting out to draw up the ambivalent balance of positive and negative features in *Civil War*, points to Enzensberger's 'dissolution of boundaries' which exposes the illusions of ideological critique and the bankruptcy of liberal optimism. She also points out that the disruption of received, 'rational' distinctions has its problematic counterpart in Enzensberger's attraction to bold assertions and the refusal to differentiate. The outcome, as she sees it, is an 'aesthetics of evasion'. The very intention of disconcerting the reader is counter-productive, since it can only reinforce passivity.

The psychological dimensions of the dissolution of the boundaries between observers and participants, engendered by the spectacle of violence, are explored by Tom Morton and Peter Morgan. Morton discerns conflicting motivations at work in *Civil War*. On the one hand, Enzensberger wants us to abandon the privileged position of the disengaged spectator and acknowledge the inadequacy of contemporary discourses on violence, which serve to construct the Balkans as the archaic barbarian other of Europe. On the other hand, at the same time as he deconstructs the *cordon sanitaire* of civilization he wants to preserve it. How is the individual to cope with the excessive moral demands raised by the recurrent spectacle of violence? Enzensberger's answer is to propose an ethics of responsibility which steers a middle way between the guilt laden impotence of moral universalism and the aggressive denial of responsibility. This requires the quarantining of the horrors of Bosnia or Somalia in order to deal with domestic conflict. But does not this redrawing of the boundaries reproduce the problem? The quarantining of the Balkans, Morton suggests, leaves us with the 'Balkanized' subject. Morgan reads *Civil War* in terms of a recovery of identity by the intellectual and erstwhile leftist. If after 1945 the *cordon sanitaire* of the Enlightenment had the task of immunizing the German Left from the *virus* of fascism and nationalism, the *retrovirus* of civil war has the paradoxical consequence of dissolving the boundaries between the detached intellectual and the German people. What the universalizing discourse of the Enlightenment separated, the universalizing counter-discourse of negative anthropology brings together. The return of violence is also for Enzensberger a return of the repressed – the memories of World War Two – which brings the recognition of the original evil in all of us and enables the intellectual to regain a sense of group identity.

Enzensberger's 'quarantining' of Bosnia and the 'negative' reconstitution of identity add up for Richard Herzinger to the contradiction of 'universalism in one country'. Behind this capitulation of thought Herzinger sees Enzensberger's ongoing polemical reckoning with the dogmatism and sentimentality of the old New Left. While acknowledging that Enzensberger's objections to an unfounded utopianism were salutary before 1989, his negative relation to the Left ends up reproducing the Left's troubled relation to pragmatic politics. Like Stavropoulos, Herzinger accuses Enzensberger of evading the political through his potent rhetorical mixture of apocalyptic vision and sober 'realism', which masks the underlying abstraction of his premise, that war and aggression are anthropological constants. Rainer Stollmann by contrast aims to restore the balance of judgment by staging in the form of a fictive interview Enzensberger's defence of his public function as a catalyst of debate. It is not the essayist's task to deliver the meta-narrative of nineteenth century grand theory or the 'scientific' treatise of twentieth century academia. Ours is the age of fractured perspectives which demands a free and fragmentary thinking, legitimized by its openness to new and as yet unthematized phenomena. Does such openness – the privilege of the essayist – invalidate the charge of escapism? Does the cognitive gain given by the dissolution of boundaries compensate for the perceived loss of differentiation? Stollmann is careful not to draw conclusions. His method of indirection, which circles around Enzensberger's delight in paradoxical turns of argument, does, however, point to an underlying focus of the other chapters on *Civil War*, which could be described as the unease engendered by the contradiction between the openness of the essay form and the pessimistic closure of Enzensberger's argument.

III *Great Migration* and the Politics of Identity

Enzensberger's vision of molecular civil war cannot be separated – for all its apparently spontaneous origin in mindless violence – from the dynamics of resurgent nationalism, xenophobia and racism set free by the end of the Cold War. Group identities – national, regional, cultural and ethnic – are at stake. Civil war and racism, inflamed by the 'great migration' of the late twentieth century, represent two of the greatest challenges to civil society and the liberal-democratic state. They are challenges which pose particular problems for a reunified Germany since they are compounded by the legacy of the past, not only the racial doctrines and exterminatory policies of the Third Reich but also by the ethno-cultural definition of German identity embodied in the still valid Citizenship Law of 1913, which means that the 7 million immigrants now living in Germany have no right to citizenship. The papers by Bernd Fischer, Klaus Bade und Stephan Castles respond to Enzensberger's *Great Migration* by placing the current debates in Germany over immigration, asylum and citizenship in the wider historical context of Western and Central European conceptions of the nation and the state.

Fischer presents these contrasting conceptions as two versions of the politics of identity. The Enlightenment idea of the constitutional state defines the 'people' in terms of the rights of citizenship and political participation, independent of race, ethnicity and national origin, as against the Romantic, Central European definition of the people as a cultural ethnicity. The German idea of the *Kulturnation* drew its legitimation not from the people as a collective of democratic citizens but from an understanding of the people as an organic community, a homogeneous natural ethnic whole, distinguished by its unique historical traditions, language and culture. Fischer sees Enzensberger as caught in the contradictions of his anti-universalistic pessimism which leads him to condemn what he actually defends: the modern Western project of identity. Without fully realizing it Enzensberger falls back into a naturalist historicism which fails to recognize the emancipatory significance of Enlightenment denaturalization, which separates the citizen from his 'natural' origins. *Great Migration* remains for Fischer entangled in the contradictory critique of universalism that is also evident in *Civil War*.

Bade interprets the xenophobic explosion in Germany after 1989 as an index of the political disorientation of the population, due above all to the refusal of the political class to admit that Germany has become a country of immigration. The government's failure to tackle the critical questions of immigration, integration and minority rights continues to hold Germany hostage to the ethnic definition of identity, codified in the 1913 Immigration Law and directed against the democratic-republican principle of identity. Both Bade and Castles attribute the underlying causes of racism to the unrealistic policies of the state and call for the urgent reform of the law on citizenship which treats resident immigrants as foreigners, a recipe for future conflict and a divided society. Reunification has not helped since it has given the question of German identity a new impetus while making it more difficult to obtain a consensus for change. The racist agitation of recent years reflects, according to Castles, an ongoing uncertainty and insecurity about national identity, for which German history offers no viable model. The Western model of 'constitutional patriotism' (Habermas) still rests on fragile foundations compared to the sense of identity derived from economic success, threatened now by unemployment. This somewhat precarious balance doubtless goes far to explain the lack of political will (Bade) to take the decisive step from an exclusionary ethnic definition of identity to the inclusive model of the political nation based on civic identity. The compromise of the 1993 asylum law, which restricts the right to political asylum but allows third generation immigrants to gain German citizenship, hovers between fear of the xenophobic fears of the population and recognition of the reality of a multiethnic and multicultural society, without solving the central problem of citizenship for immigrants.

In the light of these unresolved problems Castles, like Fischer, judges Enzensberger's contribution to the debate in *Great Migration* unhelpful. His retreat into cultural pessimism, as for instance in his fatalistic attitude to inter-group conflicts, is anything but conductive to political action. Castles opposes to Enzensberger's literary-essayistic treatment, with its tendency to substitute generalizations for analysis, Habermas' careful differentiation of individual and collective social and cultural rights as a theoretical basis for rethinking the issues of citizenship and German national identity. Thomas Wägenbaur by contrast tackles the question of the literary treatment of racism through a literary comparison. Against Enzensberger's parable of the railway compartment he sets Kafka's parable 'Fellowship', in order to deconstruct and reconstruct the self-incurred dilemmas of racism. It is the outsider, the stranger, as Kafka shows, who gives the insider his identity – a dialectical relation which the negative self-identity of racist exclusion ('The boat is full!') denies. Since the racist cannot grasp that the insiders are also strangers to each other, he cuts off the necessary circularity of self and stranger, which constitutes the condition for the maintenance of the dynamic stability of the group. Drawing on the cybernetic distinction between first and second order observation, Wägenbaur seeks to demonstrate that Kafka's presentation, critique and implied solution to the dilemma of racism escapes the perpetuation of the dilemma in Enzensberger's use of the parable form.

We could take second order observation, with its awareness of the unity of the two sides of the difference constructed by the observer, as the key to Andrzej Wirth's exposition of the other side of migration: the exit from the determinism of nativism. The *émigré*, the expatriate, chooses the cultivation of multiple identities (the utopia of multiculturalism). Wirth's autobiographical reflexions present a politics and hermeneutics of identity, premised on the circularity of outsiders and insiders, which effects the transition from the confinement of first order cultural and ethnic nationalism to the second order freedom of the citizen of the world. That second order identities also pose problems is a question pursued by John Docker, who laments Enzensberger's 'disturbingly impoverished' sense of multiculturalism. But rather than simply setting Australian multiculturalism against Central European tribalisms, Docker explores their conflictual interface in Australia today, highlighted by the controversies aroused by an award-winning first novel, *The Hand That Signed the Paper*, whose subject is the complicity of Ukrainians in the Holocaust. A novel about antisemitism or an antisemitic novel? The controversy was compounded by the fact that the author, daughter of English immigrants, claimed Ukrainian descent. Helen Darville/Demidenko's identity problem points for Docker to the other side of multiculturalism, the postmodern problem of the search for identity in and between ethnicities.

As the contributions to this volume indicate, Enzensberger's whole work is an invitation to debate. The contextualizations of *Civil War* and *Great Migration* undertaken here can be seen as a response which continues Enzensberger's own orientation to learning processes. The invocation of Sisyphus at the end of *Civil War* as the cleverest of men, the trickster who overcame Death, suggests that Enzensberger, for all his pessimism in the face of a dangerously absurd world, has not lost his faith in the capacity of human beings to refuse fatal conclusions.

I

Enzensberger's Intellectual Journey

Chapter One

Enzensberger's Iterology in the Century of Migrations

Gert Mattenklott

In the rapid chronological assessment of our century we use the wars as natural milestones. The political historians follow suit: the expressions *before* or *after* the *First* or *Second World War*, or *between the wars*, are not only chronologically unequivocal points of reference, but also categories with the sense of an historical naming of periods – yet with dubious justification. In great literature the traces of the wars commingle and overlap in a world wide migratory movement, a movement beyond comparison with anything since the exodus. Its associations are no less real than the orientation towards the wars, which are frequently – if not primarily – the cause of mass flight and expulsion. A recent study published by the UN High Commission states that there are (including refugees within nations) one hundred million migrants, refugees and expelled persons currently roaming the globe, and in the near future a potential of 1.7 billion refugees from 80 countries has been prognosticated.

This new migratory movement could provide the matter and the themes for a new epic, so universal is its magnitude. For, with this mass migration, entire cities and rural areas, their *moeurs* and their manners, are displaced and transformed; affiliations are dissolved and powers mobilized which together give rise almost reflexively to the desire for gravitation and collection, composure and security. One can scarcely imagine that the arts could survive without a loss of meaning if they fail to answer to this call. And even if this great theme, in and of itself, is not enough to guarantee great literature, coming to terms with these issues may well be the precondition for literature's continuing livelihood.

For migration has – whether expressly or implicitly – left its indelible imprint upon the literature of our epoch. The goal of many large migratory movements are the large cities. During the entire century, for this as well as for other reasons, the passage of the foreigner through the city becomes the exemplary school of perception: from the labyrinths and jungles of Joyce and Brecht to the data and symbolic systems in the novels of Barthelme, DeLillo and Pynchon. It is one of the signatures of modernism – and not only in the twentieth century – that real cities are increasingly yielded up to a transformation process at whose end we find phantasmagoric images like those in Calvino's *Le città invisibili.* This literature extends from the Irish in Paris (Joyce and Beckett), the Russians in Berlin, Paris and New York (Nabokov), the Polish in Argentina and France (Gombrowicz), Americans in Europe and Africa (Gaddis, Robben, Bowles), Caribbeans in the United States (Jamaica Kincaid and Marina Warner), to the French in China (Segalen) and the Spanish in Africa (Goytisolo). In the opposite direction, yet no less complementary, lies the path of the modern odyssey in flight from the large cities to the ethically foreign. Frazer and Mauss, Segalen, Malinowski and Levi-Strauss, Leiris and Eliade, Castaneda, Barley and Fichte are all authors of a contemporary epic that requires a new conception of world literature. Ultimately, both in the development of the sciences and in more recent literature, the conspicuous influence of the *ethnology of close observation* has increasingly become the focal point for these concerns. I mean by this the research of the most proximal living environment using the inventorial registers of ethnology and anthropology, beginning with Jean Baudrillard's *L'Echange symbolique et la mort (1976),* where the observations from the ethnological field research of Marcel Mauss on continents outside of Europe are applied towards the interpretation of the socially uprooted culture of protest in large European metropolises during the sixties and seventies. Other authors, such as Michel Certeau[1], Louis Dumont[2] and Alphonse Dupront[3], focus upon the rites of initiation, familial interaction and marriage, and especially the rites of gift giving and exchange in order to interpret behavioral patterns in urban surroundings or in small town recreational centers following the conceptual guidelines stemming from ethnic groups outside of Europe.

These remarks constitute the preface to the following discussion of Hans Magnus Enzensberger's *33 Milestones* of *The Great Migration* and its relationship to the *itérologie* of his work. Enzensberger has always devoted much attention to the relativizing of Europe during the course of this century, whether in his work on *The Exploitation of the Poverty Stricken World,* in his critique of media culture or in his comments on the loss of utopianism. In none of the phases of Enzensberger's literary activity has he shied away from seeking the large themes, even the themes occasioned by the news of the day, be it the wars in Vietnam or the Persian Gulf, or the present discussion of the laws pertaining to asylum or to the criminal acts directed against foreigners. But the 'contemporary' quality of Enzensberger's essay on our rapport with foreigners is not only its theme, but also the form in which the theme is treated: in a word, his texts are located at the peak of knowledge available to a learned contemporary, informed, too, by all the relevant arguments. No other German language author with a career of such continuity and breadth has made such rare use of the problematical concession that, particularly in Germany, is so often granted to writers so that one doesn't have to take them seriously: to pass judgment spontaneously and emotionally, and to leave everything else up to science and politics. The conviction that an author can become a companion, or even a pioneer of our contemporary society only in so far as he is in possession of sufficient factual competence is one conviction obviously deeply rooted in Enzensberger's *oeuvre*. It has contributed in no small part to the authority Enzensberger has in our literary world, an authority presently second to none.

In recent years much has been said – and justly said – about the self-neutralization of intellectuals whose otherworldliness is regularly put to shame by the more or less humble intellects of the politicians. And thus we may read with double satisfaction *The Great Migration*, a lifesaver for the sinking reputation of our trade. For one would have gladly heard a politician, one of those self-appointed advocates of foreigners, speak so adamantly in distinguishing between the right to asylum, the political conditions for immigration, and the unambiguous application of criminal justice against murder, manslaughter and arson, and to remain as sober as Enzensberger does while bringing the pious mania of a politics of wide open arms back to the basics of economic reality. I am thinking of sentences like the following on the 'inhabitability' of the Federal Republic of Germany: 'I call a place uninhabitable where a gang of thugs is free to attack people in the middle of the streets or set fire to their homes...For what is intolerable is the presence of people who undertake individual or organized manhunts' (*CW*, 140-1). But I am also thinking of the critique of the idiotic catchword 'I am a foreigner', the negative reversal of the racist cliché with all its reverent suggestions of a 'house with open doors' policy: 'Whoever calls upon his fellow citizens to offer shelter to the weary and wretched of the earth – often with reference to collective crimes stretching from the conquest of America to the Holocaust – without consideration of the consequences, without regard for political and economic mediations or whether such a project is realizable, loses all credibility. He becomes incapable of action' (*CW*, 131). Here, as elsewhere, the intended addressee is obvious enough. Far from a neo-factual pose, Enzensberger writes as an angry polemicist.

Knowledge acquired through solid research and astute argumentation, the alliance of imaginativeness and cool headed facts, and, finally, discriminating polemics are not the only recommendation for the use of the essay. The essay as thought-form is itself a form of migration and travel. In the essay, the author establishes his orientation in a field full of platitudes and precipices of which the author warns and whose outline he identifies while making his way through the history of xenophobia and xenophilia right up to the events of recent days. Here, the congruence of form and content in the motif of travel is not a coincidental product. It stands in direct relationship to the *idée fixe* of the author's works and perhaps also of the author, who seems, despite his flawless professionalism, to carry out his trade in a more or less ambulatory fashion. Even in haphazard reconstruction I recall southern Europe, Scandinavia, the USA, Mexico, South America and Cuba, but also the Far East, so that in the end perhaps no continent is missing. But beyond the traveler's biography it seems to me that a general rule can be construed from that which in particular can be said of *Great Migration:* the sense of the participation of both life and art in the idea of travel literature whose poetics seem to be – following their debut in the Enlightenment – in the process of reconstruction in our century.

Travel literature – the genre is easier to name than to define. Do not Homer's *Odyssey* and Dante's *Divina Commedia, Wilhelm Meisters Lehrjahre* and Proust's *Recherche* belong to the literature of travel? Perhaps not in the common sense of the word, though unjustly so. For one may quite seriously contend that literature is always en route, even when its heroes stay at home. Not even the authors have to be mobile. Herein lies the resemblance between travel and peace literature. If one follows the categories too closely, one impairs one's vision of their meaning. Since the beginning of history great cultures developed en route.

Travel literature corresponds to a vision of worldly experience in which traveling and writing are inextricably interrelated. The theory of travel overlaps with and is permeated by a poetics and a philosophy of life. In this conjunction, writing is just as important for the traveler as traveling for the writer, and both together become the existential metaphor for people who experience their own lives essentially as being *en route*, and the writing therein as a symbolic form of self-authorization. The consequences this has for the structure of texts, and how this changes travel and brandmarks one's understanding of life, must thereafter be ceaselessly investigated, yet not by mere addition, but rather in the analysis of each individual text. Its reader is, potentially, always also a writer in travel, so that reading, writing and travel complement one another in a triad – a triad that Michel Butor placed programmatically at the center of his work as author. In his *Le voyage et l'écriture* this complex of symbols becomes a basic anthropological equation. Those who get around in this world write their way into it. Those who read transpose their own location – out of their everyday surroundings and into a phantasmagoric *terra incognita*; when one writes, one departs on a voyage, changing location in unison with the movement of one's self. Butor quite deliberately placed this movement in the centre. Travel means becoming mobile, no less so than writing and reading. From the analysis of the various forms of movement he attempts to derive a poetical typology, or even more: his own new science, *itérologie,* which characterizes all forms of consciousness as forms of travel – following thereby the perilous course set out by Nietzsche and analogous to Ernst Bloch, who together found for their own philosophy a similar definition. For the science of iterology, the distinction between fiction and documentary is just as irrelevant a question as the hierarchical order of the forms applied.

Butor's iterology would find in Enzensberger's oeuvre a congenial object of study. This applies most notably to his worldliness. Here we recognize the fruitfulness of his translations of William Carlos Williams and Franco Fortini, Neruda and Lars Gustafsson, each a reconnaissance mission into an unknown literary world, yet not in order to conquer or to occupy, but rather to mark off a territory in his own language and to grant the foreign author a hospitable environment within it. In this fashion Enzensberger's works are traversed not so much by a path as by an imposing avenue upon which world literature has left its traces. For here we ought not to name only the many translations, but also the adaptations from, for example, Molière, or the numerous reports collected in a volume with the sighing title, *Ach Europa* (1987). Laying claim to or providing such literary hospitality has become particularly significant today since the political ideology which, during the sixties and seventies, focused attention beyond our borders under the banner of international solidarity has worn thin: even in Enzensberger's work itself for example, in the largest of his prose works of this type, the *roman de collage* on the life and death of the Spanish anarchist Durruti, *The Short Summer of Anarchy*. One can scarcely imagine what impulses might direct our gaze *away* from the narcissistic contemplation of German dispositions and *towards* the outside. Curiosity alone does not seem to be enough.

But what energies, then, effect in Enzensberger's work such relentless extroversion, even after its political and moral motivation has been extinguished? Here there seems to be an active natural reflex to cross borders, an impatience with the borders themselves, independent of who erected them and why. No imperial desire to annex lies behind this feeling, but rather the horror in the face of the identical as death. Death cannot ally itself with the longing for the foreign and the other.

At least on two occasions in recent years Enzensberger has spoken out with great resonance on the relationship between one's own and foreign culture: on the occasion of the Gulf war, where he defended the rigour against Saddam Hussein, and again recently in his *Great Migration*. In the previous work Enzensberger had to engage the arguments of the critics of the Gulf war who maintained that the West is incapable of conceding to the foreign world of Islam its own right to existence. Enzensberger's reply recommended that we place more confidence in the defense of our own Western culture, so heavily marked by the Enlightenment, and he advocated the application of moral and juridical standards that have validity in our own tradition. I recall this argument now because its twofold directedness seems to be so characteristic: both against narcissism, the tautological and the pleonastic, on the one hand, and against blindly abandoning oneself to all that is different and foreign, on the other, as if it were, simply because it is foreign, somehow better and more worthy of respect. Enzensberger's convictions, whenever he gives expression to European concerns, were formulated already at the beginning of the century by the French navy doctor Victor Segalen who traveled between Africa and China. In his *Aesthetics of the Diverse* (1910), Segalen attempted to dictate to the prevailing contemporary exoticism a new program. He wrote:

> Exoticism is thus not adaptation; it is not the complete comprehension of the non-I which one could then incorporate into oneself, but rather the sharp immediate perception of an eternal lack of understanding.
> We take our point of departure from this acknowledgment of impenetrability. Let us not boast that we can assimilate the moeurs, the races, the nations, the others; on the contrary, let us rejoice in the fact that we shall never be able to assimilate them, and retain for ourselves the lasting pleasure of feeling the diversity.[4]

In this respect, related to Segalen is Enzensberger's iterology and its continual movement back to its starting point. This distinguishes its impulses from the yearning to do away with the self, a yearning typical of the sentimentalists within the movement of European exoticism in earlier decades. Enzensberger's expeditions are conceived of as passages from which, in the end, one's own self emerges as the result of having traversed through another culture. One's own self is thus not placed at the beginning as a rigidly formed and narrow minded standard, but rather must first arise out of its pre-conscious darkness at the end in individual profile. And thus the foreign cannot be perceived by those who are, in any case, loosely tied to their own, but rather – quite the contrary – by intimate, all too intimate connoisseurs of their own. The foreign is never so sensitively recognized, one's own never so uncompromisingly interrogated, as when it is subjected to the community of traitors, renegades, dissidents and converts. As Margaret Boveri, a student of Jaspers, pointed out in her perspicacious essay on *Betrayal in the Twentieth Century*, together these elements represent the heritage of the fundamental views of liberalism. Insight does not dawn upon slumberous followers, but rather on the emotional and intellectual mestizos, the nomads between the camps; they're neither fish nor fowl, *yet not* due to their indecisiveness, but rather to their passion for the various.

And thus iterology seeks to strike up a balance between the plunge into the eternally same and identical, on the one hand, and the plunge into the completely foreign, on the other. Both are fatal to one's own independent productivity. The path between them, the small path of reason, as the essay on *The Great Migration* attempts to conceptualize it, hardly seems to appeal to any of the ingredients which, in the classical tradition of German idealism, are generally conjured up in such instances as a matter of course. Here, no ideological compromise is recommended, let alone a juridical compromise, and the author spares us the Sunday sermon on tolerance and loving one's neighbour. The reason he recommends to us in its place is the reason of self-preservation. Every intelligent system requires, if it is to endure, a certain balance between identity and alterity – not on moral grounds, but in the interest of its own survival. There is no shortage of evidence for this theorem.

Hannah Arendt is the most important sponsor of Enzensberger's second large political essay in recent years, *Civil War*. With her description of the disinterest of modern masses basking in their own prosperity (*The Origins of Totalitarianism*, 1951) Arendt delivers the foil for Enzensberger's physiognomy of 'molecular and regional civil wars'. Enzensberger develops his physiognomy as a store of reactive potential against the total loss of the self. Only this total loss can explain why the world wide aggression of an unbridled mob is not only directed against others but also, in suicidal self-annihilation, against its own life. Radically disillusioned over the role of great ideas, the mob itself has come to regard the Islamic and other forms of religious fundamentalism, the Balkan and other appeals to ethnically founded nationalism, the Afghan and other similar defensive wars against colonial intervention from outside, as little more than dubious wizardry. National liberation and revolutionary rebellion, the black power movement and religious war – so Enzensberger's diagnosis – are now nothing more than ideological trash whose remains only the desperadoes continue to pick over. Those who don't participate stand helplessly aside, vanquished by the social workers' mentality which attempts and forgives everything, or vanquished by the globally responsible universalism that collaborates whether out of sheer depression or aggressively – because it never knows where it should first inform itself, where it ought to protest most urgently or where it ought to donate money. Enzensberger's advice relies upon the desperate sobriety of a clean-up crew after the battle: hopeless cases are left to themselves; those slightly damaged are encouraged to self-help; the most difficult cases, however, so long as they seem to be curable, are supported with all the means available. The consequence? 'Our priority is not Somalia, but Hoyerswerda and Rostock, Mölln and Solingen' (*CW*, 69). Only those prone to denunciation can call that cynical.

Enzensberger's balancing act can be characterized in another way if we refer to an older opposition amongst European intellectuals. The impulse towards a continual crossing of borders which keeps him in search of the foreign as such is something he shares in common with the historical avant garde who tend to see in the other something that is closer to the origin. When Enzensberger discovered for himself Scandinavia, and later the Romanic world, then the United States, and Cuba, the literary broadening of his horizon became increasingly bound up with the political. Here his own literary and political option arose out of the critique of the narcissism of German literary culture. This same critique applies wholly to the romantic longing for the 'entirely other' and the foreign. The double opposition against tautological unproductiveness, on the one hand, and against unreflected Romanticism, on the other, seems to me to stem from one single principal aversion, thanks to which Enzensberger like very few other contemporary authors manages to participate in two political cultures which cannot be brought under one blanket category. I mean by this the democratic universalism in the tradition of the Enlightenment, on the one hand, as well as the anarchic initiatives aimed at authenticity, individuality and skepticism vis-à-vis progress, on the other. An advocate of political egalitarianism, Enzensberger favours the application of democratic traffic regulations according to the formalized rules of law and order, regardless of the situation and to whom the rules are applied. The reinforcement and expansion of the applicability of this order would imply a modest growth in reason. Nevertheless, aesthetic obstinacy and the depressing experience with the democratically managed world continuously dismantles the credibility of the liberal philosophy of the Enlightenment. As lyric poet, Enzensberger is a language critic who holds fast to the distance separating the seemingly increasing realization of the liberal norm of reason and the yearning for self-realization. This twofold liaison to the realization of the liberal concept of law and order in European democracies and, at the same time, to the tradition of anarchic individualism and its aesthetic opposition since the romantic period, impedes stable political options and solid programs. It inclines rather to irony and skepticism and leans towards nihilism.

No doubt by comparison with the utopianism of the sixties and seventies it is a melancholic-ironic position of retreat that must ultimately fail to satisfy the desire for moral confession. But here the memory looms heavily that it was precisely the practice-related impotence of such confessions that robbed them of their credibility. And here at least we must finally remark upon another *idée fixe* in Enzensberger's literary works. I am thinking of his critique of the powers of imagination. There seems to be rather too much of it than too little – so, it would seem, runs the opinion of the author. Art is no longer in a position to control such rampant fantasies. From time to time Enzensberger viewed them as the accomplices of a wild and savage phantasmagoria and liquidated them symbolically in the almanac *Kursbuch*.

This skepticism in the face of a free floating fantasy has remained right up to the most recent texts, as has Enzensberger's penchant for pouncing upon it wherever it threatens to render itself independent. In prose no less than in poetry, Enzensberger takes manifest pleasure in breaking with stylistic convention: breaking off the high tone abruptly as soon as it becomes exclusive, or knocking a tooth out of the crown of everything representative. Here the journalistic side of Enzensberger's work reappears again and again with its bag of discoveries culled together out of newspapers, lexica and encyclopedias, out of whatever he has picked up or researched along the way, returning stylistically to the report or to forms related to it. And thus Hans Magnus Enzensberger's writing – even in the last few years, where the philosophical diction has displaced the embattled political tones – has nevertheless retained its objective and factual gravitation. One can express this same thought as a description of form. But one can also interpret it in its significance as a particular type of contemporaneity and moral presence of mind which accepts the questions of our age as the most obvious occasions for literature.

Enzensberger's answers to these questions have become more reserved and skeptical over the years. And yet wherever these questions – during the decades in which he has been writing – grew dramatic, he has always appeared reliably on the scene.

NOTES

1 Michel Certeau, *L'Invention du quotidien*, Paris, 1980.
2 Louis Dumont, *La Tarasque*, Paris, 1987.
3 Alphonse Dupront, *Du sacré*, Paris, 1987.
4 Victor Segalen, *Die Ästhetik des Diversen*, p. 44.

(Translated by Brian Poole, M.A.)

Chapter Two

Gaining Positions of Distinction: On Enzensberger's Provocations

Markus Joch

How is one to define an intellectual? What do intellectuals do? What can they do, what may they do, what should they do? Pierre Bourdieu (whose terminology forms the basis of the following argument) has used the Dreyfus case to show how the term 'intellectual' first arose as writers, artists and scientists as such became involved in political life. He derives the concept of a 'bi-dimensional being'[1] from the origin of the term. Intellectuals – as the advocates of universal values – are on the one hand compelled to become involved in political matters, yet it is due to the specific nature of their 'capital' (the values connected with the strict autonomy of their fields, such as 'moral power', 'disinterestedness', 'unselfishness', 'competence', ect.[2]) that importance is given to their views.

Set against this perspective, the traditional confrontation between autonomy and commitment evolves into a relationship of preconditions. Bourdieu perceives the traditional factional conflict in the bourgeoisie as the main driving force behind the intellectuals' commitment beyond their own immediate sphere of activity ('field'). The intellectuals themselves count as part of the ruling class, but (as the dominated rather than the dominating part of the bourgeoisie) only because they possess more cultural (rather than economic) capital. The fact that they experience the latter form of capital as the decisive one in the 'field of power' (Bourdieu) means that it is unacceptable – in as far as they insist on the universal validity of their internal values in their own field, whilst at the same time denying that the dominant faction pursues these values. The position of a writer, for example, becomes intellectual when he or she tries to assert the internal values of his or her field outside that field.

Admittedly, this abstract role model only exists in individual variations, resulting in a quasi constitutive paradox for the literary intellectual, namely to be able to speak on behalf of others (on behalf of a group of interests which can be generalised) on the one hand, and on the other the need to show an unmistakable profile – in order to prevail against the competitors in the literary field. In this field of restricted production (in which the producers produce for other producers), distinction is called for – as well as the ability to differentiate oneself in a prestigious way and so gain and retain symbolic capital (prestige). The statements of an intellectual author are to be understood as individual position-takings (*prises de position*), although ones that are always relative to the field.[3] The challenge for the literary intellectual is the ability to express his or her own position in such a way that it is still consistent with the catalogue of standards described above.

Hans Magnus Enzensberger provides an example of an intellectual who has a reputation of being a chameleon and thus an interesting case study of an author's strategies of gaining distinction. Enzensberger is controversial not only because he has subjected the classical model of the intellectual to radical criticism (which in itself might just be seen as a contribution to 'late-modern' common sense). His provocative position arises from the fact that he, as a person who has accumulated his symbolic capital as a literary spokesman of the left-wing intelligentsia, is now showing these readers the very limits of their own power to define. As is well known, it was Enzensberger who, in 1968 ('Berliner Gemeinplätze'), described the political system of the Federal Republic of Germany as being 'irreparable',[4] and issued radical democratic exhortations to his colleagues to support 'the movement to make Germany politically literate'.[5] That was not all. Enzensberger, already a well-known poet and essayist at the time, drew the aesthetic consequences and rejected the artistic status of literature and began to compile documentary writings, which promised him a greater degree of broad political effectiveness. Enzensberger the socialist considered it his duty to seek an alliance with the underprivileged, and as an author become the 'ventriloquist of those who, because of the division of labour...had been denied the opportunity to express themselves'.[6] He has left this ambition well behind. Whilst his name represented literary social criticism for decades, today the name Enzensberger stands for the decisive rejection of the same. *Mittelmaß und Wahn*, his 1988 collection of essays,[7] can be seen as the climax of this break with earlier positions and as his way of settling scores with the fundamental left-wing intellectual consensus. The following discussion first attempts to describe the argumentational structures that Enzensberger uses to justify his own about-face. It then tries to show how he defends his distinction against the left-wing accusation of intellectual softness. Thirdly, it shows the points where his latest publications, *The Great Migration* and *Civil War*,[8] modify this intellectual viewpoint yet again.

At the beginning of *Mediocrity and Delusion* there is a 1974 lecture and a 1976 essay justifying the place of wilfulness in literature and the right of both to exist. Enzensberger regards it as naive to ascribe literature any further significance. If this error had previously been reserved for conservative cultural criticism and its warning of delusionary literary power, the same error is now being made by the Left – sometimes in the hope of utopian excess dressed in poetry, sometimes in the suspicion of their culinary, aesthetically anaesthetic effect that paralyses revolutionary energies. For Enzensberger, this is one of the numerous examples offered of the near convergence of conservative cultural criticism and left-wing social criticism marked by brave illusion.

Instead Enzensberger describes poetry as a micro-event that cannot be scientifically tied down. But in the Philistine hands of literary theorists and educators who strive to make individual readers' experience and schools the testing ground of their latest fashionable methods, poetry becomes a bludgeon. Who would not agree when Enzensberger mocks the inflationary jargon of educationalists spelling out 'aims and objectives', which restrict rather than give structure to school readings? Who would dispute the fact that students (under pressure to obtain marks) see interpretation as a chattel to be bartered for the necessary certificates, and not something to be experienced for the sake of enjoying the text? Who would not reject the notion that a literary creation could be reduced to a handful of handy assertions below the 'surface' of the text, to be accurately understood, corrected, ticked off, and criticised without any problem on the part of the teacher? However, Enzensberger's attacks go beyond this 'correct' interpretation (which is a demented construction in reality): 'Reading is an anarchic act. Interpretation, especially the single correct one, exists to frustrate this act'.[9] He has no desire to admit that a form of interpretation exists that is anything other than narrow-minded: Is Enzensberger really concerned about saving the poor souls of innumerable generations of defenceless students in order to provide a veneer of unselfishness, or does it rather have more to do with his own resistance to being interpreted?

This question relates to one of the central points of Enzensberger's few theoretical-poetological statements, which says far more than that the critical potency of poetry lies in its pragmatic unusability. In this context, Enzensberger's 'anarchic' position represents a complete break from literary criticism à la Adorno with its concept of mutual recognition of literary work and criticism, where criticism finds its scale in the critical content of modern literary works, with the duty of criticism being to help the latter develop.[10] The concordance of literary work and interpretation is heralded in the intention to criticise. Enzensberger ignores that the critical perception of the work is conducted analogously to the perception of reality by the literary work itself: in the reconstruction at the price of selection. Enzensberger's camouflaged plea for piety towards poetry in the name of art, based upon Susan Sontag's image of the enemy – 'to interpret is to impoverish, to deplete the world'; it is the 'revenge of the intellect upon art'[11] – resists poetry being pared to the bones of terminology.

He uses a suggestive image to formulate the mode of operation of literature in highly industrialised societies – 'the Aspirin Effect'. Poetry, once a privileged medium of non-discursive learning processes, has had to surrender its prioritised position, but has distributed its material substrate, the text, over ever more strongly competing fields – headlines, pop, advertising, etc.: that because of this 'its quality leaves something to be desired is beside the point'.[12] Feelings that had previously been unknown and new perceptions are reaching the worlds of fashion, music and the cinema. 'In this sense literature has fallen victim to socialization. It is not finished; it is everywhere'.[13] That force which drives cultural criticism into pessimistic despair (in this case the removal of literary potency) indeed has positive aspects for the more attentive observer.

Enzensberger vacillates between tearing down culturally critical findings and unsentimentally extrapolating them. Thus the undertone of the potency-removal thesis – literature is 'allowed to do everything, but nothing depends on it anymore'[14] – is only superficially melancholic. For instance, its chronicler discovers a history of decay in the development of the literary public. The genus of influential and congenial critics such as Benjamin and Sklovski is extinct. The 'circulation agents' (to do belated justice to Lukàcs' terminology) have taken their place. These critics rely on the power of their publishing houses for authority, rather than on knowledge of the subject (and certainly not on literary skill). The spoken word is only of interest for these people in so far as they can use it to identify the very latest trends. To be the first to announce something guarantees the circulation agent's status: the object of these trends becomes more and more an undisguised object of exchange to gain prestige. The space on the culture pages becomes tighter and tighter, and culture is frequently integrated into the entertainment section.

The fact that the expression 'circulation agent' was able to find approval bears witness to the term's aptness, as shown by Ulrich Greiner's use of it (albeit misunderstood, and that possibly deliberately) in his own lament on 'intellectual corruption' in *Die Zeit*. The editor of the German weekly's literary section takes an all the more serious view of this form of misguided conduct ('circulation agent' criticism), 'the more power'[15] the culture journalists obtains. However, in contrast to Greiner, Enzensberger's seemingly melancholic reminiscence does not by any means appear to recommend a reversion to the more honourable traditions of the past. He regards the decline of criticism as a further symptom that fundamental criticism has lost its classical audience – a broad public that is eager to be educated. According to Enzensberger, the decline of secondary literature will cause no suffering for the noble minority of literature and its readership. In the crisis of secondary literature that he complains about, the primary producer's claim to be literature's sole representative is celebrated once and for all. But there is a precondition: 'The writers can wipe off the representative mask which they wore for so long'.[16]

It is not the concept of 'involved thought' (Brecht) that is being undermined here, but rather the belief in expanding beyond a minority status. Criticism of everyday language for instance, which Enzensberger earlier (*Das Verhör von Habana*) performed out of critical interest in order to expose power, arose out of the necessity to ask not only whether something was ideological, but also why it was so successful. In understanding this success, questions of the tenability of one's own critical standards can arise.

This is the reasoning behind Enzensberger's reflections on 'The Triumph of the Tabloid *Bild*'. A collage of quotes is used to confront the suspicion customary amongst the Left – that the paper is simply a fascistic scandal sheet. This montage shows the paper's real recipe for success – the juxtaposition of the trivial with infernal horror, and the assimilation of the meaningless and the significant – with the effect of exchangeability of the incomparable. '*Bild* is read because not in spite of the fact that it is about nothing, liquidates every content...smashes every historical, moral, political category'.[17] True, this effect of constant exposure to the trivial can itself be placed into a political category – distraction of the masses – but the reasoning behind it all depends on the consent of both publisher and readers in a common project known as 'lack of content'. Enzensberger reminds us of the shock and disbelief of *Bild*'s opponents from the SDS (a German left-wing students' organisation of the 1960s) as they discovered that their adversaries at the newspaper marketing department had commissioned a report, which stated that one reason for *Bild*'s success was the fact that its readers identified with the superior, brutal, attacking force that the paper represented. The critics were unable to claim anything else – the company had made the accusation its own 'property'. There was nothing left to expose.

Freedom from self-idealisation of the existing reality robs ideological criticism of its basis. Enzensberger reacts to this by taking refuge in attack, resorting to the unusual tactical subversion by affirmation, which admittedly cannot hide its bitter undertones: '*Bild*'s formal model is, by contrast, radically modern. This model is the artwork of the avantgarde...*Bild* represents, in every-day terms, the break with every traditional language and with every traditional form. It is collage, montage, assemblage, it is *objet trouvé* and *écriture automatique*...the dissolution of art, the aesthetic sum total of our civilization'.[18]

Guided by a desire to exceed *Bild*'s objective scorn, the argumentation reaches its peak when he describes the tabloid not as an aberration, but rather as an extreme case of the freedom of the press, insisting on the structural equality of all journalistic media. Alongside a short-term memory fixation with topicalities, the supposedly serious press also carries on the business of 'exchangeability of all discourses' with the reciprocal encroachment of advertising and its editorial surroundings. Informativity is not seen as a contrary value, but as a bourgeois residue of journalism, stopping journalism from completely regaining consciousness – a teleological movement, typical for *mediocrity*, which can only imagine social change in the mode of extrapolation. What remains, as a historico-political relict, expresses itself with an emphatic aesthetic effect. Moments of salvational criticism are disappearing. As the theses on the tabloid *Bild* – through their assumption of inevitability – verge towards the cynical, the attestation of weakness for the intellectuals is all the more significant.

The preference for the discourse of the ruling classes counts as one characteristic of the non-literary and non-journalistically oriented work of the intellectual. Enzensberger, assuming the role of a reporter, seeks the company of bankers and financial experts in order to discuss the crisis of the economy at formal receptions or in cool, air-conditioned conference rooms. In a report on the policies of the International Monetary Fund and the World Bank, he perceptively eavesdrops on the worries and problems of their top executives. In passing, he declares their critics to be irrational.[19] Summing up, after weighing up the pros and cons, he withdraws somewhat – what remains now is a wooden sculpture, pregnant with meaning, standing in the foyer of the IMF: 'The Garuda', say the Indonesians, 'is always victorious. He looks evil, but he stands for all good things in the world'.[20]

Exceptions subtly confirm the general trend of the text. The '*j'accuse*' style used to sum up the corruptibility and 'help yourself' attitude of the ruling class in response to scandals like the Flick affair (a major political corruption scandal which engulfed nearly all of Germany's political parties in the 1980s) sticks out like a sore thumb. On the one hand Enzensberger confirms that investigative journalism is indispensable, yet on the other he comments on the danger of the role of 'moral deputy' while unable to count on the unlimited interest of the reader: 'The venerable tradition of muckraking in journalism presupposes a reader who can be disappointed. But only a person whose face can be distinguished from their mask can be unmasked'.[21] This could be the revealing paraphrase of a quotation from Büchner. With regard to this Jacobin phrase, one would have to tear the masks off the faces of the depraved and corrupt aristocrats. As Danton says to his comrade-in-arms Lacroix: 'The faces will come off too'.[22] Whilst Robespierre's moral fervour was able to receive support from the angry people, Enzensberger meanwhile sees the public as being disillusioned. The more it devotes itself to Philistine imperatives,[23] the less its moral outrage about the selfish carryings on of its (in this sense thoroughly representative) representatives. Here, the praise of the *petite bourgeoisie* reaches its limits: 'Noone, or almost noone, would like to be seen as a utopian dreamer or blue-eyed idealist aiming to improve the world'.[24]

Enzensberger's own position could hardly be put more succinctly. The absence of social criticism is characteristic for *Mediocrity and Delusion*. A deeper reason for this lies in Enzensberger's belief in the self-regulation of society in Germany. Accordingly, the political parties owe their election to the desire of the electorate to avoid a one-party system and less and less to an ever smaller loyalty to sets of beliefs. The widespread apathy about the political confrontations in Bonn shows that in any case, decisive impulses no longer come from the once so hotly contended political power centres. What is meant here is not the interest of capital. Instead, society has split into a plethora of special interest groups, the concept of 'control from the centre' is obsolete, and the parties have lost their leading role in forming opinions. The political is reduced to specific, local areas, with commitment only in some particular areas which touch on the life of the individual in an immediate way: 'Today the state is faced by every possible kind of group, by minorities of every kind...You can discover 10,000 instances of power in our society. The result is an impenetrable confusion'.[25]

According to Enzensberger, a clearly definable political power centre forms the precondition for an oppositional response, the traditional territory of the intellectual. By spiriting this away by sleight of hand, the role of the opposition is also removed. Conversely, the political rulers in Germany had stigmatised and suppressed the intellectuals through the never-ending assumption that they (the intellectuals) were a disruptive political element that ought to be taken seriously. Thus both sides in the traditional contest between intellect and power tended to find their former function as representatives taken over by society itself, their permanent feud diminishing in substance. Social conflicts arise outside both camps. The former adversaries, it seems, see themselves restricted to tasks of the same or similar nature. If politics plays the role of repair workshop within capitalism, then the role of the intellectuals is to provide cultural compensation for the damage to life caused by modernisation. Their new task would then not leave the terminology and form of the cultural untouched – the empty dynamic of diversionary culture would profit rather than contemplative, written culture. 'After all, on this new terrain quite different talents can develop from those poets and thinkers, critics and teachers. The more uncomfortable the surroundings, the more urgently do we need environmental artists and video magicians'.[26]

Mediocrity and Delusion, the title essay of the *Collected Diversions*, introduces the two quintessentially 'complementary'[27] terms. Enzensberger believes he can systematically and genealogically grasp the Federal Republic of Germany's ability to stand up to crises and that he can make a focused judgement on forty years of social criticism: 'Their interpretations have not only proved to be impotent, they were wrong'.[28] According to this thesis, the total collapse of the German Reich formed the basis of the successor project, the Federal Republic. The republic (though delayed by the Adenauer era) has thrown off a heritage of submission to authority, and has institutionalised class-compromise through a period of lasting economic prosperity. Left-wing social criticism has become usable by the system that is itself being contested. The Left's permanent warning of authoritarian tendencies can be seen as a 'self-refuting prophecy; the point of its statements would then consist of providing for their own refutation'.[29]

According to Enzensberger, not only the political mean is golden, but also cultural mediocrity. The supremacy of the *petite bourgeoisie* is reflected both in levelling and pluralising, as it is not possible to discern a cultural elite, i.e., lifestyles cannot be differentiated vertically along the lines of social strata. 'The rich...dispose of no class consciousness of their own, have no style of their own, no ideology of their own, no prestige outside the economic sphere'.[30] However, the result is not a homogenous mash, but a horizontal variety of lifestyles within the limits of the mediocrity of taste. The 'average deviant'[31] dominates the picture. Supposed expressions of personal originality are limited to participation in the 'high' of current fashion, trips and subcultures, yet here the triumph is the triumph of mimicked individuality, departing from any criticism of the illusionary nature of individualisation. Enzensberger never tires of attacking the superfluousness of criticism.

Where mediocrity itself becomes excessive, claims its eulogist, radical artistic dissidence can no longer expect its need for demarcation to be satisfied. It can no longer rely on the bourgeoisie's time-honoured aversion to modern art, which provided its creators with a gain in distinctiveness. Modern art is now met everywhere with a tolerance oscillating between an absent-minded sort of interest and indifference, which appreciates the provocative as entertainment value, subsided by the state and privately sponsored.

Enzensberger explains the blemish on his (otherwise sympathetic) portrait of the Federal Republic as the non-contemporaneity of the subsystem of institutionalised politics and its limited ability to learn, so that political opposition still has to face repression by the state. In the process, the radical catalogue of demands gains systematical functionality – maximisation of the input of ideas guarantees minimum output from the state: 'The political outsider becomes the specialist in the overdose, without which no noticeable feedback would be registered in the apparatuses at all'.[32] Enzensberger blames the political minority's self-alienating delusion for its rejection by the majority. The one-size-fits-all-explanation of intellectual allergy to political normality prevents him from recognising that the political dissidents feel the limits of normality, without having to seek self-exclusion themselves. Enzensberger's judgement on the German political system in 1968 was: 'We can either consent to it or replace it with a new system. There is no other possibility'.[33] In the *Mediocrity* essay, the pendulum swings most unambiguously back to the first of these alternatives.

The same basic message, if radicalised, informs the central model of *Politische Brosamen* (1982): vertical ideological conflicts like those between the bourgeoisie and the 'toiling masses', are replaced by horizontal ones: correspondingly, the *petite bourgeoisie,* the 'neither nor class',[34] dominates – a class that gives rise to its own, powerless critics, the intellectuals. There is a clear division of roles: here the pragmatic majority, concerned with securing its own affluence, and there the outsiders, concerned with gaining distinction. The latter (though themselves well-nourished by prosperity) cultivate their own revulsion against popular taste and at the same time untiringly (and just as unsuccessfully) belabour their contemporaries with questions of *Sinnstiftung* and utopia. Enzensberger revalues the attitude of the majority as being one of a wide-awake common sense, a typical social democratic outlook which rejects political experiments for good reason: 'They suspect that the alternative would be...barbarism and self-destruction'.[35] On the other hand, he vigorously attacks the attitude of the critics: 'Hatred of affluence is one of the existential lies of the West German intelligentsia'.[36] In addition, they presume themselves arbiters of culturally valuable property, but the silent majority rightly opposes the 'enlightening' rationalisation of aesthetic discrimination.

The intention (one that does not shrink back from daring generalisation) to blame intellectuals' disgust at consumer culture and mass culture as being precisely the attitudes that alienate them from the mass of the population (a population on whose behalf the intellectuals claim to agitate) was due to a strategy of gaining distinction in the intellectual field: sarcastic and downward-looking rejection of the 'normal' habitus[37] of the 'specials' made it possible to remain special in the company of the 'specials'. Thus, in Enzensberger's own symbolic schema, we can recognise the field-related intention to be distinctive – the very thing that he accuses others of.

Politische Brosamen can also be understood as self-criticism, which understandably distances itself from the author's own earlier disgust at normality.[38] This did not change the fact that the praises sung for the happily consuming, social democratic mainstream did meet with rejection from left-wing writers. Wolfgang Pohrt faulted the tame way that all problematic social areas are ignored; he suspected that Enzensberger was unable to put a distance between the governing practical norms and himself.[39] Hermann L. Gremliza reminded his readers that Enzensberger, only ten years earlier, had seen the Federal Republic of Germany as a state of 'masked Fascism', and he condemned 'the manoevrability of such *Harlequin* turncoats as Enzensberger'[40] as profit-oriented, opportunistic ingratiation to the dispositions of the dominant faction.

This field conflict also bears an influence on the later *Mittelmaß* theses – it sharpens their intent. Especially in Enzensberger's case the question brought up by Bourdieu can be answered in the affirmative, whether the necessity exists, even for an author who claims to write independently of popular expectations, to reckon with 'the social situation of his work...and its mirror which his audience, critics and interpreters hold up to his eyes', and whether he has to revise 'his original project...in view of this reflex'.[41] The struggle for symbolic capital has the effect that Enzensberger's attempts to seek the reasons for the limits of intellectual power of definition changes into a general rejection of the concept of political opportunities – a rejection which does not draw back from a general attack on the opponents which calls their sanity into question. After the attacks on Enzensberger's power of persuasion, indeed on his integrity, his burning desire to prove the superfluousness of his own and the republic's critics has become his actual, new symbolic purpose – even more than presenting a differentiated view of the situation in Germany. Now he consciously occupies the affirmative position he has been accused of occupying by the competing field forces, holding it to be the only position that can be taken seriously.[42] This leaves the touches of self-critical modesty contained in the *Brosamen* collection behind, in a kind of forward defence (so to speak), resembling the arguments in *Gemeinplätze* in its dogmatic gesture – a spiralling movement.

However, this gain in distinction can only be achieved at the price of an internal-habitual conflict: though Enzensberger superficially rejects the habitus of those possessing a high degree of cultural capital, he himself has incorporated this behaviour to a great extent. Nowhere is this ambivalence more apparent than in his spectacular estimation of television as being intellectually out of question on the one hand, and on the other hand a completely ineffective 'zero medium'. The rejection of ideology-critical objections guarantees the gain in distinction, without Enzensberger being able to hide his own disgust at the medium ('the cotton wool in front of one's eyes').[43] A sarcastic playing down of the perils of television offers itself as an alternative, both to the standardised 'no' to the medium and to apologies for it. It is particularly on the question of the media that Enzensberger makes a sarcastic U-turn: in 1970, he developed the vision of an emancipatory usage of audio-visual media, which promised collective political learning processes, because (in contrast to serious literature) they were capable of breaking the bourgeois educational privilege. He now holds this position to be outdated: in a society in which – even amongst the elites – the 'secondary illiterates'[44] dominate, the privilege of education is no longer recognised. No one is outclassed anymore. However, serious literature can be rehabilitated. It has lost its guilt, it is no longer a class privilege in a class society.

Certainly, the *Mediocrity* theses can be read as a seismograph indicating an objective cultural shift. It should however be noted just which conclusions the analyst draws from his diagnosis of the time. It is one thing to take note of an altered, de-hierarchicalised definition of culture, it is another to accuse the supporters of cultural dissidence of having a yearning to dictate taste, in other words to equate aesthetic wilfulness with rules adressed to 'mediocre' contemporaries. The same mechanism can be observed in the political considerations: to go from a position of seeing a general satisfaction with a prosperous consumer capitalism to one of completely de-legitimising alternative political concepts is not something that should be taken for granted. The polemic element of the diagnoses owes everything to a heretical habitus and to the desire for dissent which is above all due to the intellectual field's implied standards of taste. The traditional habitus in the intellectual field represents, on the one hand, autonomy from powers that possess no specifically intellectual legitimacy and, on the other, the opposition to the dominating factions of the ruling class. Maintaining his right to autonomy now against the latter disposition and trying thus to gain acceptance[45] for his heretical habitus, Enzensberger's position becomes an explosive one. This makes him the principal witness for the conservative forces in the field,[46] making him all the more suspicious to the Left.[47]

It would be a mistake, though, to extrapolate the tendentiously anti-intellectual position at the end of the 1980s into the present time; as a motive for writing, anti-intellectualism fades into the background in the more recent essays. Again, this renewed change can be explained by the interrelation between subject aspect and field aspect. The fact that Enzensberger saw in the old Federal Republic a civil society of cultural mediocrity, shying away from utopias, but stable and acceptable to a large part of the population with a reassuring level of liberalness, made it easier for him to assume the mantle of serene observer posing as the man sounding the all-clear to a moralizing intelligentsia's well-rehearsed gesture of admonishment and warning. As *Civil War* and *Great Migration* reveal, this serenity has meanwhile given way to worry: in the new Germany, the civil substance of society threatens to erode, allowing new barbarism to gain ground. In a changed political climate where it has become part of normal life that foreigners have to fear for life and limb, because it so pleases an unleashed mob, and cannot feel certain of protection by the state's monopoly of force, restitution of a committed attitude becomes Enzensberger's duty – a committed attitude, however, of the unpretentious kind; its objective is the defence of a bare minimum of civilization.

We find ourselves below this minimum, the sarcastic diagnosis tells us, if the state apparatus shows 'sympathetic lenience for killers', if politicians become social therapists in the face of arson and homicide, making allowances for the 'regrettable deficiencies in the education system, especially in the former GDR', 'the harsh reality of unemployment', and 'the killer's cultural disorientation': 'All in all, we were dealing with "poor souls" who had to be treated with the utmost patience. It was hardly possible to expect such underprivileged persons to realize that setting fire to children is, strictly speaking, not permissible' (*CW*, 143, 142).

The altered situation does not, however, lead him to confuse morals with politics; a mistake he continues to accuse the indigenous protest milieu of making. The literary intellectual sees his task much more in intervening in an intellectual field of forces that has dangerously shifted centre – in a way that demonstrates learnedness and a readiness to enlighten while distancing himself from the discourse that has been systematically deformed by the relevant party headquarters and opinion leaders, as in the case of 'foreign infiltration'. For Enzensberger, objectifying protest against the creeping barbarism constitutes a political act. It is not multicultural idylls that *Great Migration* mobilizes against the ever less disguised appearance of xenophobia but unobtrusive representation of the situation and historical memory; as when proving that the ethnic homogeneity of the German nation has always been fictitious, that the local population has been much more the historical result of huge migration movements. Seen in this light, the widespread hysteria in the immigration question can only be explained by collective amnesia. Of course it is easy enough for Enzensberger to draw attention to the grotesque contradiction of chauvinist delusions: on the one hand, to announce 'the boat is full', and on the other hand, to paint a bleak picture of the Germans becoming extinct – a case of 'demographic bulimia' (*CW*, 117). More important, because more difficult, is his own description of the problem which strives for materialist rationality. Enzensberger stresses that it is not the case that dubious imaginary values such as 'cultural identity' are at stake in the immigration question, this being what conservative propagandists try to make us believe. First and foremost it is a matter of struggles over the distribution of material resources. Not the strangers as such are the object of aggression in the Western nations but poverty as a characteristic property: 'The Indian astrophysicist, the star Chinese architect, the Black Nobel Prize-Winner are welcome all over the world. The rich are also never mentioned in this context; no one questions their freedom of movement...Where bank accounts look healthy, xenophobia disappears as if by magic...But strangers are all the stranger if they are poor' (*CW*, 121).

For the observer socialized by Marxism the migration movements are the inevitable consequence of the world market that condemns entire groups of people to economic redundancy, thus compelling them to emigrate. He calls the common distinction made by the state apparatus between acceptable and illegitimate asylum seekers, i.e. between those who are persecuted for political reasons and those who are 'merely' economic refugees, mendacious and anachronistic: 'Corruption, indebtedness, flight of capital, hyper-inflation, exploitation, ecological catastrophes, religious fanaticism and sheer incompetence can reach a level which provides just as solid reasons for flight as the direct threat of prison, torture or shooting' (*CW*, 127).

Avowedly, Enzensberger does not possess simple solutions to the political dispute about immigration any more than any other person. He also feels no desire to identify with one of the conflicting political camps. On the contrary, he attempts to avoid the fixations of the present debate in the media, 'the contradiction between deliberate underestimation and denunciation, idyll and panic' (*CW*, 135). He does not venture to predict exactly to what degree the Federal Republic, for instance, can become what it is known to be: a country of immigration. The historical and current experience of nations of immigrants and multinational states seems ambivalent to him and cannot, therefore, furnish unequivocal conclusions. Structural unemployment and the considerable reluctance on the part of locals to extend their solidarity to people foreign to the country make him feel rather sceptical; both factors that a serious political discourse plainly cannot ignore. Still the diagnostician does not act fatalistically towards them but confronts the widespread exclusion mentality with this account: 'The more fiercely civilization defends itself against an external threat and puts up barriers around itself, the less, in the end, it has left to defend. But, as far as the barbarians are concerned, we need not expect them at the gates. They are already with us' (*CW*, 138).

Enzensberger's new alarmism is a 'castling' of objectifying (*Great Migration*) and dramatizing (*Civil War*) strategies. Characterized by carefully considered dramatizing, for instance, is the speech about the molecular civil war, which totalizes a leitmotif, reducing most disparate phenomena like hooliganism on the one hand, and the atrocities in Bosnia on the other, to a common denominator that, if looked for, is readily found as well: autism, self-destruction, lack of conviction and purpose of the perpetrators, devoid of ideological trimmings. The text works in the manner of pre-programmed self-affirmation, akin, in its unmistakable allergy to clear differentiations, to the formation of quite a few postmodern theories. But its thrust is not purely directed, as often assumed, towards cultural pessimism. Enzensberger constructs a complexity of terror in order to diminish it pragmatically in a second step. He shares and represents a collective perception that finds itself overtaxed by the media-transported ubiquity of horrible pictures. From this situation he derives the inevitable necessity to select from the terrors and establish one's priorities. 'Everywhere we look the war is on our own doorstep' (*CW*, 69): but only at one's own doorstep commitment is credible, because only there it promises success. In this sense, the aesthetics of oppressive totalization surprisingly leads to an ethic of the local.

The dismissal of an ethical universalism that feels responsible for everything is not motivated cynically (any more), but pragmatically, because only that dismissal sharpens one's senses for the possibilities and duties: 'Our priority is not Somalia, but Hoyerswerda and Rostock, Mölln and Solingen' (*CW*, 69). It is this setting of ethical universalism against the more 'doable' ethic of graded responsibility that distinguishes Enzensberger from the present intellectual field. The objection put forward against ethical universalism during the times of *Mediocrity* emphasized its superfluousness, the current one, however, its action-blocking effect – a change of angle that marks the transition from an anti-intellectual to an intellectual position. This primary motive now overlaps signals of delimitation against a merely sermonizing protest, which he does in fact attack as being on a zero level of political thinking.

Meanwhile, Enzensberger does not distance himself from the Left as such, but from its moral narcissism that contents itself with portraying violent criminals as victims of their environment and thus relieving them of the responsibility for their deeds. As he does in *Great Migration*, he sets the analytical tradition of Marxism against 'political kitsch' (*CW*, 34) as well as against the conservative complaint about the decay of values, and identifies the perpetrators all over the world as the losers of the capitalist modernization process. Whoever wants to denounce Enzensberger as an ideological turncoat should at least take note of that. However, he does not derive a revolutionary perspective from the Marxist method: 'The losers, far from regrouping under a common banner are hard at work on their own self-destruction, and capital is retreating from the battlefields wherever possible' (*CW*, 34). What remains is a sober semi-Marxism that has to do without an edifying utopia.

The double delimination against the prevailing discourse and a disorientated Left can also be gauged from the way in which Enzensbergers shows off to his advantage his specific capital as a literary intellectual. He intervenes in the form of linguistic criticism when, watchful against misleading collective symbols, he not only dismisses the assertion that 'the boat is full' as being far from reality but also tracks down its imprinted phantasm that it is oneself, and not at all the migrants, who are threatened with destruction. Besides that 'classical' way of criticism – proof of false consciousness – he perfects the more subtle one of threading into his own speech a literary subtext that allows for vicious elucidation of a problem in a flash. Varying the words of another literary intellectual, he phrases his criticism of the self-hatred of German political Protestantism to which large parts of the Left – in his opinion – have regressed: 'Would it not be easier/For the preachers/ To dissolve the people/And elect another one?' (*CW*, 132). Employing this subtext, Enzensberger signals not only the relevance to the current situation of literary cognition in general, he also refers, laden with distinction, to a truly political habitus that does not confuse commitment with (multicultural) wishful thinking. That literary subtext functions as a trump card in the struggle for power of definition in the intellectual field: to allude to Brecht in such a way means to snatch him from the milieu under attack.

The literary intellectual achieves the highest gain in prestige if he succeeds in talking more illuminatingly, because differently, about political problems. Enzensberger elevates the 'story of the railway carriage' to a lucid parable on the relationship of the Germans to their new fellow citizens wherein the passengers, hardly having secured seats for themselves, behave toward newcomers as though they had been there all along. But it is a sign of intellectual honesty to limit the suggestion of comparability at once. The consequences of xenophobia, the master of metaphor admits, 'go beyond a reluctance to move closer together in the first class compartment. Since 1991 they have reached the dimensions of organized manhunt' (*CW*, 129). Making the problem literary is not an ideal path. The essayist is acting politically everytime he allows the lyric poet to inspire him, but not to entice him into imaginary solutions to the problems.

NOTES

1 Pierre Bourdieu, *Die Intellektuellen und die Macht*, Hamburg, 1991, p. 42.
2 Bourdieu, *Die Intellektuellen und die Macht*, p. 42.
3 This point is argued in greater detail in Pierre Bourdieu, 'The Field of Cultural Production, or The Economic World Reversed', *Poetics*, 12 (1983), pp. 311-56. 'Every position-taking is defined in relation to the space of possibles which is objectively realized as a problematic in the form of the actual or potential position-taking corresponding to the different positions; and it receives its distinctive value from its negative relationship with the coexistent position-takings to which it is objectively related and which determine it by delimiting it. It follows from this, for example, that a prise de position changes, even when it remains identical, whenever there is a change in the universe of options that are simultaneously offered for producers and consumers to choose from' (p. 313).
4 Hans Magnus Enzensberger, 'Berliner Gemeinplätze', in *Palaver. Politische Überlegungen (1967-1973)*, Frankfurt/Main, 1974, pp. 7-40, here p. 14.
5 Hans Magnus Enzensberger, 'Gemeinplätze, die Neueste Literatur betreffend', in *Palaver. Politische Überlegungen (1967-1973)*, pp. 41-54, here p. 53.
6 Interview mit Hans Magnus Enzensberger, in *Weimarer Beiträge*, 5/1971, p. 77.
7 Hans Magnus Enzensberger, *Mittelmaß und Wahn. Gesammelte Zerstreuungen*, Frankfurt/Main, 1988 (abbreviation: *MW*). All quotations in English are from the English edition, *Mediocrity and Delusion. Collected Diversions*, London, 1992 (abbreviation: *MD*).
8 Hans Magnus Enzensberger, *Civil War*, London, 1994 (abbreviation: *CW*).
9 *MD*, p. 11.
10 Cf. Theodor W. Adorno, *Ästhetische Theorie*, Frankfurt/Main, 1992, p. 194: 'Zugleich ist das Bedürfnis der Werke nach Interpretation als der Herstellung ihres Wahrheitsgehalts Stigma ihrer konstitutiven Unzulänglichkeit'.
11 Susan Sontag, *Against Interpretation and Other Essays*, London, 1966, p. 7.
12 *MD*, p. 26.
13 *MD*, p. 26.
14 *MD*, p. 29.
15 Ulrich Greiner, 'Stichworte zur geistigen Korruption der Zeit', in *Die Zeit*, 7.10. 1988.
16 *MD*, p. 33.
17 *MD*, p. 55.
18 *MD*, p. 56.
19 *MD*, pp. 104-105: 'Today there is no longer any life outside what was once, in 1968, called "the system" and today goes by the more modest name of "the world market"...Only someone who seriously hopes for the collapse of the global economy, with all the consequences that entails, and who is capable of thinking another option through to its conclusion, can expect something good from the abolition of the two monsters'.
20 *MD*, p. 105.
21 *MW*, p. 134.
22 Georg Büchner, 'Dantons Tod', in *Sämtliche Werke nebst Briefen und Dokumenten*, Berlin, Darmstadt, 1985, pp. 37-113, here p. 57.
23 *MW*, p. 135: 'Die aberwitzigen steuerlichen und sozialstaatlichen Regelungen, die wir den Bonner Parteien verdanken, haben die Deutschen zu einem Volk von Trickbetrügern gemacht. Wer sich nicht darauf

versteht, nach Strich und Faden abzuschreiben, einzuklagen, rauszuholen, abzusetzen, der hat hier nichts zu lachen'.

24 Ibid., p. 138.

25 *MD*, p. 141.

26 *MD*, p. 129.

27 *MD*, p. 188.

28 *MD*, p. 168.

29 *MD*, p. 169.

30 *MD*, p. 177.

31 *MD*, p. 179.

32 *MD*, p. 185.

33 Quoted in *MD*, p. 170.

34 Hans Magnus Enzensberger, *Politische Brosamen*, Frankfurt/Main, 1982, p. 195.

35 Enzensberger, *Politische Brosamen*, pp. 19-20.

36 Enzensberger, *Politische Brosamen*, p. 193.

37 According to Bourdieu, this ist the unified perception, thought and action pattern of a social agent in all fields of activity, the individually anchored, experienced and observable but class-specific acquired generation principle of 'klassifizierbarer Praxisformen und Werke zum einen, der Unterscheidung und Bewertung der Formen und Produkte (Geschmack) zum anderen'. Bourdieu, *Die Feinen Unterschiede*, Frankfurt/Main, 1982, p. 278.

38 'Du riechst nicht gut. Dich gibt's zu oft': 'An einen Mann in der Trambahn', in Hans Magnus Enzensberger, *verteidigung der wölfe*, Frankfurt/Main, 1957, p. 74.

39 Wolfgang Pohrt, 'Loblieder auf die Inkonsequenz', in *Der Spiegel*, 52, 1982, p. 108: 'Die Verharmlosung der Realität infiziert das Denken selber mit einer Kraftlosigkeit, welche den beschworenen Verhältnissen angemessen ist, den wirklichen freilich nicht'.

40 Hermann L. Gremliza, 'Journal des Luxus und der Moden', in *Literatur Konkret*, 1980, p. 8.

41 Pierre Bourdieu, *Zur Soziologie der symbolischen Formen*, Frankfurt/Main, 1974, p. 89.

42 Cf. Bourdieu, 'The Field of Cultural Production', pp. 312-313: 'The literary or artistic field is a field of forces, but it is also a field of struggles tending to transform or conserve this field of forces. The network of objective relations between position subtends and orients the strategies which the occupants of the different positions implement in their struggles to defend or improve their positions (i.e. their position-takings), strategies which depend for their force and form on the position each agent occupies in the power relations (rapports de force)'.

43 *MD*, p. 69.

44 *MD*, p. 41.

45 Cf. Pierre Bourdieu, *Sozialer Raum und 'Klassen'. Zwei Vorlesungen*, Frankfurt/Main, 1985, p. 75: 'Der Antrieb [of a social agent, M.J]...steckt weder im materiellen oder symbolischen Zweck des Handelns, wie der naive Finalismus, noch in den Zwängen des Feldes, wie die mechanistische Sicht es will. Er steckt in der Verbindung von Habitus und Feld, so daß der Habitus selber das mitbestimmt, was ihn bestimmt'.

46 Cf. Frank Schirrmacher, 'Verteidiger der Wölfe', in *Frankfurter Allgemeine Zeitung*, 13.11.1989: 'Wenn man eines Tages die psychische Konstitution Westdeutschlands als etwas Unverständliches und Fernes notiert, wird man in ihm den Archäologen deutscher Befindlichkeiten sehen'.

47 Cf. Eberhard Falcke, 'Märchen vom goldenen Mittelweg', in *Der Spiegel*, 4, 1989, pp. 198-190: 'Und angesichts der Tatsache, daß der Essayist Enzensberger bar jeder Lust scheint, andere Themen als derartige

Salonspäße [tv as 'zero medium', M.J.] zur Beschäftigung seines beweglichen Geistes aufzutreiben, ist auch die Frage, ob er das denn wirklich alles ernst meint...hinfällig, ganz abgesehen davon, daß die Einfälle, die er auf seiner Zauberbühne der Geistesblitze inszeniert, in den Feuilletons der Republik gern unbesehen als Beweisstück gehandelt werden...Er setzt an zum Staatsdichter, der den historisch heimatlosen und von Gewissensqualen zermürbten Bundesdeutschen eine wunderschöne Republik zusammenreimt'.

Chapter Three

What's Left? – Enzensberger and the Role of the Intellectual in Germany

David Roberts

In 1962 Jürgen Habermas published *The Structural Transformation of the Public Sphere*, his account of the emergence of the bourgeois public sphere, its normative function and its disintegration in the society of mass culture and mass communications. In the same year Hans Magnus Enzensberger, born like Habermas in 1929, published *Einzelheiten*, which opened with the short but influential essay 'Consciousness Industry'. Habermas's book and Enzensberger's essay are both responses to Adorno's essay on the culture industry in *Dialectic of Enlightenment*. Both pose the question of the role of the intellectual in relation to structural changes to the public sphere, a question that Habermas returns to in his 1986 essay, 'Heinrich Heine and the role of the intellectual in Germany'.[1] We can perhaps best approach this essay through the literary debates sparked off by the collapse of the German Democratic Republic. The caesura of 1989 offered the inescapable and irresistible occasion for historical revisions of East and West German literature since 1945 as represented most prominently by the one postwar generation in both East and West, that is, the contemporaries of Enzensberger. A key focus of these literary-historical retrospectives was the literary opposition of the 1950s and 60s in West Germany (*Gruppe 47*) and the literary dissidents of the 1970s and 80s (Heym, Müller, Wolf, Braun) in East Germany, bundled together under the one heading, justification and accusation: *Gesinnungsästhetik* (aesthetics of conviction).[2] This term, derived from Max Weber's famous distinction between *Gesinnungsethik* and *Verantwortungsethik* (ethic of responsibility), is difficult to translate and is in this sense indicative of a specifically German phenomenon, the long tradition of the antagonistic relationship between intellectuals and the German state. It is Habermas's contention in his essay on Heine that the conflict between *Geist* and *Macht* is a consequence and reflection of the absence of a functioning political public sphere in Germany up to 1945.

If 1945 signified a new beginning for West Germany, this of course was not the case for East Germany. The one party state conserved the negative symbiosis of *intellectuals and power* up to 1989, with all the accompanying intellectual deformations of an heretical literary opposition, more royal and loyal than the king to the dream of a true socialism, the dream of a republic of the intellectuals.[3] The East German public sphere remained fixed at the stage of its historical genesis, the literary public sphere. We can thus ask whether it makes sense to place East and West German literature under the one heading of *Gesinnungsästhetik*. The answer must be yes, insofar as the democratization of West German society was necessarily a slow process, apparent only in retrospect. In the 1950s and 60s it seemed as though the *Gruppe 47* was the moral-critical substitute not only for an effective political opposition but also for a public sphere as yet unsure of itself. In fact the 1960s was the crucial decade for the consolidation of the public sphere – indeed, one might almost say, of the birth of the public political sphere from the spirit of literary opposition. On the one hand we have electoral support by prominent members of the *Gruppe 47* for the Social Democrats, on the other the apparent crisis of democracy precipitated by the Grand Coalition and the accompanying radicalization of protest in the student revolt. The happy end of the story comes with the victory of the Social Democratic Party in 1969 and the election of Gustav Heinemann as President of the Federal Republic. For Günter Grass and Jürgen Habermas, 1969 represented an historical turning point: the moment of the symbolic reconciliation and defusion of the conflict between *Geist* und *Macht*. Democracy had proved itself; West Germany had at last (re)joined the Western world.[4]

The democratic normalization of political life, that is, the constitution of the public sphere as the mediating instance between state and society is, as Habermas reminds us in 1986, the condition of the normal role of the intellectual and of the acceptance of this role by the public. Habermas contrasts the post-1945 process of normalization with the incipient civil war of the Weimar Republic, where all the intellectual groupings, for all their bitter differences, had one thing in common: they were intellectuals, who did not want to be intellectuals, all defined in their different ways by an arrogant fetishization of *Geist* or a cynical adulation of power. Neither the Weimar Republic nor the Second Empire can offer Habermas a model for the engaged intellectual. As he observes, the Second Empire took from the Dreyfus Affair only the negative stereotype of the public intellectual, propagated by the French nationalist right, but not his positive embodiment in such figures as Zola, Anatole France or Jaurès – the heros of the 'un-German German', the *Zivilisationsliterat* Heinrich Mann. Habermas proposes as his model of the public intellectual Heine, whose union of German romanticism and French enlightenment endeared him neither to the right nor the left. Heine's exile from 1844 to 1856 stands as the index of an absent public sphere in Germany.

Why is Heine the representative intellectual for the second German republic? Habermas's answer – to simplify – is the following: between 1830 and 1848 Heine responded to the new situation of the writer after the end of the *Kunstperiode*, the new situation, that is, of the emergence of a political public sphere from the literary public sphere in the wake of the 1830 revolution by solving in exemplary fashion the crucial question of the relation between art and politics. Rejecting the false alternatives of identifying or dissociating art and politics, inherent in the unmediated opposition of *Geist* and *Macht*, Heine was able to combine political engagement with a respect for literary autonomy. Habermas stresses Heine's sensitivity to the power of the new medium of the press and his awareness of the consequences of this structural change for the writer and his communicative strategies.

The Heine of Habermas's essay is of course a Heine in Habermas's image. The 1986 essay could be read as an overture to the 'Historians' Debate' of the same year: Habermas speaks of the normalization of the public engagement of the writer and intellectual which has occurred since 1945 as the precondition for the formation of a post-conventional national identity, which has assimilated Heine's own painful, critical and self-critical relation to Germany. For Habermas the normative and normalization go together. It enables him in 1986 to span the gap between the idea of the bourgeois public sphere in the eighteenth century, Heine as the embodiment of the public intellectual in relation to the emerging public political sphere between 1830 and 1848, and the Federal Republic. In 1962, however, the idea of the public sphere in *Structural Transformations of the Public Sphere* served as the critique of its disintegration under the impact of structural change, i.e., the society of mass communications, which has replaced cultural reception by cultural consumption, the printed by the visual image, publicity in the original Enlightenment sense by public relations, opinion polls and market research. This tension between the normative and normalization brings me back to Enzensberger, hailed by Alfred Andersch in the late 1950s as a new Heine. Is Enzensberger, with his combination of poetry and publicity, his romantic and enlightenment allegiances, the new version of the old model of the intellectual in the age of the consciousness industry? Does he manifest a comparable sensitivity to structural changes in the public sphere? I would like to suggest that Enzensberger's trajectory from normative beginnings to the defence of normality and the praise of mediocrity[5] in the 1980s charts in its own way a representative story, in which he plays through the rise and fall of the public intellectual in the Federal Republic.

This alternative version of normalization starts from the transformation of the public sphere into an omnipresent consciousness industry against which the intellectual is pitted as the critical voice of dissent. If 1969 signified for Habermas the moment of the reconciliation of *Geist* and *Macht*, 1968 for Enzensberger signifies the moment of their apparently irreconcilable opposition, which sets in train, however, a self-critical dissection of the role of the intellectual, whose outcome is the reversal of his original normative self-understanding. By the 1980s, Enzensberger has come to understand normalization as the process by which society has emancipated itself from its intellectuals. Up to 1968 the task of the intellectual was conceived as that of liberating the benighted mass of the population from false consciousness, culminating in the 'gigantic project' of the political alphabetization of Germany, a project, which Enzensberger hastens to assure us, will also involve the 'long and painful process' of the self-education of the educators.[6] The conclusion of this painful process is the realization that intellectuals can liberate themselves from their own false consciousness only by learning from the silent majority, which prefers normality and mediocrity to the blind uncompromising idealism of the committed. An indication of the distance Enzensberger has travelled since the 1960s is given by his 1988 gloss on the antithesis of *Geist* and *Macht*, which is dismissed as 'a German game of cowboys and Indians'.[7] Intellectuals and politicians like to think of themselves as enemies even though they share the same narcissistic conviction that they are responsible for the public good. The truth of the matter, however, is that they have fallen victim to the structural transformations of society which have dethroned *both intellect* and *power*. A self-organizing society[8] – or in Niklas Luhmann's terminology, an autopoietic social system – no longer needs a normative public sphere. Enzensberger echoes here Luhmann's 1971 debate with Habermas, where Luhmann argued that a functionally differentiated society cannot form a rational identity, indeed cannot even be thought of in terms of identity. There is no privileged vantage point of observation above and outside society which could justify the supposedly superior insight of critical theory.

Luhmann's enlightenment of the enlighteners, which continues the post-1945 attacks on intellectuals by Helmut Schelsky and Arnold Gehlen, discussed by Habermas in his Heine essay, could be taken as the end point of Enzensberger's revisionism. Enzensberger's progression from the 1960s to the 1980s appears in this light as an odyssey of the self-critical intellectual who finally arrives at an ironic reconciliation with normality. There is another reading of Enzensberger's progression – which I shall call the romantic as opposed to the enlightenment version – but before considering this I would like to outline the four stages and the three self-critical leaps of Enzensberger's work up to 1989.

Stage One (1957-1964): Here we have an Enzensberger, the literary intellectual in Heine's image negotiating in assured fashion the borderlines between poetry and politics, while skilfully playing the 'dangerous game' with the intellectual's partner and enemy, the consciousness industry.[9] We could call this first stage Past Present, since the poet's self-understanding is overshadowed on the one hand by the Third Reich and on the other by the sense of the historicity of modern poetry and the avantgarde.

Stage Two (1965-1974): Enzensberger's first self-critical leap catapults him out of the ranks of the literary opposition into political activism. The time has come for time-tables (*Kursbücher*) instead of aesthetic proclamations. Now that the political irrelevance of literature, co-opted by the market, has become manifest, cultural revolution will be a revolution without literature, aimed at the cultural apparatus of the consciousness industry. We may call this stage, whose highpoint is 1968, Future Present. Is is succeeded in

Stage Three (1975-1980) by the return to poetry. Enzensberger's second self-critical leap takes him from the Future Present to the Future Past. After surveying the archeology of modernity in the mausoleum of progress and sinking the *Titanic*, Enzensberger renames his muse the 'Fury of Disappearance' and announces 'I like to recall the future'.[10] But he also observes: 'But even catastrophe isn't what it used to be'.[11] This third stage is an extended meditation on progress and apocalypse, temporality and transience, presided over by Benjamin's Angel of History, which opens the way to

Stage Four (1981-1989) and Enzensberger's own secular version of Benjamin's *Jetztzeit*, accomplished by the third self-critical leap out of the Future Past into the Present Imperfect. The principle of a normal, i.e., imperfect present, is the principle of life, that is, compromise, correction, revision. History carries a salutary warning for all intellectuals, for all German fetishists of the spirit: adapt or perish! Survival demands 'the end of consequentiality' (1981) and the recovery of the freedom of movement which only opportunism can assure.[12]

This gives the cue for an alternative reading of Enzensberger's progression, which replaces the odyssey of self-enlightenment and its ambiguous version of survival with a romantic game of masks – romantic in the sense intended by Carl Schmitt's critique of romantic occasionalism in his *Political Romanticism*. In this perspective Enzensberger appears as a master of metamorphosis but also as a faithful mimic of the times.

In stage one he presents a model Adorno-style intellectual, who walks the tight rope of poetic autonomy and political engagement, flanked by the museum of modernism on the left and the consciousness industry on the right.

In stage two he transforms himself into a model Sixty-Eighter, agitator, ideology-critic and preceptor in one, denouncing with scorn the alibi function of a morally 'engaged' literature, which hides its political regression behind the gestures of avantgardism and attempts in vain to square the circle of autonomy and engagement.

In stage three Enzensberger throws away the mask of cultural revolution to become the model of leftist melancholy. Documentary agitation mutates into poetic elegy as the erstwhile revolutionary swims away from the wreck of the future that was, surrounded by the flotsam of history: 'difficult to say why, crying I swim on' (*...schwer zu sagen, warum, heule und schwimme ich weiter*). There is no need to despair, however. *The Sinking of the Titanic* is subtitled *A comedy*. Enzensberger has another surprise in store for us. Just as stage two delivered the rhetorical self-critique of stage one, so stage four will mock mercilessly the apocalyptic melancholy of hope abandoned.

In stage four Enzensberger declares that the game of public intellectual is over. The masks have been used up and the time has come to reveal the plain face of common sense. And what common sense tells us is that opportunism is the best cure for melancholy. But before we take our romantic occasionalist to task, we should recall that common sense has solved the riddle of the consciousness industry. If literature has lost its social function, the same fate has befallen the consciousness industry. A self-organizing normality can do without either. Literature has been granted a nature reserve to share with the happy few. And the consciousness industry has at last found its true hygienic purpose – brain washing. Television is the ultimate Nirvana-machine. We switch on in order to switch off.[13]

Where does this leaves us? If we take Enzensberger as our example, we are left with the self-abdicating intellectual. If we take Habermas as our example, the public intellectual continues to play his normative role in relation to a normalized public sphere. The post-1945 process of democratic normalization, which for Habermas has enfranchised the public function of the intellectual, is interpreted by Enzensberger as the normality which has disenfranchised the intellectual. In Habermas's case, it is clear, modernity remains an incomplete project: the idea of communicative rationality supposes personal autonomy and a social subject, and thus the intellectual who carries on his modern role. In Enzensberger's case, social normality serves to register the reality of a self-sufficient process of rationalization, which no longer needs a social subject and accordingly has made the public intellectual superfluous. Enzensberger's conclusion, which completes his account of the process of normalization and the rise and fall of the public intellectual between the 1960s and the 1980s, poses two questions. Does this make the intellectual who has survived his own demise the voice of the unspoken consensus of the silent majority? What happens when the social normality of the 1980s disintegrates in the 1990s?

Civil War (1993) can be seen as responding to both questions, while at the same time seeming to confirm the two readings of his progression – the self-critical enlightened realist and the romantic occasionalist – sketched above. Enzensberger's sudden discovery that the real existing utopia of *civil society* is in reality riven by the all pervasive violence of *civil war* appears as a volte-face of a quite alarming rhetorical occasionalism. But then again we can read his 'polemical pamphlet against the universalism of human rights' as the continuation of his campaign against the unrealistic convictions cherished by public intellectuals.[14] Enzensberger's version of an 'ethic of responsibility' (*Verantwortungsethik*), which declares ethnic cleansing in the former Yugoslavia none of our business, articulates a 'realism' which is a faithful echo of the changing times: his proclamation of the liquidation of the normative reflects all too accurately the 'responsible' consensus of a German and European normality in search of an alibi for its own self-willed unwillingness to defend human rights in Bosnia.

NOTES

1 Reprinted in Jürgen Habermas, *Eine Art Schadensabwicklung*, Frankfurt/Main, 1987.
2 See D. Roberts, 'Gesinnungsästhetik? Günter Grass, "Schreiben nach Auschwitz" (1990)', in *Poetik der Autoren*, ed. P.M. Lützeler, Frankfurt/Main, 1994, pp. 235-261.
3 See D. Roberts, 'The GDR, Dissidents and the Redemptive Paradigm', *European Studies Journal* X, 1/2 (1993), pp. 313-332.
4 See D. Roberts, 'The Historikerstreit. The Self-Understanding of the Federal Republic and the Self-Understanding of a Generation: Jürgen Habermas and Günter Grass', *Thesis Eleven*, 30 (1991), pp. 33-55.
5 'Zur Verteidigung der Normalität' (1982) in H. M. Enzensberger, *Politische Brosamen*, Frankfurt/Main, 1982; 'Mittelmaß und Wahn. Ein Vorschlag zur Güte', in H. M. Enzensberger, *Mittelmaß und Wahn*, Frankfurt/Main, 1988.
6 'Gemeinplätze, die Neueste Literatur betreffend' (1968) in H. M. Enzensberger, *Palaver. Politische Überlegungen* (1967-1973), Frankfurt/Main, 1974, p.53.
7 'Macht und Geist. Ein deutsches Indianerspiel', in H.M. Enzensberger, *Mittelmaß und Wahn*.
8 See 'Vermutungen über die Turbulenz', (1989) in H.M. Enzensberger, *Der fliegende Robert*, Frankfurt/Main, 1989.
9 'Es handelt sich nicht darum, die Bewußtseins-Industrie ohnmächtig zu verwerfen, sondern darum, sich auf ihr gefährliches Spiel einzulassen', in H. M. Enzensberger, 'Bewußtseins-Industrie', *Einzelheiten*, Frankfurt/Main, 1962, p. 15.
10 H. M. Enzensberger, *Gedichte*, Frankfurt/Main, 1983, p. 394.
11 'Randbemerkungen zum Weltuntergang', (1978) in *Der fliegende Robert*, p. 281.
12 'Das Ende der Konsequenz' in *Der fliegende Robert*.
13 'Das Nullmedium oder Warum alle Klagen über das Fernsehen gegenstandslos sind', (1988) in *Mittelmaß und Wahn*.
14 Axel Honneth, 'Universalismus als moralische Falle. Bedingungen und Grenzen einer Politik der Menschenreche', *Merkur*, Sept/Oct. 1994, pp. 867-83.

Chapter Four

Can the Republic Be Lived In? Enzensberger's *Great Migration* and *Civil War* Viewed Against the Background of His Literary Development Since 1960

Horst Domdey

I 1960: Pluralism and 'Community' in Italy

Enzensberger was already talking about the 'Civil War of the Century' in 1960, before he turned to Marxism – admittedly in a completely different way than thirty years later in *Aussichten auf den Bürgerkrieg*. The Italian 'civil war' of the fifties appeared tolerant and liveable. In his contribution to the anthology *Ich lebe in der Bundesrepublik. Fünfzehn Deutsche über Deutschland*, edited by Wolfgang Weyrauch and published in 1960, Enzensberger accentuated his disassociation from the Federal Republic: 'I don't live in the Federal Republic'.[1] He emphasized: 'I don't like the cafés in Düsseldorf. Gulping down whipped cream on the set of a *Ufa* film from the mid-thirties, a nightmare in three-four time. They still won't take any responsibilty for items of clothing left in the cloakroom. It's a sinister remake, somewhere between *Serenade* and *Wunschkonzert*, between *Bel ami* and *Jud Süß*'.[2] But Italy was another story. A person could live in a place like Lanuvio, near Rome: 'In the Pasticceria Mazzini we can play lottery and win a piglet, we can weigh ourselves, we can make phone calls, buy Easter Bunnies and stamps...We can pass on our regards to *signor il dottore*, flirt, argue, read Adorno, play rock 'n' roll, have coffee roasted, make a contract, debate about the Holy Trinity or the art of boxing. We can ogle at Sophia's breasts, order a barrel of wine or a taxi, write poetry, bribe the tax collector, organise christenings, catch the latest gossip, booze with the drivers and send the *Democrazia Cristiana* to Purgatory with the blessing of All Saints. In our café on the corner we've got a community, a civil society (*Gesellschaft*)'.[3] Even here, Enzensberger adds, 'the civil war of the century is brewing, but both parties are not blowing on the fires...Here, no-one is more Russian than the Russians, nor more American than the White House. Here, communists are people too; yes, there are even capitalists here who are people, and you can make fun of the fascists without getting goosebumps while you're at it. So even the fascists are people. A country where everyone sees everyone else as being people could never be divided'.[4]

The time would come when Enzensberger would attribute to a pluralized and mentally relaxed Federal Republic the quality of being a *civil society, or community*, of living and letting live, of carrying on social intercourse across the borders of differences and even contrasting views. But that was to be thirty years later, in 1988.[5] Shortly thereafter, in 1993, he was to return all the more vehemently to the subject of 'civil war', in a universal sense, not just referring to Germany and Europe. But there was no more talk of an Italian-style liveability of such a war. The 'civil war' of the nineties appears to Enzensberger to be unconstrained, destroying any liveability.

II Materialist Perspective

A look at the path taken by Enzensberger since 1968 should be illuminating. It will show not only the illusions and disillusionments he had to experience, but also which of his ideals and perspectives have remained stable, in spite of his flexibility. In *Great Migration* and *Civil War* this meant, amongst other things, retaining a grasp of the materialistic grand view:

> Only an idiot would argue that just because Marxist analysis is out of fashion, it is no longer useful. Few dispute that the world market, now that it is no longer a vision of the future but a global reality, produces fewer winners and more losers as each year passes. This is not confined to the Second and Third Worlds, but applies equally in the core capitalist countries. Where, there, whole countries, or even whole continents, drop out of the international exchange system, here, increasing sections of the population can no longer keep up in the competition for advantage that gets more brutal by the day. (CW, 34)

Whether the statement that the global market produces more losers than winners is true or not is neither here nor there. This thesis is a prerequisite for understanding Enzensberger's warnings of the 'great migration' and 'civil war'. The statement represents one point of consistency since 1968: the conviction that the capitalist world market is a reality and must therefore be the basis for every analysis.

In 1993, Enzensberger is playing again the role of Cassandra, conjuring up a vision of the great crisis of capitalism which, according to him, is losing all its power of social and economic integration. He feels that whole areas of the world's population are being excluded and pushed to the margins. This was the classic point of view in the 1960s as well: it was the base from which world revolution was imagined. But now Enzensberger resists the temptation to draw up plans for a revival of the revolutionary horizon, in spite of his adherence to a basically Marxist view. But, even in view of the looming global crisis, so tempting to the anti-capitalist theorists' urge to speculate, Enzensberger has remained consistently faithful to his programme of disillusionment since 1969/70.

The differences in his attitude between '68 and now are immense. They concern above all the interpretation of the Federal Republic of Germany, which was considered fascist by the Left then. One can see how Enzensberger, in 1992/1993, avoids anything which would still appear to support such a view today, even though his 'footnote' to *Great Migration*, entitled 'Peculiarities of the Manhunt', identifies the Federal Republic as the area of the hunt. According to Enzensberger, the neo–Nazis' attacks on people and property did not make the Republic fascist.

III 1965 to 1968: The 'masked fascism' of the Federal Republic

In June 1968, Enzensberger had discerned an ongoing continuity since 1933:

> The old fascism was a parody of revolution. It lived on robbery, what it had stolen from socialism after ambushing it, in terms of tactics, strategy and psychic impetus. It understood itself as a movement which was mobilizing the masses. It depended on those on the margins of society, the non-integrated and the prevaricators
> Neo-fascism is a parody of counter-revolution. It exists on what was built up during the time of the 'economic miracle'. All that is available to it in terms of tactics, strategy and psychic impetus are the left-overs from the era of anti-communism and the Cold War. It considers itself to be a besieged fortress. It dare not mobilize the masses, but must keep them in check. It depends on the centre stratum of society, those who are integrated and hang on grimly to what they have. This neo-fascism is no longer just a threat, it has been reality for a long time: it is an everyday, monolithic, introverted, institutionally secure and masked fascism. A long–forgotten cigarette smoker in the late 50s found the words for its slogan and placed them in newspapers at the cost of those whom it was meant to stupefy: 'The class struggle is over'. After history has been purified, in other words done away with, all that should remain is the new guarantor of the future: the centre as the extreme.[6]

Twenty years later the centre appeared to be anything other than extreme to Enzensberger. But in the period of the criticism of the capitalist system during the early years of *Kursbuch*, he considered it impossible that the system could reform itself. Because the ruling class had supposedly regenerated itself, its core remaining intact: namely, financial and industrial capital wealth, ministerial and legal bureaucracy, the Churches and the military top brass. Only the big landowners could complain of having suffered losses for geographical reasons. The growth in the numbers of top officials of the Social Democrats and the union bureaucracy had not only *not* weakened the ruling class, it had strengthened it. The class consciousness of the latter was 'completely unbroken' at that time. Enzensberger paid his respect to this 'victory of the counter-revolution in West Germany': 'A ruling class which is capable of ruining the nation, without anyone resenting their having done it, and who can continue to rule it almost unharmed, deserves to be taken seriously'. He added: 'It deserves the respect of each and every cynic amongst us'.[7]

IV Revolution instead of Reform

Such sentences reveal the source of energy for the student movement; they mark the determination to break with the older generation. Here was a deep-rooted suspicion that the ruling class, the capitalists, had only accepted the rules of formal democracy under pressure from the Allies in order to survive, while they had 'never come to terms within themselves with this restriction'.[8] Thus, Enzensberger's acceptance speech on receiving the Culture Prize from his home town of Nuremberg, which he received in March 1967, turned out to be a vehement condemnation of 'class justice' in the Federal Republic. Based on documents received from the lawyer Heinrich Hannover, Enzensberger drew attention to 'the thousand or so criminal investigations (at least) instigated every year against politically motivated activists' – as a rule, of course, against communists or socialists. He announced the setting up of an aid fund for the legal costs of those accused, which he opened with the 6,000 DM he had just received for the culture prize. This speech created a scandal and eventually led to a question at Question Time in the *Bundestag* (which had to be answered by the then Minister of Justice, Gustav Heinemann, who was later to become President of the Federal Republic).[9]

Enzensberger was of the opinion that the *Grundgesetz,* given as a 'gift' to the Germans by the Allies had only been accepted by the ruling class under duress. It still had to be incorporated into society by a 'revolution from below', firmly anchoring the process of democratization and only then making the republic a place fit to live in. As a consequence, every reformist tendency (the most scandalous expression of which was, to the Left, the Grand Coalition of 1966) appeared to him to be a betrayal of 'real democracy'. For twenty years the bourgeois-left intellectuals in the Federal Republic, those 'model pupils of the reformists' had only made suggestions for tinkering with the inner workings of the system, but had 'not come up with any radical counter-proposals'.[10] However, this fools' paradise was now over, Enzensberger suggested, the period of self-deception had come to an end. Enzensberger's support of the 'revolution' grew out of his disillusionment with the reformism of the bourgeois moderates.

Consistent with this were the ominous opening words of his *Berliner Gemeinplätze* from 1968: 'There is a spectre haunting Europe, the spectre of revolution'. In the cultural/political magazine *Kursbuch,* which he had been editing since 1965, Enzensberger organized the discussion of the theoretical and practical possibilities of this revolution.[11] How the revolution was to appear in West Berlin and internationally was discussed in a critical but future-oriented manner.

Enzensberger tended to be reticent in his attitude towards 'existing' socialism and did not – as for example Peter Weiss had done – draw the conclusion that he should bang the drum for the GDR. In a documentary on the Kronstadt Rebellion of 1921, which had already been published in *Kursbuch* in 1967, Enzensberger quoted from Rosa Luxemburg's *The Russian Revolution* (1918) and drew attention to her demand for the democratization of the revolution. According to Luxemburg, general elections were necessary, not just *soviets*. He also quoted from the fliers put out by the Kronstadt student movement: 'What the workers and peasants need above all is freedom. They do not want rules and regulations handed down by the Bolsheviks. They want to decide their own lot. We demand the release of all detained socialists and party-neutral workers; the lifting of the state of emergency; freedom of the press, speech and the right of assembly for all workers; we demand freely-elected Works' Councils, union employees and freely-elected soviets'.[12] Socialist countries which took their lead from the Soviet Union – as for example the GDR had done – had no chance of being recognized as alternatives to capitalism. Not just that, Enzensberger went to Cuba in 1969. Only the Third World appeared to make the wholly Other real: the connection between socialism and democracy, the only acceptable kind of anti-capitalism.

V 1978: Disillusionment (*The Sinking of the Titanic*)

> Back then in Havana the plaster was peeling
> off the houses, a foul smell hung immovably
> over the harbour, everything from the old days
> was withering luxuriantly, night and day shortage
> was desperately gnawing away at the Ten Year Plan,
> and I was busy writing *Der Untergang der Titanic.*
> ...
> It'll be better tomorrow, and if not tomorrow,
> the day after tomorrow. Ah well – maybe not
> necessarily better, but different, completely different,
> at any rate. Everything will be different.
> A wonderful feeling.
> ...
> I am writing this in Berlin...
> I am freezing. I remember (hard to believe that it's not even
> ten years ago) the peculiarly light days of euphoria.
> ...
> And I was distracted and looked out over the harbour
> wall at the Caribbean Sea, and there I saw it, much
> larger and whiter than white, way out there, only I
> could see it and nobody else, in the dark bay, it was
> a cloudless night and the sea was black and smooth
> as a mirror, and there I saw the iceberg, unbelievably
> high and cold, like a cold fata morgana it was heading
> slowly, unstoppably, white, straight for me.[13]

While still in Havana in 1969, confronted with a crumbling Cuba, the process of 'unstoppable' disillusionment set in. The iceberg of demise – Enzensberger puts the open secret into words – comes from the warm waters of the Caribbean Sea and is the result of his experience in Cuba. The 'tropical festival', the time of euphoria, the projections – as if the Third World would reveal the beginning of the utopian Other – were at an end. Enzensberger ironises the projections of the socialist dreamers in his allegory of the exotic salon paintings of his *Titanic*. By using the symbol of sinking, he declares that the leftist ideas of the nineteenth century had made fools of themselves by becoming reality in the twentieth. All that remained was the devastating self-criticism of 1968: 'Prophets with their backs to the present.'

VI 1988: In Praise of Mediocrity

Twenty years after 1968 the 'centre stratum of society', 'those who were integrated', were once more at the centre of his attention. But his point of view had completely changed. Not the 'centre as an extreme' but the centre as the *middle* is now the object of his reflections. In his essay 'Mediocrity and Delusion' (1988) revolutionary tendencies, for example the terrorism of the Red Army Faction, appear as insanity – basically as an attack against the majority of the population. Enzensberger praises the mediocre; he values it as a plus for the state of civilization: '*This society is mediocre*. Its holders of power are mediocre, as are its works of art, its representatives and its taste, its joys, its opinions, its architecture, its media, its fears, its vices, suffering and traditions'. Of course this insight was not new: Enzensberger was only stating what was already a widely held opinion in 1988. But according to Enzensberger it was an insight that had 'something redeeming' to it, or so he provocatively put it.[14] And thus he enumerates the advantages of mediocrity:

> The majority of the population want to have nothing to do with political adventures, they reject all ideological fanaticism, any kind of utopia, and they are profoundly suspicious of totalitarian dreams. Their attitude is: 'Don't get carried away! We've already seen where that gets us'...This majority prefers to show its moderate side in the face of conflict. The class struggle is reduced to the level of national pay talks. The soft solution to questions concerning minorities is preferred. It has become a habit to appeal to tolerance and understanding...Social civil war has become unimaginable for this society. It is founded on pluralism and its highest virtue is indifference.[15]

The result of this social and cultural levelling is 'not the much-vaunted drab uniformity which had previously been described, but an exceptionally multi-faceted society': Enzensberger points out the tremendous growth in freedom, opportunity and choice. In such a society, politics is no longer 'experienced as the need to "make history" – an ambition which has regularly caused the Germans to fall flat on their faces –, but as an expression of the need to save your own scalp, and mainly against your own chiefs at that'.[16]

VII Can the Republic be lived in?

The turbulence caused by the new national and civil wars after 1989, the flood of refugees and the devastation caused by right-wing radicals have all forced this point of view into a crisis. Of course Enzensberger did not paint the 1980s as an idyll. In 1979 he had explained the 'secrets of German democracy' to a New York audience and pointed out the ambivalence inherent in a modernization of the German police in terms of psychology, ideology and technology:

> [The modern policeman] does not harbour any hate against intellectuals, not least because he counts himself as one of them...He is hardly interested in the past at all: he considers himself to be future-oriented. He usually feels politically most at home with the Social Democrats and sometimes with the liberal party. An excellent representative of this type is Dr. Herold, the President of the West German Federal CID. His power does not stem from the barrel of a gun but from the software of his computer. Based in his 40 million DM headquarters in Wiesbaden, he has available to him the most modern police data processing system in the world. From this 'situation centre' he can access (in the shortest of access times) the computers of the individual state CID offices, customs, border and immigration services, justice and prison authorities, central federal registry, the JURIS legal documentation system, the computers of the state prosecutors, and the data net of Interpol; in addition, by way of 'official support' (which in Germany means the *ad hoc* and unregulated exchange of information between official agencies of different areas of competence) the data banks of the vehicle registration offices, the central registry of foreigners, the communal registrars, tax, social security, health offices, the building authorities, libraries, Federal Pensions Agency, the Military Counter-Intelligence Service, the Federal Intelligence Service, and the Federal Office for the Protection of the Constitution .[17]

Enzensberger writes that there is no question that the population of West Germany is 'subjected to a degree of surveillance today that is historically unprecedented'; the 'Gestapo could only have dreamed of such a range of technical equipment'. He reaches the conclusion that 'the civil rights and freedoms once promised by the bourgeois state recede into the distance in a community organized in such a way'. But then he continues: 'But we cannot overestimate the value of what is left [of those rights] nor defend them too fiercely, because what is left still is considerable. This rest is what makes the Federal Republic inhabitable'.[18]

The crisis scenarios of 1992/93 must be interpreted against this background. Their pessimistic energy feeds from the historical experience of German reconvalescence, from the fear of what will be seen to have been lost when looking back during a period of normalization. The development starting with sheer desperation at not being able to live in the republic of the 1950s and 1960s, leading to a growing sceptical trust in the 1970s, culminating in what can almost be called confidence in the 1980s, now seemed to be getting out of control. This development would appear to be under serious threat from the consequences of the development of the global market. And that would mean in Enzensberger's view that not only what was gained during a favourable period of German history would be under threat, but the inhabitability of countries, territories and cities all over the world.

VIII 1992/1993: Wars without Aura

In 1968 Enzensberger did not yet see a Europe as it would be in 1992, flooded with refugees, with people fleeing from political and economic catastrophes. Back then it was more the dead, the victims of the war in Indochina, who had descended on Europe:

> The shadow of the revolution is the shadow of another, bigger, starving, plundered world, ripped to shreds by bombs. Its dead are with us. The revolution in Europe is to this day but a shadow of the revolution that Europeans tried in vain to crush. Nowadays they leave this work to the United States of America, out of weakness – not because they realize their mistakes. Every victory and every defeat in this struggle dips us deeper and deeper into the shadow of the revolution. What keeps on coming back, disturbing the peace, and will not be turned away, is the future.[19]

In 1992/93, on the other hand, Enzensberger sees the old *Realpolitik* confronted with the 'ruins of an imperial style of thinking that belongs in the nineteenth century'. Since the end of the Cold War, he suggests, word has got round even in Washington that brotherly aid costs more than it earns and that substitute wars are not worth it. What is more, from the point of view of the capitalists, war is becoming more and more a loss-making activity, with armament exports only amounting to .006% of global trade. Countries involved in civil war are said to be punished by withholding investment. However, Enzensberger concludes, it is still an unusual sight to see capitalists as liberators and peace-makers (*CW*, 16,17).

More decisively important than his realization that the 'West' is now only marginally interested in using wars for its own ends, is Enzensberger's refusal to elevate riots, rebellions and wars to the status of revolutions, as the Left had done for decades. ('The children are on the march', wrote for example Heiner Müller with reference to Pol Pot's guerillas.) Enzensberger's disillusioned view of the Third World, which had begun in 1969 in Cuba, culminates in this refusal, in that he deprives 'wars of liberation' of their aura of a revolutionary future. According to Enzensberger, civil wars have supposedly carried the mask of the struggle for national liberation or revolutionary uprising until recently. But since the end of the Cold War they had shown their true faces. Civil wars ignite spontaneously, from within, they are 'endogenous', led by gangs. Even the 'integrity of the nation' or the 'true faith' have turned out nowadays to be simple excuses. The 'war of all against all' is running its course. Enzensberger of course does not question that skinheads are an expression of social relationships; however, his sobered view made the aggressor visible again as the perpetrator.

That the global market is the definitive scale of reference remains for Enzensberger a fixed part of his point of view. Freedom of capital has the tendency to free up labour as well. Thus, the migratory movements are taking on a new quality with the globalization of the market. In this respect Enzensberger is basically following Marx : the victory of capitalism *qua* market and exploitation, as foreseen in the *Communist Manifesto*, has already taken place world wide. In his view, electronic money only follows its own logic and has no difficulty in overcoming any resistance. However, the 'political consequences the Marxist theoreticians predicted have not come about' (*CW*, 34). The international class struggle is not taking place. The theory of *revolution* has been refuted. In Enzensberger's view, Marx is still quite usable for diagnosis, but not for therapy.

Where, in 1968, Enzensberger preached revolution in criticizing the establishment, and saw it coming, he now makes the defensive demand that the republic be kept inhabitable: 'I call a place uninhabitable where a gang of thugs is free to attack people in the middle of the street or set fire to their homes' (*CW*, 140). Enzensberger is afraid of our losing the minimum of what makes civilization and demands that the state monopoly of power be established and maintained. In this process he sees a danger of 'setting the limits of the *Limes*', of inward protection becoming a fortification against the outside: 'Those who don't flee wall themselves in' (*CW*, 45).

This minimum demand for inhabitability is a result of his disillusionment with the grand design. Enzensberger's scepticism regarding the *rhetoric* of universalism, vis-à-vis the, in principle, limitless commitment to human rights is one more step in the suspension of historio-philosophical thought. His plea for 'setting priorities' emphasizes 'that our scope for action is both finite and relative' (*CW*, 66, 67). A concrete relationship thus takes the place of abstraction. Enzensberger also recognizes as a problem of ethics that any such a setting of priorities becomes a problem of *triage*.

Enzensberger finishes his essay with a look at the 'true heroes of the civil war'. Their appearance is unheroic. They do not get noticed, and they are never seen on the screen. They are beginning to make the world liveable again. Enzensberger compares them with the figure of Sisyphos:

> In an improvised workshop, artificial limbs are being made for amputees. A woman is looking for rags to use as nappies. Shoes are fashioned from the tyres of a bombed-out car. The first water-pipe is patched together. A postman appears from no-where. A mother who lost her children hangs a hand-painted sign outside her hut and opens the first café in the neighbourhood. (*CW*, *70)*

'The persistence of these people', Enzensberger continues, 'is close to miraculous. They know they cannot put the world to rights. Only a little corner of it – a roof, a wound. They even know that the murderers will be back, in a week or in a decade. Civil war doesn't last for ever, but it constantly threatens to start again' (*CW*, 71).

NOTES

1 Wolfgang Weyrauch, *Ich lebe in der Bundesrepublik. Fünfzehn Deutsche über Deutschland*, Munich, 1960, p. 30. Enzensberger's sentence was used as the title for an answer to Weyrauch's volume, namely Hermann Kesten's anthology with the title *Ich lebe nicht in der Bundesrepublik*, Munich, 1964.
2 *Ich lebe in der Bundesrepublik*, p. 25.
3 *Ich lebe in der Bundesrepublik*, p. 25-26.
4 *Ich lebe in der Bundesrepublik*, p. 29-30.
5 'Mittelmaß und Wahn. Ein Vorschlag zur Güte', in Hans Magnus Enzensberger, *Mittelmaß und Wahn. Gesammelte Zerstreuungen*, Frankfurt/Main, 1988.
6 Enzensberger, 'Berliner Gemeinplätze II', in *Kursbuch*, 13, June 1968, p. 191. The reference to the author of the sentence regarding the supposed end of the class struggle is an allusion to Helmut Schelsky.
7 Enzensberger, 'Berliner Gemeinplätze', *Kursbuch*, 11, January 1968, pp. 155, 156.
8 Enzensberger, 'Berliner Gemeinplätze', *Kursbuch*, 11, p. 155.
9 Hans Magnus Enzensberger, 'Staatsgefährdende Umtriebe', *Voltaire Flugschriften*, No. 11, ed. Bernward Vesper, Berlin, January 1968.
10 Hans Magnus Enzensberger, 'Staatsgefährdende Umtriebe', *Voltaire Flugschriften*, No. 11, p. 158.
11 See for example Hans Magnus Enzensberger, 'Ein Gespräch über die Zukunft mit Rudi Dutschke, Bernd Rabehl und Christian Semler (Oktober 1967)', in *Kursbuch*, 14, August 1968, pp. 146-174.
12 Hans Magnus Enzensberger, 'Dossier I, Kronstadt 1921 oder die Dritte Revolution', in *Kursbuch*, 9, June 1967, p. 12.
13 Hans Magnus Enzensberger, *Der Untergang der Titanic. Eine Komödie*, Frankfurt/Main 1978, pp. 14-5.
14 Enzensberger, *Mittelmaß und Wahn*, p. 258.
15 *Mittelmaß und Wahn*, p. 260.
16 *Mittelmaß und Wahn*, p. 263.
17 Hans Magnus Enzensberger, 'Unentwegter Versuch, einem New Yorker Publikum die Geheimnisse der deutschen Demokratie zu erklären', in *Kursbuch*, ed. Karl Markus Michel and Harald Wieser, in collaboration with Hans Magnus Enzensberger, June 1979, p. 10.
18 Enzensberger, 'Unentwegter Versuch, einem New Yorker Publikum die Geheimnisse der deutschen Demokratie zu erklären', p. 14.
19 Enzensberger, 'Berliner Gemeinplätze', p. 151.

Translated by Colin Hall (Berlin).

Chapter Five

'Middle Way' and 'Recognition': Enzensberger's Essays on the Political Culture of the Federal Republic

Gerhard Fischer

I

1968 was the year in which, as Hans Magnus Enzensberger wrote, the 'imaginary has built its nest'.[1] Six years later, Alexander Kluge and Edgar Reitz released a feature film, *In Danger and in Deep Distress the Middle Way Spells Certain Death*. In the title, the two 'new wave' German film directors referred to the short time of hope around 1968 when there was a widespread belief that the embarcation for Utopia was imminent. It was a reminder, not without ironic, self-distancing undertones, of a mode of political and social–cultural critique, which had become dominant at the time, based on the belief in a decisive historical caesura: contemporary events were seen as an expression of extreme crisis which called for radical political intervention and change, for the revolutionary transformation of the complete societal system. In 1968, Enzensberger, who had just come into prominence in a second career as political essayist and editor of a trend-setting journal, wrote: 'The political system of the Federal Republic is irreparable. We can either agree with it, or we must replace it with another system. *Tertium non dabitur*' (MW, 253).

Around the turn of the decade from the 1970s to the 1980s, Enzensberger took up the title of the Kluge/Reitz film, quoting it with a characteristic change that announces his departure from the thinking of the New Left of '68: 'In Gefahr und großer Not/ist die Konsequenz der Tod'.[2] In a programmatic essay, 'Das Ende der Konsequenz', Enzensberger admitted that his earlier critique was in error. He now proclaimed the 'joys of undogmatic thinking' (*die Freuden der Inkonsequenz*) and asserted that there was a 'new situation' which presented dangers of a different kind. What was required now was exactly the opposite of what was demanded before, namely an understanding that the radical and polarized way of thinking – 'You're either part of the problem, or you're part of the solution' – had turned out to be ideology: *false consciousness*. The times, in fact, did not require radical action and extreme measures. Rather, they called for the *middle way*. Now, salvation was seen to lie in compromise, consensus, and pragmatic muddling through, rather than strict and consequential adherence to dogma and principle, of either the left-wing or right-wing variety. This self-correction was repeatedly confirmed by Enzensberger. In 'Mittelmaß und Wahn', a similarly programmatic essay of 1990, he wrote that the 1968 call for the abolition of the Federal Republic and the announcement of the imminent end of the 'bourgeois-capitalist' system had turned out to be, like so many proclamations of the time, 'self-refuting prophecy'.[3]

Enzensberger's political essays, from the mid-1970s to the early 1990s, can be characterized by a growing inclination towards the 'middle way', both in terms of his political philosophy and with regard to his analysis of the political culture of the Federal Republic. The essays, with characteristic titles such as 'In Defense of Normality' or 'Mediocrity and Delusion', argue in favour of policies of common sense, scepticism, modesty and self-limitation. Enzensberger's philosophy of the 'middle way' proclaims an ideal of 'averageness', also translatable as 'mediocrity', and it does so with irony and satire, by playing on the double meaning of the word; but in the last instance the concept of the 'middle way' is proposed in earnest and without apology. Enzensberger finds his legitimation in a tradition of Stoic and Epicurean philosophy, in the praise of moderation as a cardinal virtue of Christian theology – underpinned by references to Plato – and, most importantly, in the model of the thinkers of the European Enlightenment where the idea of a *juste milieu*, first formulated by Voltaire, was a positive concept (before it acquired its derogatory sociological connotation relating to petty bourgeois mentality and values).[4] In particular, Enzensberger cultivates an image of himself in the likeness of his literary role-model, Diderot; it is in the intellectual tradition of the *encyclopédiste* that he locates the roots of his own political philosophy: scepticism, irony, common sense, undogmatic and unideological thinking, and the role of the critical intellectual free from political attachments. Enzensberger's essays signal a movement away from the left of the political spectrum to a liberal-democratic centre. This also implies a move away from a critique aimed at the destruction of the political system to one that accepts its legitimacy: Enzensberger's critique is an integral part of the socio-political discourse *within* the Federal Republic. At the same time, he stays clear of any involvement in party politics. He rejects his previous engagement for the left, including a brief appearance for the Social Democrats,[5] because he considers that the social-democratic reform policies are no longer relevant, and he equally rejects the positions of the political right because he considers the 'value'-debates of the patriarchal elites in the tradition of German cultural conservatism as even more hopelessly anachronistic. Enzensberger's essays provide an unexpected answer to an old German question: *Wo steht der Geist?* In the case of Enzensberger, the answer could be: neither on the left nor on the right but in the centre, or perhaps: above the centre, critically.

Enzensberger's analysis of the socio-political culture of West Germany, in the 1970s and 1980s, stresses the notion of 'averageness'

(*Durchschnittlichkeit*); he describes a society which praises ordinariness and normality and whose political ambition is to steer a middle course of consensus and compromise. Of course, averageness does not apply only to the Federal Republic. Rather, Enzensberger sees the extension of the 'average' middle classes as a world-wide phenomenon; he speaks of the 'hegemony of the middle class' and, elsewhere, of the 'hegemonic culture of the petty bourgeoisie' which supposedly spreads like an 'oil spill' around the globe.[6] But it is in the Federal Republic 'that the average (*Mittelmaß*) has found a true home, more so than elsewhere'.[7] This is seen as a positive development: it means the end of the peculiar, and dangerous, German way of doing things, the notorious *Sonderweg* of German development towards modernity as the 'late nation' to which German history owes its catastrophes. In the 1970s, as a result of a long but eventually successful learning process, the citizens of the West German republic have finally caught up with the democratic societies of Western Europe and North America. They have managed to discard traditional and stereotypically 'German' values and attitudes: their fatal inclination towards *Weltpolitik* and towards imperial-hegemonic ambitions in foreign policies, for example, or the proverbial *Obrigkeitshörigkeit* and *Untertanendenken*, i.e. a willing subservience to the authoritarian state. This emancipatory act is a result of the mentality changes caused by the cultural revolution of '68: for Enzensberger an 'achievement in civilisation'.[8]

Enzensberger's attitude to this 'average', civilised, republican society is one of ironic distance and satirical exaggeration, on the one hand. But it is also one of acceptance and critical affirmation, even of cordial agreement. Indeed, there is a distinct sympathy for the 'normality' of this society, particularly for the average 'little' people who are not presented as 'heroes' but as a motley lot of individuals. On the whole, Enzensberger's approval rating of the West German population and society is remarkably favourable, even though he also insists that, behind the common–sense approach towards a mediated consensus and the generally prosperous, contented 'normality' of the population, there is a complementary, darker side, driven by an irrational force which he calls 'madness' or 'delusion'. To cite only one example provided by Enzensberger of what he sees as an uncanny *Wahn*: the West Germans' fetishistic attachment to their automobiles and to the principle of individual freedom of movement at unregulated speeds transforms the middle majority into suicide and killing commandos the moment they turn onto the freeways of the republic. In *Civil War* there is a similar comment when Enzensberger reminds his readers of the schizophrenic turn-coat potential of his fellow citizens who, in the air raid shelters during the last months of World War II, had already forgotten their enthusiastic veneration of the *Führer* of the Third Reich in view of their new devotion to the Allied victors. Could it be, Enzensberger seems to say, that in Germany a 'healthy common sense' might still not be so far away from what was once called a 'healthy *Volksempfinden*'?

The notion of a nation of individuals who are no less individualistic in fact than the most critical intellectuals raises, of course, the question of the role of the critical intellectual in this society, and thus of Enzensberger's own position. This is a topic which he studiously avoids addressing in his essays and which he apparently prefers to leave to his interpreters. Is there a need for the special role of the intellectual in such a society? Does not the idea of the cultural hegemony of a midle class that is operating on a world wide basis preclude the idea of a 'free-floating' *intelligentsia*? The concept of the petty bourgeoisie as an 'experimental class' appears to rule out the notion of the *avantgarde*, but it also seems to make the job of the cosmopolitan, self-employed cultural producer and commentator, e.g. the essayist of the German *feuilleton* as spokesperson of a cultural elite, an anachronistic redundancy.[9] Enzensberger's praise of the 'average' people is, of course, also part of a literary strategy of demarcation, an ironic role-playing which aims at delineating his own contributions vis-à-vis those of other intellectuals and competitors, and thus to increase his own exclusivity. Enzensberger's criticism is typically directed against his own colleagues and, generally, against people involved in the production and administration of cultural 'meaning' in the Federal Republic. He is less than generous to the professional cliques of journalists, talk-show hosts, politicians, lobbyists, unionists, social workers, teachers, or clerics in the Republic, and he has no qualms including these groups in his list of 'secondary illiterates',[10] one of the favourite categories in his remarkable litany of invectives. The essays reveal a measure of intellectual curtness and arrogance with which positions of competing intellectuals are disposed of and which make Enzensberger's friendly and benevolent (if ironic) approval of the 'average' people appear all the more apparent.

It might be of interest to isolate three aspects of Enzensberger's description of the Federal Republic in the 1970s and 1980s, because they will be useful in the analysis of *Great Migration* and *Civil War*. The first is the phenomenon of de-politicization and de-centralisation: in a highly developed, complex society, political processes are no longer controlled by a single centre. The political authorities, e.g., the Federal Government, are losing influence and control vis-à-vis a multitude of organized interest groups of all kinds, from institutions of the European bureaucracy to Greenpeace and to multinational industrial concerns, the media or local citizen's initiatives, to nation-wide consumer or other lobby groups. The political centre suffers a loss of power and of political–social relevance, as more and more important and innovative decisions and processes are initiated and developed at the periphery of a self-organizing society. As a consequence, the whole system of official politics is becoming an uncontrollable, 'stochastic process', and the central authority less dangerous (or more normal), i.e., less likely to resort to (traditionally German) authoritarian, undemocratic measures. Again, this development is regarded quite clearly as positive: it is one instance of the success of the 'cultural revolution' of '68 and of the practice of the new social movements which are characterized by an increase in democratic participation within a society that is happily on the way to anarchistic self-regulation. Enzensberger, who likes to recall and to play with the metaphors of '68, speaks of the government that has become 'a paper tiger'.[11]

The second aspect is the development of a very heterogenous population, held together by the umbrella of 'averageness', yet characterized by a 'maximum of variation and difference'. The increase in social mobility, in individual freedom and in disposable income, has created a culturally diverse society of 'average deviants'. Enzensberger, fond of providing lists, constructs one long litany of typical West Germans who populate the average small towns and villages of the Republic: 'Golf-playing butchers, spouses imported from Thailand, secret service agents cultivating their front yards, Turkish mullahs, pharmacists (female) who chair solidarity committees for Nicaragua, vagrants driving Mercedes-Benzes, Tamil ice-cream sellers, militant lesbians, computer-freaks who commute between data banks in California and nature parks in the State of Hesse', etc., etc.: the list goes on.[12] The essay reveals the author as a realistic observer of everyday life. With friendly irony, he describes the globally-linked, affluent and multicultural world of the average citizens of the Federal Republic of Bonn. Perhaps surprisingly, the analytical concept of multiculturalism does not appear in this panoramic view: a deficiency to which we need to return later.

The third aspect of Enzensberger's analysis of the 'average' Republic concerns the notion of mediation as a pervasive principle in the resolution of conflicts. This does not only apply to the solution of industrial disputes (characteristically, the West German concept of 'tariff autonomy' makes government involvement in this area all but superfluous) but to social and political differences generally. According to Enzensberger, the West German preference for 'balance' and 'dialogue', for mediation and the concept of 'social partnership', is yet again the result again of an historical learning process: the average West Germans are highly suspicious of political fanaticism and adventurism; they reject all kind of utopian dreams and radical ideologies because the lessons of recent history as well as of the current example of life in the other German republic are too painfully obvious. As a result, this society is capable of generating an enormous integrative capacity. It is also thoroughly peaceful. Enzensberger explains the 'German Autumn' of 1977 which pitted the terrorism of a few dozen members of the Red Army Faction against a state apparatus armed to its teeth with computers and military hardware, as a 'last relapse' and the 'atavistic return of suppressed phantasies of violence', a kind of final armed shoot-out about and in the Republic. But this 'ghostly regression' is now a closed chapter in the history of the Federal Republic. In 1991, Enzensberger writes: 'There has never been such a high degree of ultra-stability in German history...Social civil war has become unimaginable for this society'.[13]

In *Great Migration* and *Civil War*, then, an entirely different story is told: the 'turbulence' of movements of migration and displacement as the 'normal' state of human affairs throughout history, violence and civil war as an all–pervasive phenomenon, both global and local or 'molecular'. It seems as if, in Enzensberger's perception of the impact of the collapse of the socialist states and the return of inter-ethnic warfare in Europe, a new period of 'danger and deep distress' has arrived. The removal of the Iron Curtain ushers in another era of mass migrations; the end of the Cold War does not bring peace and liberation from the threat of nuclear annihilation; rather, the end of a forty–year period of *pax atomica* leads to intensified ethnic tension and social disintegration, to new sources of unrest and regional conflicts. Without the protective shelter of Cold War containment, the 'middle way' of capitalism has triumphed and become the norm. A difference between crisis and averageness can no longer be made. However, the norm no longer reads 'peacefulness', 'mediation', 'consensus', but rather upheaval, displacement, terror, conflict and violence. The mechanisms of the capitalist market economy as the overriding instrument of societal development create and re-create the conditions for what Enzensberger terms 'civil war', constantly and continuously, on a global scale. So, which way is the right way to take now? Is this a time where radical political measures and interventions are called for? And what might they be, following the loss of utopian certainty and belief in a historical telos that was seemingly built on scientific principles? The critical observer from Western Europe who, once before, had shouted 'Wolf!' only to find that no one listened, has this time learned his lesson. He prefers, quietly, to find his theory of averageness confirmed and, with an ingenious dialectical trick, declares the dangerous times the normal times. Radical measures or decisive political mangement are neither possible nor called for; the 'middle way' as the only way is now defined as the defense of a 'minimum of civilisation'.

II

Enzensberger's essays respond to the historical changes of the early '90s with a fundamental shift in perspective. Rather than focusing on the socio-cultural micro-environments of Germany and Europe, as he basically did in the essays of the 1970s and 1980s, and on a relatively short period of European history (from the seventeenth century), he now adopts a global and anthropological point of view. The essays of 1992 and 1993 cover enormous ground, indeed. They include a history of the whole of humanity, from the archetypical myths of nomadic pre-history to the Los Angeles riots, from the Peleponnesian Wars to the debate on asylum-seekers in today's Europe. This big picture, sketched with meticulous attention to detail, reflects the global dimension of Enzensberger's thesis in the two essays: in the wake of the dissolution of the bi-polar world with its clear and fortified ideological boundaries we now experience a tremendous growth of regional power centres and conflicts, the weakening of the traditional centres confronted with a dynamic periphery. Enzensberger does not see the historical situation of post-1989 as one of passing turbulence, as a transitory era of adjustment or as a particularly dynamic phase in the world-wide process of modernisation; he rather sees the dawn of a new 'world disorder'[14] of uncontrolled and uncontrollable violence, as a secular paradigm change of unpredictable consequences. The globalisation of the market economy and of the labour market is responsible for the fact that more and more individuals are becoming 'superfluous', that whole groups of people are left out of the economic process; this in turn intensifies the dynamic of international migration movements and the development of 'autistic' violence as people who struggle for recognition in a desperate, self-destructive bid for self-assertion.

In *Great Migration* and *Civil War* Enzensberger takes up ideas which alreday featured prominently in earlier essays. There is, however, a paradigmatic change in emphasis and evaluation. The 'stochastic' process of politics, for example, which was previously used as an argument to demonstrate increased democratic participation in the context of the development of a 'civil' society in West Germany, is now judged negatively. In 1992/93 the accent is clearly on the disintegration of traditional state politics and forms of community or communal experiences. Neither the positive pictures of the new social movements nor the citizens' initiatives with their practice of grassroots democracy are being emphasized. Enzensberger seems to have forgotten about the heterogenous, multi-ethnic society that is peacefully living its multicultural diversity. Instead, he focuses on the disruptive power of world wide migration movements and, in its wake, the development of xenophobic hate and violence which is declared an 'anthropological constant' (*CW*, 106). And while the earlier essays underscore the integrative capacity of the West German welfare state which assures a balance of interests between 'social partners', the emphasis is now on the atavistic, eternal battle between master and servant.

The master-servant dialectic is essentially a problem of 'recognition'. It features as a central concept in both essays even though it is dealt with explicitly only in *Civil War*. Recognition is also a theme to which Enzensberger has devoted a great deal of attention in previous works. His 'radio–novel' *Jakob und sein Herr* (1963-1979) is in fact an extended literary treatment of Hegel's famous historical–philosophical parable which Enzensberger has adapted from the work of Diderot (*Jacques le fataliste et son maître*, 1770s).[15] In *Civil War* Enzensberger discusses recognition in the central chapter V of his essay: 'The longing for recognition is a fundamental anthropological fact' (*CW*, 38). The discussion of recognition is underpinned with a reference to Franz

Fanon's classic account of the Algerian War of Liberation, *The Wretched of the Earth* (*Les damnés de la terre*). The dialectic of the master–servant relationship, in the context of anti-colonial violence, explains the cycle of revolt and self-destruction which Enzensberger develops as a key thesis of his essay: once the victims of colonization have overcome their rulers, 'the old resentments, buried deep in the collective memory, come to life again in tribal feuding...the conquered throw themselves into acts of revenge'. What follows is the 'literal self-destruction of a collective' as a way 'in which the colonized vent the physical strain of colonization' (*CW*, 38). Enzensberger finds in Fanon the confirmation of his thesis concerning the self-destructiveness of today's perpetrators of violence: the losers in the modernisation process turn against each other and against their own group as much as against outsiders, not in pursuit of concrete political or ideological aims but in a rage of blind, 'autistic' self-destruction.

Enzensberger's comments about violence that 'has freed itself from ideology' (*CW*, 20) propose an interpretative perspective which appears particularly relevant and convincing in view of the increasing number of inter-ethnic conflicts around the world. The reference to Fanon seems equally pertinent and prescient in view of the recent escalation of violence in Algeria. But nevertheless it must be asked whether Fanon's analysis, of thirty years ago, of the peculiar psychological make-up of the Algerian freedom fighters confronting their rulers after 130 years of brutal colonial oppression, justifies the sweeping conclusions Enzensberger draws. One might point to the recent developments in South Africa as a counter-example; significantly, South Africa is a country that has both a tradition of colonial rule and repression and of institutions of a constitutional democratic liberalism (which the successful Algerian FLN did not manage to establish after their victory over the French) which may provide the basis – it is to be hoped – for a continuing process of peaceful negotiation, or mediation, of the demand for recognition of a people who successfully overcame the humiliation of apartheid.

Enzensberger apodictically states: 'The longing for recognition is never satisfied' (*CW*, 39). In a sentence missing in the English translation, he doubts whether such realization is possible in principle.[16] It becomes clear here that a principled anthropological pessimism has taken the place of Enzensberger's earlier sceptical and ironic-optimistic view. The struggle for recognition appears to him as an eternal cycle that replaces Hegel's historical-philosophical project: since there will never be a society of equals, there will always be distinctions and privileges as well as people who will not accept discrimination and the non-recognition of their rights. The problem with this argument seems to be that Enzensberger understands recognition as an unhistorical anthropological construct disassociated from the political sphere. It is conceived in abstract-categorical terms, as a 'condition' rather than a process. He does present it in the context of 'struggle', but it is curiously a confrontation that allows only an 'either/or' solution; there are no provisions for mediated or negotiated political outcomes, for the 'middle way' of democratic compromise.

What Enzensberger does not recognize is a 'politics of recognition' in the sense that Charles Taylor employs the term.[17] Taylor's widely-discussed essay, which appeared the same year as Enzensberger's *Great Migration* and in German translation at the same time as *Civil War*, also takes Hegel as its point of departure: 'Due recognition...is a vital human need'.[18] The decisive difference between Enzensberger and Taylor is that the latter speaks of recognition in the context of a theory of human and civil rights. Taylor's essay is part of a discourse on recognition that has developed as a result of a development towards multiculturalism in some Western liberal-democratic societies over the last few decades, notably in Canada, the United States and in Australia, and more recently in Western Europe including the Federal Republic. According to Taylor, who also refers to the thinkers of the European Enlightenment, recognition is closely linked to the issue of identity, including ethnic and cultural identity, and to the question of the dignity of the human being. The demand for recognition of a person involves, in a dialogic process, his or her quest for a specific identity as the expression of that person's unique individuality. This happens both on a personal, intimate and a public, collective level, i.e., as part of a larger socio-cultural and/or ethnic group. Out of this quest arises a 'politics of difference' to complement the traditional 'politics of equality' which was previously used as the main instrument in realizing the goal of a fair and just society. Habermas, in his response to Taylor, speaks of the 'struggle for recognition' which takes place as part of the public discourse within the framework of the democratic–constitutional state, and he makes the important point that 'a correctly understood theory of rights requires a politics of recognition that protects the integrity of the individual in the life contexts in which his or her identity is formed'.[19]

The discourse on recognition is a precarious balancing act; it attempts to negotiate seemingly contradictory demands (e.g., equality for all versus the acknowledgement of differences), and it has led to a heated debate between the proponents of a 'procedural' liberalism (Dworkin, Rawls) and the adherents of a 'communitarian' liberalism to which Taylor subscribes. The politics of recognition, according to Taylor, are designed to create policies, institutions, social measures, and a political culture, generally, which are based on the principle that the quest for recognition is indeed a fundamental human need which must be treated by society and the state with the same seriousness as the demand for equal rights. The politics of recognition is thus part of the politics of human rights, and it concerns a central problem of today's liberal-democratic societies: the balancing act between universalism and particularism. In countries with ethnically diverse populations, such as the Federal Republic with its motley collection of 'average deviants', a politics of recognition would facilitate the development of secure but complex, fluent, hybrid socio-cultural identities within a pluralistic, open society characterized by what Gadamer calls a 'fusion' of cultural 'horizons'[20] or what Paul Michael Lützeler describes as overlapping 'identity circles'.[21]

It is interesting that Enzensberger, who deals with the question of recognition very prominently in *Civil War*, pays very little attention to it in *Great Migration*. There is no attempt to think through the question of the recognition of ethnic and cultural differences within societies characterized by immigration and by ethnically diverse populations; nor is there any discussion of a specific 'politics of recognition'. Rather, Enzensberger employs the theory of an anthropological 'longing for recognition' to support his argument about the self-destructive forces of today's societies; he does not use the concept to explain how in some multicultural societies the quest for identity has become the imperative for putting into place measures designed to mediate and to negotiate social and cultural conflicts arising out of the need for recognition. Enzensberger makes a very perceptive point when he refers to the struggle over 'imaginary resources' (*CW*, 108), but there is no perception at all that the imaginary process of identity formation is part of a struggle for recognition. In the political discourse on multiculturalism the distribution of the imaginary resource 'identity' plays a very prominent part indeed. How otherwise could we understand the political dimensions of the struggle over recognition of ethnic and cultural identities and the formation of hybrid identities as a typical feature of societies in a postmodern and post-national stage of development? How is, to give a concrete example within the realm of experiences of the Federal Republic, the 'anthropological longing' for recognition of a child to be fulfilled who is born of Turkish immigrants in Germany and who has grown up bilingually or biculturally but who is denied the status of a citizen of the Federal Republic? To Enzensberger, the norm seems to be xenophobic exclusion rather than integration based on the development of complex identities or the fusion of cultural traditions. Despite the considerable integrative potential of the socio-political system of the Federal Republic, which Enzensberger underlined previously, he cannot imagine the struggle for recognition as the pursuit of a common political goal which understands ethnic diversity as an 'imaginary' resource which is negotiated within the parameters of a democratic process and as part of a societal discourse, under the rule of law, and which is – finally – essential to the wealth and security of contemporary societies. Enzensberger can imagine the struggle for recognition only as violent confrontation.

Enzensberger's failure to develop the discussion of recognition to include a consideration of a politics of recognition reveals, it could be argued, his lack of a clear understanding of the concept of ethnicity and of ethnic identity and its importance within the context of a multicultural society. This 'blind spot' amounts to an analytical deficiency which is a symptom of the generally 'underdeveloped' state of 'multicultural thinking' in Europe, as Lützeler has observed,[22] and perhaps also of the peculiarly German tradition of a denial of immigration policies.[23] It explains why some passages in his essays are open to misunderstanding as well as in need of critical evaluation. It explains, for instance, the very unproductive discussion in *Great Migration* of the idea of a multicultural society which is dismissed as a 'confused slogan' that is supposedly 'taboo' as far as conceptual clarification is concerned (*CW*, 134). In *Civil War*, Enzensberger speaks rather condescendingly of the 'folkloristic costume ball of ethnic groups' in the context of what is called 'fictitious formation of traditions'.[24] Enzensberger's paradigm for understanding multi-culturalism is, strangely enough, defined by the dubious example of the Soviet Union. He makes a link between the Soviet state's 'great efforts to instil in its citizens a sense of identity and of common goals in a "multicultural society"' and its subsequent 'implosion' (*CW*, 135): blaming multiculturalism for the demise of the Soviet empire seems extraordinarily biased. But Enzensberger's comments on multicultural societies in the West are equally indefensible: it is doubtful whether the readiness of immigrants to integrate is decreasing, as Enzensberger summarily maintains, or that minorities 'are cutting themselves off' by allegedly 'insisting on their "identity"'(*CW*, 136). And, in the case of Germany, it is rather problematic to claim that 'the distinction between natives [*Inländer*] and foreigners [*Ausländer*] is irrelevant' (*CW*, 140) in the context of a discussion about the prevention of xenophobic violence. In societies where 'foreigners' or 'aliens' are *not* automatically associated with notions of underclass and cultural underdevelopment but are considered citizens with full equal rights, 'there can hardly be any across-the-board discrimination'.[25] Conversely, the state promotes xenophobic exclusion through its policy of non-recognition of immigrants as citizens and thus, unwillingly, encourages violence against 'foreigners' which, as Enzensberger complains, should be its duty to prevent because of its monopoly on the use of force. The official government policy towards foreigners in Germany [*Ausländerpolitik*] is an example of non-recognition *par excellence*: that Enzensberger does not refer to this in his discussion of recognition as a 'fundamental' anthropological fact is indeed remarkable.

In his parable of the travellers in the railway carriage, Enzensberger does seem to acknowledge a sphere of politics. He speaks of 'an institutional code', 'norms of behaviour' and 'a system of rules' (*CW*, 105) which the passengers employ to accomodate each other. But he does not develop the subject at all: in his application of the parable, the emphasis is on what he calls the 'anthropological constant', e.g., xenophobia as something that pre–dates all forms of social organisations, or the 'territorial instinct'. The discussion is then wound up in images suggesting 'turbulence', 'chaos', and violence. In a similar vein, he describes the 'development of stationary populations' over 'the millenia' as 'exceptions' (*CW*, 104), in contrast to the never–ending instability of migration which allows him to emphasize again the notion of 'turbulence'. But should the formation of 'stationary societies' not be seen as the other side of migration movements, as a dialectical process in history in which ever new forms of political arrangements between different ethnic or national groups are being worked out? Enzensberger seems to make quite a crude distinction here: ethnic groups which develop, as it were, naturally, and which thus seem to belong to a somehow pre–modern era, and modern nation–states which are created 'consciously', even 'artificially' (*CW*, 107). The English translation of *Great Migration*, incidentally, does not fully grasp the complexities involved here. Enzensberger speaks of ethnic groups which supposedly come into being by a process of 'organic growth', which is rather different from 'semi–spontaneous', as the English version has it (*CW*, 107).[26] On the same page, Enzensberger speaks of an 'organic development' of some states. The use of similes of nature and organic growth is quite uncharacteristic for Enzensberger who otherwise takes a dim view of biological explanations of human behaviour. In *Civil War*, he takes issue with the 'biological argument', calling it 'intellectually defective' and pointing out its 'moral debility' (*CW*, 41). In *Great Migration*, the organic-biological metaphor is a characteristic slip that shows up the weakness in Enzensberger's own argument.

III

A discussion of the 'politics of recognition' is not only relevant in view of the complex problems of migration, ethnicity and multiculturalism. It also ought to find an application with regard to the question of violence, in particular in view of Enzensberger's comments on young people as the 'avantgarde of civil war'. Enzensberger's description of the causes of violence of young radical extremists amounts to a complex picture of psycho-social contexts and political-economic developments. The 'cauldron of violence' (*CW*, 43) is the result of many ingredients: the 'normal pent-up physical and emotional energies of adolescence', the 'incomprehensible legacy' of the 'destructive mania' of their parents (usually manifest only in 'socially tolerated forms' such as drug abuse and violence at home) which in itself is a symptom of the affluent society and its 'irreconcilable problem of wealth that brings no joy' (*CW*, 42, 43). Enzensberger describes the frustration of a disillusioned generation of young people, without perspective and hope, who are growing up in a period characterized by 'de-industrialisation', whose life world is characterized by the humiliating experience of exclusion from the work process to which they react with desperate and aggressive defiance. He also describes the temptation of an aesthetic experience of ecstacy which he finds confirmed in the 'self-experimentation' of the American journalist Bill Buford (*CW*, 47). And there is also the hopelessness of young people whose self-destructive violence in a decisive phase of their personal development suggests that they have not succeeded in finding a secure sense of identity and belonging because, in their struggle for recognition, they have received too little support by parents or teachers or the societal system in general.

Enzensberger's complex analysis of this network of cause and effect is supported by the findings of social scientists and psychologists. The 'disposition to radicalism'[27] among young people can lead to acts of violence which are perpetrated behind the façade of political or ideological ideas but in reality have no significant relationship to any political content. In these processes, the demand for recognition always plays an important role. Violence is always a symptom of hurt feelings of self-esteem and of 'disturbed relationships',[28] whether in the family, at school or at work, or in peer-age groups. It is always also a symptom of processes of dysfunctional identity formation within the complex net of social and communicative interaction in the peer groups of young people. The failure of such processes of identity formation, however, is not an anthropological constant – as Enzensberger claims – but a characteristic feature of modernity. Charles Taylor writes: 'What has come about with the modern age is not the need for recognition but the conditions in which the attempt to be recognized can fail'.[29]

As in *Great Migration*, the author's use of a specific metaphoric language, characterized in *Civil War* by medical imagery and terminology, points to the weakness of the argument. Enzensberger discusses violence using terms such as 'virus' and 'infection'; he finds in civil war the 'characteristics of a political retrovirus', elsewhere he speaks of the 'epidemics of war' and 'metastases' of civil war. But above all he speaks of 'autism' – the central metaphor of his essay – as the 'common denominator' of combatants of civil war around the world (*CW*, 20, 30, 47). There is no place here to include a discussion of the medical-scientific issues involved in the research on autism. There is very little clarity and even less consensus among scientists about what autism actually is. There are no clear findings to suggest that this is a neurological or a psychological dysfunction nor is there agreement on diagnosis or therapy. Autism is often diagnosed at an early phase of childhood development ('early infant autism' as a symptom of childhood schizophrenia). Generally, autism is seen as a basic symptom of schizophrenia which is characterized by a lack of contact with the outer world, both in terms of cognitive and intellectual processes and in terms of socio-communicative interaction. The autistic patient is concerned with himself or herself, with his or her own body, without apparently having a consciousness of 'self'. The thinking of such patients is not logical and consequential or oriented towards the outer reality.[30] But how does the description of such an illness establish a connection with the psycho-social realities of teenage perpetrators of violence?

Enzensberger seems to use autism as a metaphorical synonym for *selflessness*, for an underdeveloped or non-existent consciousness of one's self, and at the same time for an extreme self-centredness; his use of the term seems to suggest failed processes of identity formation and socialization as well as a disturbed capacity for communication and social interaction. But the image of the autistic patient, caught within his or her own world and hermetically shielded from the outside world, neither appears to fit that of violent youths and their dependence on youth group (or *gang*) interaction, nor does it correspond to the longing for recognition which Enzensberger describes as centrally important. The connection between the failed wish for recognition, insufficient identity formation and acts of violence, as an expression of compensatory action born out of frustration and self-destructive energy, is found in the context of dialogical processes with and inside peer-age groups which offer a notion of collective identity and belonging to boost the weak individual self and to assume the responsibility for actions in lieu of the independently responsible individual. How can this social-pedagogical explanation, which is essential for an understanding of young people tending to extremist violence, be reconciled with the diagnostic image of 'autism'? It is also questionable whether the literary use of the term provides an appropriate analytical-theoretical tool to advance the understanding of the motives for violent acts, with which the young perpetrators formulate their claim for recognition, if these acts are born out of social disaffection and anomie, as Enzensberger also postulates. One might also question the cognitive value of autism as metaphor when, to use yet another theoretical model of explanation, the violent potential of young men is understood – following the ideas of Theweleit's *Male Phantasies* – as a manifestation of a 'fascistic, hallucinatory practice of body preservation' which is about the creation of 'feelings of completeness' in order to 'save' the young person form 'being swallowed up by threatening realities: located in politics, the economy or the family'?[31]

The literary value of Enzensberger's autism-metaphor seems to lie rather in its scintillating inexactitude. What it appears to suggest is a vaguely threatening message concerning the helplessness of modern society in view of mysterious diseases for which there are neither cures nor scientific explanations. It is no coincidence that Enzensberger's metaphorical language establishes a connection to the debate on the AIDS phenomenon (e.g., the references to 'epidemics' or the 'political retrovirus'), suggesting a kind of viral invasion inside the 'body politic' which goes on to destroy the societal immune system from within. The medical metaphors with their ominous vagueness evoke the ghostly apparition of dreadful, incurable diseases with symptoms of neurotic-psychological dysfunctionality: the consequences are feelings of fear, helplessness and despondency. There is also an obvious link to apocalyptic scenarios of destruction.[32]

While Enzensberger's literary strategies are in need of critical evaluation, it is equally important to point out that his analysis fails, again, to provide any meaingful suggestions as to what should be done with the patients diagnosed as 'autistic'. Even if the diagnosis, and the conceptual framework used, is acceptable: should the analysis not be followed up with further ideas concerning therapy, perhaps even strategies of prevention? And even if there is or cannot be a cure, the obvious next step would be to think about the social and medical management of this psycho-social dysfunction. Enzensberger does not offer any ideas at all how to deal with the 'autism' of his young civil warriors. There is no attempt to think through a possible 'politics of recognition' which would be based on an analysis of the life experiences of young perpetrators of violence and which might provide the basis for preventing the failure of processes of identity formation. What seems lacking in Enzensberger's essay, in short, is a more advanced instruction manual, as it were, i.e., a programme or an outline of a 'politics of recognition' to respond to the problem of unfulfilled recognition. Or, to quote Klaus Theweleit: what is needed, 'since – as a rule – we have no access to their life world, is that we continue to work towards creating political conditions in which the "depraved"... young people...who are susceptible to the temptation of fascist slogans, do not need to acquire the feelings of beauty and wholeness – which they need – from neo-fascist neo-poppers'.[33]

It might of course be argued that it is not the role of the intellectual observer to provide a blue-print for political action. However, such a reservation would certainly not apply to Enzensberger who has stated repeatedly that he does not want to be considered an 'idealistic (*weltfremder*) dreamer' and who has never shied away from making practical policy suggestions, most recently in an article which proposes a number of concrete cost-cutting measures to overhaul the foreign cultural policy of the Federal Republic with the aim of increasing both its relevance and its efficiency.[34] An example of a similar kind, relevant to the present context of a debate on young people and their disposition to violence, can be found in an essay on educational reform. Enzensberger's plea for the return of the 'private tutor' is one of his wittiest and most entertaining satires, but it is equally a serious work that makes an innovative and original contribution to educational debate.[35] In its utopian and democratic implication it is no less radical than Walter Benjamin's 'Programme for a Proletarian Children's Theatre' of 1929, but its ideological implications are altogether different.[36] Enzensberger suggests that his 'modest proposal', namely to abolish schools and to replace them with classes conducted in the homes of pupils in small groups under the supervision of 'private tutors' (*Hauslehrer*), is feasible and manageable within the existing political and administrative structures of the Federal Republic. The return of the *Hauslehrer* of feudal times as the 'normal' teacher of the middle class Federal Republic would resolve all educational problems, Enzensberger claims with customary immodesty, tongue-in-cheek and with an ironic twinkle in his left eye. But the satirical attack against entrenched bureaucratic interests, both of the teachers' unions and the state education authorities, does not hide the serious intention of his essay.

Read in conjunction with similar ideas put forward by educational theorists, teachers and social workers concerning the development of strategies to assist young people who have shown a disposition to radical violence, due to failed recognition processes at home and at school, the article provides a stimulating and thought-provoking contribution to a difficult sector of educational and social policy. Furthermore, Enzensberger takes great pain to back up his proposal with thorough research – even though it may appear totally over the top at first sight. The reform package is presented with breathtaking pragmatism: there is scrupulous attention to detail, sober cost efficiency calculation and rigorous application of advanced principles of human resource management. The point to be made here is that Enzensberger is indeed very well capable of – and usually also interested in – developing concrete sugestions and realistic proposals concerning political reforms in a number of areas. In *Civil War* and *Great Migration*, he offers instead a rather undifferentiated broadside against his old friends of the left; he accuses them of being responsible for making demands based on an ethical universalism devoid of concrete political content. But Enzensberger's position is essentially no less fundamentalist than that of his favourite bogeymen, the social workers, therapists and engaged laypeople and clergy, who he accuses of making unrealistic demands. How relevant, or realistic, is Enzensberger's critique, it must be asked, if it takes as its point of departure the universal anthropological 'longing for recognition' but then fails to take the next step, namely to consider a 'politics of recognition'?

Enzensberger's pragmatic contribution is restricted to suggest the concept of *triage*, of graduated ethical responsibilty, as a guiding principle. But this pragmatic solution falls short off the mark: essentially, *triage* means nothing else but compromise, the 'middle way'of liberal-democratic societies. It is practised daily wherever political decisions are being made, on local and state levels as well as in international organisations. The German 'asylum compromise' is a prominent example of *triage* in action. But whether the constitutional amendment of the *Bundestag* represents a solution that is acceptable according to principles of a human rights policy is rather doubtful. *Triage* as a political prescription remains vague and largely meaningless, as Wolfgang Huber has argued, if it is not accompanied by political argument and debate which would make the criteria for graduated responsibility transparent.[37] The discussion of human rights in *Civil War* displays a similar absence of concrete political application: the universal principle of human rights, according to Enzensberger, stipulates that 'we should all be responsible for everyone else' (*CW*, 58). Enzensberger sees the demand for universal human rights as an abstract, moral imperative; his emphasis is, rather fundamentalist, on 'humanity' and not on 'rights' as in a 'politics of rights' guaranteed by constitutional liberal-democratic principles which, in turn, need to be realized in political practice. According to Huber, Enzensberger's 'departure from the universalism of human rights' is based on a 'grotesque misunderstanding': 'The core of human rights is not the claim that every individual human being is responsible for the fate of every other human being. The core is rather a universal legal principle: every human being is endowed with an unalienable dignity...this legal principle binds the power of the state first of all'.[38] Huber continues:

> The Germans, according to Enzensberger, are ill-advised to play the role of 'guarantors of freedom and champions of human rights'. Well roared, lion! But even more to the point: a person who is concerned about the international credibility of the Federal Republic should not only talk about new forms of deployment for the *Bundeswehr* but should, above all, work towards formulating new concepts for a policy oriented towards human rights and its implementation.

IV

Enzensberger's solution is not to call for decisive political measures or radical intervention but to insist on the state to guarantee the 'minimum prerequisites of civilisation' (*CW*, 138) by strictly enforcing its monopoly of power and by scrupulously observing the rule of law. These minimum prerequisites are defined with reference to basic democratic and civil rights: freedom of speech, the power of the courts to settle disputes, personal liberty (with women receiving a special mention), and the inviolableness of the individual person. Enzensberger's 'middle way' solution corresponds most closely to the 'dry' or 'proceduralist' liberalism, or the libertarianist position of the American tradition, which propagates 'as forcefully as possible' the rights of the individual while demanding 'a decidely neutral state...without its own religious or cultural projects...or, indeed without any collective aims which go beyond the preservation of the personal liberty and physical safety...of its population'.[39] But Enzensberger's liberal position is not ideologically founded, and he is thus no 'true' liberal. He does not argue that the state should not take up any creative-political role beyond the defense of a 'minimum of civilisation' because it is not the function of the state, in the liberal understanding, to assume such tasks and power. Rather, Enzensberger argues that the 'stochastic' process of politics and the 'turbulence' of uncontrollable social and economic developments in the contemporary global situation make any political intervention impossible or meaningless. It is a defensive position in view of a particular historical situation, experienced after 1989, which is seen as posing seemingly unsolvable problems for 'not just the individuals involved but existing political systems as well'. Both are, in the end, 'overwhelmed' (*überfordert*) by demands that create 'too heavy a burden' (*CW*, 62, 65).

Enzensberger's argument in both *Great Migration* and *Civil War* culminates in the demand for a minimum standard of democratic civilisation. It is a position which clarifies the democratic-liberal core of his critique, the defense of democratic and republican values; it insists on the active role of the political institutions of the constitutional state under the rule of law, and it emphasizes the state's responsibilities in the support of the civil society. Enzensberger's position is thus characterized by a continuing commitment to the ideals of liberal democracy and the traditions of the Enlightenment. As such, it needs to be fully supported. On the other hand, however, one must ask whether this 'minimalist' position does not fall behind a standard reached already, in particular in view of Enzensberger's earlier comments on the successful democratic learning processes within the Federal Republic, the de-facto multiculturalism of its society, its integrative potential and the general consensus prevalent in its democratic political culture. There is a concern that the appeal to the state to use its monopoly of force just might not go far enough, as expressed by Theweleit in a formulation which seems to be addressed to Enzensberger: 'Nothing but a call for the courts. Daddy the State is supposed to play the Good Guy and thrash the backside of the right-wingers'.[40] What should be possible above and beyond the call for the rule of law and the state's monopoly of force is the call for a politics of recognition which would take as its point of departure the anthropological longing for recognition formulated by Enzensberger. The 'politics of recognition' need to be developed for example in the area of immigration and integration policies (a policy of recognition in view of ethnic-cultural identities on the basis of constitutional equality and civil rights), but also with regard to the special status of young people who are susceptible to extremist violence (an integrative policy of recognition that would address the need for specific educational, social and labour market reforms). Such policies of recognition, which in Germany could only be formulated on the basis of an historical tradition regarding the principles of the 'social market economy', are not only indispensable but also 'realistic': they only conform to the 'middle way', the broad social consensus within the society of the Federal Republic which Enzensberger portrayed with such enthusiasm only a few years prior to his last two essays.

Enzensberger's poetic presentiment of the 'twilight of social democracy' (*CW*, 32) provides the clue to an understanding of his anthropological pessimism. The Spenglerian language of the metaphor signals the break with a tradition of the European democratic Left for which Enzensberger sees no future – in a sense he comes perilously close to a position that is reminiscent of the pessimistic nihilism of Heiner Müller who reduces capitalism to the 'Auschwitz principle' of 'selection'.[41] The concept of the social market economy – the backbone, as it were, of the political success of the Federal Republic after 1949 – stands at the core of an experience of liberal democracy which is not possible without the essential contribution of social democratic principles. But the claim that 'social democracy' has outlived its historical use-by date is made neither on the basis of supporting evidence nor on the ground of substantiating argument. The post-war

'German' model – with its uniquely successful fusion of entrepreneurial capitalism, state-mediated social welfare and the participation of the organized labour and union movement, complemented by a growing democratic participation of individuals and groups at grassroot level within a differentiated, pluralistic and muliticultural society – is of course not restricted to Germany alone or to its Western European and Scandinavian neighbours. In the wake of new tensions and the upheaval following the collapse of the Eastern European bureaucratic-socialist societies with their 'planned economies', this model is certainly under pressure. But the suggestion that it is about to be thrown onto the dungheap of history, to be superceded by a globally victorious 'dry' liberalism that parades as unadulterated economic rationalism driven by nothing but the 'pure' market, is merely speculative: it is the doomsday prognosis of a pessimistic clairvoyant rather than sober historical and political analysis.

Enzensberger's anthropological pessimism can be traced back to at least the early 1970s: to the experience of shock and disenchantment in the wake of the political defeat of the New Left, as described in *The Sinking of the Titanic*, and to the profound disillusionment expressed in his radical questioning of the 'history of progress' in *Mausoleum*. It reappears in the essays of 1992 and 1993 which reflect upon the breakdown of the postwar order of the world in which Enzensberger had found for a time the assurance of a peaceful, integrative civil society – albeit under the ominous shadow of a past of irrational 'delusion'. Enzensberger's anthropological pessimism is most striking in the last passage of *Civil War* which resurrects the myth of Sisyphus as a paradigm of *la condition humaine*. His reading of the myth, unlike the experience of existentialist liberation stressed by Camus, underlines the ordinariness of the everyday hero's struggle to maintain a minimum of civilization in view of the 'anthropological constant', i.e., permanent civil war. In the last poems of his most recent collection, *Kiosk*, the emphasis on the idea of social practice gives way to melancholia and millenial introspection. The titles of these texts are characteristic enough: 'Of Life after Death', and 'The Interment'. In the latter poem, the question of the 'core' of the individual human being is described as something that resists explanation, even after all theoretical models have been tested: '[It] belongs to a species/of which we know nothing'.[42] The other poem provides an apocalytic yet serene image of twentieth century civilisation that has come to an end and is being reclaimed by a triumphant nature in hypertrophic growth. The relics of the industrial society – concrete, power plants, neon lights – are shown to disappear in an impenetrable jungle like the age-old temples of Angkor Wat while the melancholic voice of the lyrical persona laments the absence of an artist like Piranesi whose *veduta* might have filled the ruins and decaying landscapes with an imaginary life, preserving it for a posterity which can by no means be taken for granted.

NOTES

1 Hans Magnus Enzensberger, 'Erinnerungen an einen Tumult. Zu einem Tagebuch aus dem Jahre 1968', in *Hans Magnus Enzensberger, Text und Kritik,* Vol. 49 , ed. Heinz Ludwig Arnold, Munich, 1985, pp. 6-9, here p. 6.

2 Hans Magnus Enzensberger, 'Das Ende der Konsequenz', in *Politische Brosamen,* Frankfurt/Main, 1985, pp. 7-30, here p. 19. The essay was written in 1981.

3 Hans Magnus Enzensberger, 'Mittelmaß und Wahn. Ein Vorschlag zur Güte', in *Mittelmaß und Wahn,* Frankfurt/Main, 1988, pp. 250-277, here p. 252.

4 Cf. 'Mittelmaß und Wahn', p. 261.

5 'Fünf halbherzige Seiten in einem Taschenbuch': Enzensberger about his political engagement for the SPD in 1961, cf. 'Das empfindliche Ungeheuer. Ein Wahlkampf-Unterhaltung aus dem Jahre 1987 mit Hellmuth Karasek', in *Mittelmaß und Wahn,* p. 227 (reprint of an interview first published in *Der Spiegel,* 4/1987).

6 Cf. 'Mittelmaß und Wahn', p. 259, and 'Von der Unaufhaltsamkeit des Kleinbürgertums. Eine soziologische Grille', in *Politische Brosamen,* pp. 195-206, here p. 205.

7 'Mittelmaß und Wahn', p. 259. In *Diderots Schatten* Enzensberger gives a literary portrait of Diderot as an intellectual which is a self-portrait at the same time. He questions the concept of *Engagement* and emphasizes instead a notion of *Hilfsbereitschaft,* of 'naive curiosity' and an interest in 'daily practice' – rather than a feeling of 'ideological duty' – as the essential qualities of the intellectual. The public intellectual is driven by a desire for 'new experiences' - which is why he involves himself in every problem - but is also conscious of his own problematic position: 'ein wohlmeinender Menschenfreund...der sich seiner eigenen Fragwürdigkeit innegeworden ist': Hans Magnus Enzensberger, 'Nachwort', *Diderots Schatten,* Frankfurt/Main, 1994, pp. 382, 383, 385.

8 In the last scene of the play by Volker Ludwig and Detlef Michel, *Eine linke Geschichte,* which follows the biographies of three 'sixty-eighters' through the seventies and eighties, the protagonists quote from an interview with Enzensberger to sum up the achievement of their generation: cf. Hans Magnus Enzensberger, 'Ich will nicht der Lappen sein, mit dem man die Welt putzt', Interview mit André Müller, *Die Zeit,* 20.1.1995.

9 Cf. 'Von der Unaufhaltsamkeit des Kleinbürgertums. Eine soziologische Grille', p. 204.

10 Cf. the essay 'Lob des Analphabetentums', in *Mittelmaß und Wahn,* pp. 61-74, here p. 67. See also 'Über die Ignoranz', pp. 9-22.

11 'Das empfindliche Ungeheuer', in *Mittelmaß und Wahn,* p. 229.

12 *Mittelmaß und Wahn,* pp. 263, 264, 265.

13 *Mittelmaß und Wahn,* pp. 274, 261.

14 Hans Magnus Enzensberger, *Aussichten auf den Bürgerkrieg,* Frankfurt/Main 1993, p. 10. The English translation has 'new world order': cf. *CW,* 12.

15 Enzensberger, *Diderots Schatten,* pp. 153-258.

16 Cf. *Aussichten auf den Bürgerkrieg,* p. 45.

17 Charles Taylor, *Multiculturalism and 'The Politics of Recognition',* Princeton, 1992. See also the German edition *Multikulturalismus und die Politik der Anerkennung,* ed. Amy Gutmann, Frankfurt/Main, 1993, which includes responses to Taylor by Gutmann, Steven C. Rockefeller, Michael Walzer, Susan Wolf, as well as an essay by Jürgen Habermas, 'Anerkennungskämpfe im demokratischen Rechtsstaat'.

18 Charles Taylor, *Multiculturalism and 'The Politics of Recognition',* p. 26.

19 Jürgen Habermas, 'Anerkennungskämpfe im demokratischen Rechtsstaat', in Taylor, *Multikulturalismus und die Politik der Anerkennung*, p. 154.
20 *Wahrheit und Methode*, Tübingen, 1975, pp. 289-90, quoted in Taylor, *Multiculturalism and the Politics of Recognition*, p. 67.
21 Paul Michael Lützeler, 'Vom Ethnozentrismus zur Multikultur. Europäische Identität heute', in *Multikulturalität. Tendenzen, Probleme, Perspektiven im europäischen und internationalen Horizont*, eds. Michael Kessler and Jürgen Wertheimer, Tübingen, 1995, pp. 91-106, here p. 95.
22 Paul Michael Lützeler, p. 103.
23 Cf. the chapter by Klaus J. Bade in the present volume.
24 *Aussichten auf den Bürgerkrieg*, p. 43. The English version (cf. *CW*, 36) fails to convey the complexities involved here.
25 Heribert Adam, 'Fremdenfeindlichkeit, Einwanderungspolitik und Multikulturalismus in Deutschland und Kanada', *Leviathan*, 22, 1 (1994), pp. 60-77, here p. 67.
26 Cf. Hans Magnus Enzensberger, *Die Große Wanderung. Dreiunddreißig Markierungen. Mit einer Fußnote 'Über einige Besonderheiten bei der Menschenjagd'*, Frankfurt/Main, 1992, p. 15: 'Ethnien entstehen quasi naturwüchsig, "von selbst"; Nationen sind bewußt geschaffene...Gebilde'.
27 Cf. Ute Benz, 'Rechtsradikalismus – Merkmal einer neuen Jugendkultur?', in *Gewalt – Faszination und Furcht*, eds. Frauke Meyer-Gosau and Wolfgang Emmerich, Leipzig, 1994, pp. 120-139, here p. 120
28 Ute Benz, p. 120.
29 Charles Taylor, *Multiculturalism and the Politics of Recognition*, p. 35.
30 This is not the place to discuss the scientific literature on autism. Two useful introductory works are *Autism in Adolescents and Adults*, eds. Eric Schopler and Gary B. Mesibov, New York, 1983, and Uta Frith, *Autism: Explaining the Enigma*, Oxford and Cambridge, Mass., 1989.
31 Klaus Theweleit, 'Jetzt gehts loo-ooos? Ein Gespräch mit Klaus Theweleit', in *Gewalt – Faszination und Furcht*, pp. 150-171, here p. 159.
32 Cf. Cora Stephan, 'Eine deutsche Hysterie', *Der Spiegel*, 4/1995, pp. 174–8.
33 'Jetzt gehts loo-ooos? Ein Gespräch mit Klaus Theweleit', p. 158.
34 Hans Magnus Enzensberger: 'Da in Bonn jeder als weltfremder Träumer gilt, der ein wenig Beweglichkeit erwartet, möchte ich mit ein paar praktischen Vorschlägen schließen': 'Auswärts im Rückwärtsgang', *Der Spiegel*, 37/1995, pp. 215-221.
35 'Plädoyer für den Hauslehrer. Ein bißchen Bildungspolitik', in *Politische Brosamen*, pp. 161-176.
36 Cf. Gerhard Fischer, 'Benjamin's Utopia of Education as a *Theatrum Mundi et Vitae*: On the Programme for a Proletarian Children's Theatre, in *'With the Sharpened Axe of Reason' – Approaches to Walter Benjamin*, ed. G. Fischer, Oxford and Washington, D.C., 1996, pp. 201-217.
37 Wolfgang Huber, 'Menschenwürde und Menschenrechte als Grundelemente einer zukünftigen internationalen Ordnung', *Leviathan*, 1/1994 (March 1994), pp. 47-59, here p. 59.
38 Wolfgang Huber, p. 59.
39 Michael Walzer, 'Kommentar', in Charles Taylor, *Multikulturalismus und die Politik der Anerkennung*, pp. 109-117, here p. 109.
40 'Nichts dahinter als ein Ruf nach den Gerichten. Papa Staat soll der Gute sein und den Rechten den Arsch versohlen': 'Jetzt gehts loo-ooos? Ein Gespräch mit Klaus Theweleit', p. 160.
41 Cf. Heiner Müller, 'Auschwitz und kein Ende. Ein Gespräch mit jungen französischen Regisseuren', *Drucksache*, 16, 1995 (Berliner Ensemble GmbH); reprinted in *Communications–IBS*, 24, 2 (December 1995), pp. 54-60.

42 Hans Magnus Enzensberger, *Kiosk. Neue Gedichte*, Frankfurt/Main, 1995. Cf. the poems 'Vom Leben nach dem Tode' and 'Die Grablegung', pp. 128, 129.

II

Civil War and the Politics of War and Violence

Chapter Six

Eliding Politics: Enzensberger and the Aesthetics of Evasion

Pam Stavropoulos

I Confronting Ambivalence

The enormity of post-Cold War developments has re-ignited intellectual debate about nationalism, and re-appraisal of the conceptual currency, and even relevance, of liberal democracy.[1] In different but also mutually reinforcing ways, critique broadly described as post-modernist has problematized the notions of reason and progress, highlighted the totalizing tendencies of universalist theorizing, and contested the privileging of the human subject.[2] Since a recurring tenet of contemporary critique is to dispute the legitimacy of dichotomies and binary oppositions (as between, for example, 'high' and 'popular' culture) it would be erroneous to see such debates as the preserve of the academy. Yet a range of factors (of which the sophistication of much contemporary intellectual discourse, and the always problematic role of the intellectual are two) can combine to limit the direct intervention of intellectuals into the sphere of 'public' debate.

It is in this context, and against this background, that the recent essays of Hans Magnus Enzensberger, *The Great Migration* and *Prospects of Civil War* – collected in the London edition of 1994 under the title of *Civil War* – assume wider significance. Revealingly (and to the extent that anticipation of a charge is an attempt to deflect it, disarmingly) Enzensberger admits that one enters the public realm of discussion at one's 'own risk' (*CW*, 139). His essays are succinct and abbreviated; at one level they do not readily permit the more nuanced exposition alternative modes of expression might facilitate. To the extent that they succeed in dramatizing urgent contemporary issues, it might also seem misguided, and even churlish, to subject them to analysis.

Yet polemic is potent precisely because it eschews qualification; the writer's ability to mediate constraint is itself a theme of contemporary critique. As a lettered and even celebrated male European writer, Enzensberger is assured (and with the Penguin release of his *Civil War* essays, virtually guaranteed) a wide readership. This being the case, and in light of the gravity of the issues with which he deals, these essays arguably need to be taken seriously and not absolved from the sustained analysis his longer critical work has received. Indeed, for the reasons I have outlined, there are grounds for arguing that his recent work should be subject to more, rather than less, scrutiny, and that whatever his intentions in the *Civil War* essays (intentionality, of course, itself problematic) we must again and necessarily take him at his word.

In the *Civil War* essays, Enzensberger writes arrestingly about confronting topics. So arrestingly, in some places, that the effect is akin to a kind of psychic assault. But he also writes authoritatively, and this authoritativeness partly accounts for the ambivalence I feel in relation to his recent work. I am aware, of course, that the capacity of his critique to elicit unease is intimately related to the assertiveness with which he assembles and presents his case. Perhaps my objections and ambivalence are themselves manifestations of the defence mechanisms he is successful in evoking. But in this chapter I want to try to dissect my ambivalence, as I feel there may be more important questions at issue than those pertaining to my personal reaction.

An initial comment on 'ambivalence' may be appropriate. The word seems to have become a shorthand term to denote a reaction or state in which the negative outweighs the positive, and to which almost everyone has recourse. In this way, ambivalence has permeated the *Zeitgeist*; has become a popular synonym for contemporary *Weltschmerz*. In contrast, I want to endorse the need for dissection of ambivalence as a possible means of saving it from the fate of normalization. In a review of Kate Millet's recent study *The Politics of Cruelty*, Anthony Elliott (1994:34) contends that ambivalence 'should not necessarily be seen as an obstacle to political knowledge and action', since 'the capacity to tolerate feelings of confusion and anxiety are essential to reflective political judgment'. The danger, he goes on to say, of attempting 'to short-circuit ambivalence, or to transcend it...is that such a strategy plays into the hands of a culture that already jerks its knee at the very mention of ambiguity'. In any case, and as Bauman (1991:16) has elaborated, 'efforts to dissolve the ambivalent category result in yet more ambivalence and prove in the end to be counterproductive'. In what follows, I will attempt to locate the sources of my ambivalence about Enzensberger's *Civil War* theses. I will also argue that far from confronting the painful dilemmas he lays bare, Enzensberger actually evades them. He does this, I contend, principally (though not exclusively) through evasion of the realm of the political. And in such evasion, his style and mode of expression will be shown to play a central role.

II 'Positive' Features of Enzensberger's Critique

To the extent that my reservations about Enzensberger's critique are in some ways the corollary of what I regard as its strengths, it is artificial to extrapolate out respective dimensions. Yet not to do so is also problematic, and, in the context of this chapter, would further entrench the more 'negative' reading of ambivalence I also want to contest. So I will begin by highlighting what for me are some of the extremely powerful and in many ways persuasive features of Enzensberger's analysis (which I need to make explicit in any case, since I cannot assume we find the same things persuasive).

My aim in this first part of this chapter is less to engage in sustained consideration of particular points than to isolate broad themes of the *Civil War* essays. This will serve as a prelude to the subsequent focus on what I will argue to be much less persuasive elements of Enzensberger's critique. There is no particular order in my presentation of these points; of themselves they strike me as powerful. Yet the often implicit relationship between them enhances their potency, and they are especially powerful in combination.

The paucity of 'useful' theory on the topic of civil war, and the inadequacy of political theory more generally

Enzensberger's contention that 'the mad reality [of civil war] eludes formal legal definition' (*CW*, 12) is surely correct. In the context of his corresponding contention regarding the absence of a 'theory' of civil war, the general lack of material on the topic of civil war *per se* is both indictment and revelation.[3] Where do we turn, of what do we avail ourselves in the perhaps misguided but nonetheless compelling attempt to 'understand' contemporary (post-Cold War) developments?

The possible irrelevance and inapplicability of much conventional political theory to this topic is no less disturbing. In the reading of Enzensberger, 'we have always regarded politics as a struggle between opposing interests, not only for power, for resources and for better opportunities, but also in pursuit of wishes, plans and ideas'. Yet when 'no value is attributed to life – either to one's own life or to the lives of one's opponents – this becomes impossible, and all political thought, from Aristotle and Machiavelli to Marx and Weber, is turned upside down'. All that is left, he suggests, 'is the Hobbesian ur-myth of the war of everyone against everyone else' (*CW*, 30, 31).

Foucault (1979:66) has spoken of the 'normalising discourse' of the human sciences. To the extent that to theorize is to normalize, critique which points to the limits of 'theory' is salutary. But whether consciously aware of it or not, we all engage in 'theory'; the dichotomy between 'ideas' and 'action' is itself a fallacy. So if much of what passes for 'political theory' is no longer relevant, where does this leave us in apprehending not only the numerous civil wars which are currently raging, but the contemporary 'politics' over which they are fought? Even if wanting to dissent from Enzensberger's unequivocal reading, in posing such questions so starkly he challenges complacent assumptions and forces their re-examination.

A corrective to the naivety (and even bankruptcy) of liberal optimism

I want to be careful in relation to this point, both because liberalism is a complex and variegated doctrine, and because (conservative?) pessimism is no less problematic. But Enzensberger's critique of 'the curious notion that man is basically good' (*CW*, 33) seems to me to be as important as it is sobering. In another of his deceptively simple formulations, Enzensberger tells us that 'there are now no criminals, only clients', and exposes the 'insane attributions' of responsibility everywhere other than to the proponents and perpetrators:

> All in all, we are dealing with 'poor souls' who [have] to be treated with the utmost patience. It is hardly possible to expect such underprivileged people to realize that setting fire to children is, strictly speaking, not permissible. Attention must be drawn all the more urgently to the inadequate supply of leisure activities available to the arsonists. (*CW*, 42).

What will/does it take, Enzensberger challenges, to dislodge the residual belief that despite (and perhaps *because* of) all the evidence to the contrary, people are 'basically good'?

The critique of ideology

Implicitly linked to both his broad critique of political theory, and more specific critique of liberalism, Enzensberger sees ideology as an unhelpful and even irrelevant concept with which to address contemporary developments: 'Violence has freed itself from ideology'; 'the complete absence of conviction is striking'; 'the ideological label is no more than a charade' (*CW*, 20, 21, 23).

Against 'restrictive ideological analysis', Enzensberger counterposes 'the telling physical detail' (*CW*, 84). With something of the flavour of Sontag's 'Against Interpretation', he contends that while 'the leading articles and polemics of the [early post-war period] have a strange mustiness about them...eyewitness reports remain fresh'; 'The specialists in perception are at their best when they generalize least, when they do not censor the fantastic contradictions of the chaotic world they have entered, but leave them as they are' (*CW*, 84). The point is disarming, even as it is problematic in implying the possibility of unmediated apprehension.

The critique of ideology (which in a different way comprised a major theme of early post-war criticism) is, of course, a tenet of postmodernist analysis.[4] In *Anti-Oedipus* (1972:104), Deleuze and Guattari declared that 'it is not a question of ideology...It is not an ideological problem, a problem of failing to recognize, or of being subject to, an illusion'. And Foucault has argued that 'the notion of ideology' is 'difficult to use' on several grounds.[5] While critics such as Spivak are salutary in indicting attempts to de-emphasize ideology,[6] Enzensberger's questioning of its capacity to illuminate contemporary developments is as confronting as it is necessary. Is 'the telling physical detail' – in all its starkness and squalour – all we have? And given its potentially paralyzing effect, is it even enough?

The critique of artists (in addition to intellectuals) as unworthy guides

If several of the themes in Enzensberger's *Civil War* essays are not novel, it is part of the power of his critique that they are restated with particular urgency. His indictment of the role of artists is a compelling illustration of this. For again despite (or because) of evidence to the contrary, there are seductive incentives to preserve the (precarious?) boundary between 'politics' and 'culture'; to deny that art can be complicit in, and even perpetuate, power relations.

Bourdieu (1993:43) declares 'the most disputed frontier of all' to be 'the one which separates the field of cultural production and the field of power'. But our investment in denying the possible overlap between the two can still scarcely be exaggerated. No less a figure than Edward Said (1993:xiv) has said that 'as someone who has spent his entire professional life teaching literature, yet who also grew up in the pre-World War Two colonial world, I have found it a challenge *not* to see culture in this way – that is, antiseptically quarantined from its worldly affiliations'.

Enzensberger is confronting because he does not flinch from the nexus, so that we, as readers, cannot avoid recognition of it: 'Happy the man who can talk himself into believing that culture can safeguard society against violence'. Indeed, for Enzensberger, 'the production of hatred and the preparation for civil war is still one of the principal concerns of the creative artist' (*CW*, 52, 53). If, as Nietzsche expressed it, 'Apollonian consciousness' is 'but a thin veil hiding the whole Dionysian realm' and 'what we call culture is entirely composed of...beguilements', such starkness is, again, potentially too much for most of us, who need illusion and 'the remedy of art' (1956: 28, 109, 95) to render existence bearable.

The dissolution of boundaries

Attempts at containment of the affronting or unacceptable within strictly defined limits constitute further consolations of which Enzensberger divests us. Indeed, most forms of delineation are presented as problematic in his analysis. Thus 'aggression and defence become indistinguishable' (*CW*, 47). Implicitly evoking Peter Gay's resonant phrase 'alibis for aggression' (1995:35), he speaks of 'a destructive mania that dares not express itself except in socially tolerated forms' (*CW*, 2-3).[7]

In his pioneering study of the coercive functions of stereotypes, Gilman (1985:240) concedes that it would be 'the task of Sisyphus' to 'stop the production of images of the Other, images that demean and, by demeaning, control'. We need crude representations of difference,

Gilman argues, 'to localize our anxiety, to prove to ourselves that what we fear does not lie within'. Enzensberger is similarly lucid: 'As far as the barbarians are concerned, we need not expect them at the gates', since 'they are always already with us' (*CW*, 138). Attempts at rationalization of the unpalatable are revealed for what they are. Psychological escape routes are sealed off.

An excoriating style

As is apparent from the brief quotations I have cited, Enzensberger's style of writing is a further weapon in his capacity to confront. In her suggestive study of receptivity to the thought of Lacan, Sherry Turkle (1992) highlights the respect accorded *style* in Europe (and specifically France) in contrast to a broadly American attitude which sees style as antithetical to 'substance'. There is, of course, a large literature on the politics of writing (eg. Barthes, 1977) which it is not possible to discuss here. In my reading of Enzensberger, 'style' is inextricably related to 'substance'; his forceful and yet dispassionate – even resigned – expression both reflects and underlines the vision to which he gives voice.

Enzensberger's facility and talent for synthesis of disparate contexts is so succinctly expressed that one might wonder whether the material he links up is really disparate at all: 'Where, there [ie. the 'Second' and 'Third' Worlds] whole countries, or even whole continents, drop out of the international exchange system, here [ie. the 'First', 'developed' World] increasing sections of the population can no longer keep up in the competition for advantage that gets more brutal by the day' (*CW*, 34). As I will go on to elaborate, I am not uncritical of Enzensberger's style (which is simultaneously apocalyptic and laconic) or of certain rhetorical devices by which he seeks to seduce – though at times to bludgeon – the reader. But there is no denying the power of his choice and use of language, his mode of argumentation, or his sheer relentlessness.

Moreover, it is part of the power of his phraseology that these characteristics apply irrespective of whether he is equating the barbarism of 'First' and 'Third' World economies, or describing his own more personal reactions and responses:

> Just the mention of civil war sooner or later turns into a kind of self-experimentation...I am not neutral. I have been infected. I feel the rage, the fear and the hate building up inside me. I am deeply involved in my subject. My brain is flooded with chemical messengers I know nothing about. I am in danger of losing control of the thoughts that come into my head.

'It is impossible', he goes on to assert,

> to have a linear discussion on this theme. Merely stating your own position fans the flames of conflict. There is no Archimedean point. I have stepped into an intellectual and moral minefield. I have to move with great

> care. But I know that although I might, if I'm lucky, find my way through, I'll never be able to clear the field. I don't see eye to eye with anybody, not even with myself. (*CW*, 49)

To quote Turkle from her study of Lacan (1992:236), 'the search for the real can lead to a kind of delirium – or in any case to a delirious discourse'. The above passages from Enzensberger clearly partake of 'delirious discourse'. To the extent that we, as readers, are borne along by it (and there are surely senses in which it is difficult to remain immune) we, too, risk invasion and 'infection'.

Personal confrontation

The combined effect of Enzensberger's critique of theory, of ideology, and (more specifically) of liberalism, his indictment of art and culture as well as intellect, his dissolution of boundaries, and his arresting and evocative style, is potent. Nor do these features of his analysis exhaust the critical avalanche to which we are subjected. I have said little, for example, of his reference to our lack of preparedness for the post-Cold War scenarios which are unfolding, or of the desolation the single sentence *'No one knows what to do'* (*CW*, 14) can elicit. His critique posits challenges not only intellectually, but emotionally, psychically and existentially.

The 'thousand and one things we take for granted in a functioning civil society' mean that however we may like to suppose otherwise, we are not morally exempt. On the contrary, we are complicit in 'the barbarity of the everyday'. Enzensberger speaks of 'deliberate self-deceptions'; of how 'the best intention is frustrated by the cosiness of the seminar room' in that 'no one can credibly declare how he would behave in an emergency' (*CW*, 69, 123, 113). The essays evoke, at one level, remarks made by Foucault (1984:374) in the interview 'Politics and Ethics', that 'at every moment, step by step, one must confront what one is thinking and saying with what one is doing, with what one is'.

III 'Negative' Features

And yet: my contention that to read Enzensberger is to be powerfully and personally confronted *at one level* is advised. Having suggested some of the ways in which Enzensberger throws down intellectual and emotional gauntlets to his readers, I now want to argue that the strength of the challenges he poses is blunted and undercut. This may seem paradoxical, and even contradictory. But I want to argue that far from following through and delivering on the critique he so skilfully mounts, Enzensberger actually abrogates its most confronting challenges. In this charge lie the sources of my ambivalence. In the second part of the chapter, I thus attempt to locate omissions, evasions and distortions in Enzensberger's critique, many of which are corollaries of the strengths I have elaborated.

A problematic location of violence

In his account of civil war, Enzensberger is unequivocal about where to locate the violence and aggression from which we seek to avert our eyes: *'It comes from within'* (CW, 20; emphasis added). This attribution both suggests a salutary corrective to unreflective liberalism, and revives notions of responsibility which (partly because of the challenge they can pose to belief that man is 'basically good') are of dubious popularity. But locating the sources of violence within individuals *per se* (Enzensberger declares that 'it is probably enough if one person in every hundred wants to make civilized co-existence impossible'; CW, 20) is less persuasive in its failure to acknowledge what Turkle (1992:248) calls 'the presence of social forces within the individual, in the interpenetration of individual and society'.

While the nature of this interrelationship is beyond the scope of this chapter, I do want to stress its importance, and in the sense that Enzensberger fails to engage with it explicitly, a shortcoming of his critique. Even if he did not wish to address it in detail, there exists a burgeoning literature on the 'interpenetration' of these two dimensions (eg. Elliott, 1992) to which Enzensberger could have pointed. In her probing exploration of the question 'Where to locate violence?', Jacqueline Rose (1989:25-39) criticizes approaches which are predicated on an 'inside'/'outside' dichotomy. Rose argues (1989:28) that such approaches are inadequate to address the complex interrelationships at issue: 'For a theory that pits inside and outside against each other...wipes out any difference or contradiction on either side: the subject suffers, the social oppresses, and what is produced, by implication, is utter stasis in each'.

To the extent that Enzensberger is clearly not insensitive to the broader social context (although I would argue that he gestures toward it rather than engaging with it[8]), the above criticism may seem illegitimate when applied to him. But I would argue that in his constant reiteration of the potential and actual barbarism of *individuals*, he both shifts the conceptual terrain from the need to explore interconnections *between* individual and social context, and implicitly rationalizes his failure to do so. Interestingly, he seems in this way to have sacrificed some of the sophistication of his own earlier work – eg., in *Raids and Reconstructions* (1976) – which was careful to preserve the links between 'inner' and 'outer' reality.[9]

One does not have to be a Lacanian (emphasizing the extent to which 'each of us is inhabited by society through use of language'; Turkle, 1992:249) to have reservations about critique which does not specifically allude to (much less systematically explicate) *the nexus between 'individual' and 'societal' aggression*. In a provocative essay which seeks, among other things, to expose the limits of the view that cruelty 'is just a fact of life: some people *are* that way', Mary Maxwell (1991:87-113) suggests that cruelty cannot occur without societal sanctioning (and thus complicity). Enzensberger is clearly impatient of attempts to evade the reality of cruelty. But his own failure to engage with its overlapping and interpenetrating dimensions contributes to the very simplifications he ostensibly opposes.

The limits of 'spontaneity' and the evasion of politics

A consistent emphasis on the 'spontaneous' eruption of violence is no less problematic. This is because it leads to a lack of emphasis on, and even attention to, the processes by which the most destructive potential of violence is made possible. Enzensberger tells us that 'today's civil wars ignite spontaneously from inside' (*CW*, 17), that violence 'can escalate at any time to epidemic proportions' (*CW*, 20), and that 'the seeds of brutalization...may escalate to raging aggression' (*CW*, 61). In contrast, I would like to emphasize the limits – and even illegitimacy – of the 'spontaneity' argument, in that it deflects attention from the specific, and often carefully orchestrated, triggers which ignite the most rampant forms of destructiveness.

No one could deny the snowball effect of aggression; its rapid inflammation of tension, and direct relationship to (via the courting of) retaliation. Indisputedly, cycles of violence are unleashed, and unpremeditated ('spontaneous') aggression a reality. Yet how far can this argument be taken before it becomes insensitive to the calculated *politics* of aggression; to the deliberate fuelling and fostering of violence? And what happens to notions of agency and responsibility, which Enzensberger (*CW*, 64-5) also wants to assert?

To take just one example, while it would be naive to deny the alacrity with which *some* formerly peaceable citizens of the former Yugoslavia have engaged in the most barbarous atrocities, to deny that 'nationalist' leaders like Milosevic, Karadzic and Tudjman have ruthlessly exploited and encouraged such behaviour for their own perceived interests and purposes is scarcely tenable. To contend, as does Enzensberger, that contemporary civil wars 'are waged without stakes on either side, that they are wars *about nothing at all*' (*CW*, 30, original emphasis[10]) is to be wilfully blind to the perceived interests and investments ('rational' and otherwise) with which they are endowed. It is also to abrogate the realm of the political (and particularly of so-called 'elite' politics) almost entirely.

A persistent denial of the realm of the political (and, as I have suggested, of *agency*, even as it is simultaneously and contradictorily asserted) is both a disturbing and incipiently coercive feature of Enzensberger's critique. To take another example, he declares that 'sectional self-interest and xenophobia are anthropological constants which predate every rationalization', and that 'their universal distribution indicates that they are older than all known societies' (*CW*, 106). But once again, this is to divert much needed attention from the societal and cultural sanctioning without which they could not be so destructive. Enzensberger thus comes alarmingly close to passivity and fatalism, which, while related to pessimism, are not its necessary corollaries.

He rightly notes the limits of an emphasis on 'biology' in the understanding of civil war (1994:141). But if he is going to invoke the findings of anthropology, he should consult more recent work which – as the very title of one contemporary collection, *The Social Dynamics of Peace and Conflict* (1988) suggests – is attentive to the social and cultural underpinnings of aggression. His own analysis is not. Enzensberger is implicitly beholden to the view (for which, of course, there is considerable evidence) that given the right (or perhaps one should say the wrong) circumstances, there are few limits to the barbarisms people will inflict. But the former part of this contention needs at least as much emphasis as the latter. Without corresponding attentiveness to its politics and cultural sanctioning, emphasis on the 'spontaneous eruption' of violence is not only one-sided, but dangerously so.

The denial of innocence

Also disturbing (and directly related both to the evasion of politics and the contention that all human beings possess the potential for bestial behaviour) is Enzensberger's contesting of the notion of 'innocence'. Implicitly related to his critique of boundaries (eg., 'perpetrators' versus 'innocent civilians', even as this, too, is problematic in terms of notions of agency and responsibility) Enzensberger insists upon the complicity and even culpability of those we may seek to exempt from acts of commission and aggression: 'But who was it who fed and nourished the perpetrators, who applauded them and prayed for them, if not the "innocent civilians"' (*CW*, 51)?

As intimated previously, narrowing the gap between – and even dissolving – conceptual boundaries and demarcations is both necessary and persuasive in some contexts. Yet, in this particular case, collapsing distinctions between 'guilt' and 'innocence' is extremely problematic. For it betrays an *illegitimate* dissolution of distinctions – as between, for example, the somnolent automaton who orders the razing of a village, those who carry out the order, and the children who will be destroyed by its execution. The distinction between adults and children should perhaps be particularly emphasized. As eloquently conveyed by the character Ivan in Dostoevsky's *The Brothers Karamazov* (1968:243), there surely exists a distinction between 'grown up people' who have 'eaten the apple' and 'go on eating it still', and the children 'who haven't eaten anything, and are so far innocent'.

The tendency to 'react psychotically by striking out blindly in all directions' is, in Enzensberger's reading, 'at work everywhere': 'Even apparently ordinary people take it upon themselves to do away with the superfluous masses...The steps they are prepared to take *differ only in degree*, and depend on the means at their disposal' (*CW*, 39-40;

emphasis added). Specificity is collapsed into generality; important distinctions between omission and commission, between complicity and instigation, are discredited in advance. Enzensberger speaks of 'contempt for human life' (*CW*, 40). But his own contempt for *degrees* of participation is disturbing. Dissolving – as distinct from problematizing – distinctions between guilt and innocence entails inability to mediate *levels* of participation, which is again as coercive as it is problematic.

Style as power

In all these contexts, Enzensberger's style of writing plays an important and problematical role. I have noted what, in my reading, is the inextricable relationship between 'style' and 'substance' in Enzensberger's critique. And of course attentiveness to the way in which we express ourselves – our mode of argumentation – assumes considerable, and even crucial, importance in post-modernist critique. What is particularly interesting and relevant in this context is the extent to which, even in an attempt to extricate ourselves from power relations (the power of the critic over the subject on which s/he writes) we can remain wedded to them.

In his essay 'What is An Author?', Foucault (1984:103) contends that 'a certain number of notions that are intended to replace the privileged position of the author actually seem to preserve that privilege and suppress the real meaning of his disappearance'. This point seems pertinent to Enzensberger's writing in *Civil War*. For while in some respects 'democratic' in his treatment of the broad issues he canvasses, Enzensberger implicitly – and at times explicitly – partakes of the privileged position of 'author'. Here I would contend that his style of writing – which is simultaneously forceful and iconoclastic; laconic and diffident – is a weapon by which he does this.

Much of the forcefulness of Enzensberger's critique derives from bold assertions with which, it is intimated, we could not possibly disagree. A consistent rhetorical ploy utilized in this context is attribution of illegitimacy to views contrary to the writer's own. Thus we frequently come across such formulations as 'Only an idiot would argue...', 'No rational person believes that...' and 'Even the most stupid person should grasp...' (*CW*, 34, 35, 144). In Enzensberger's hands, such formulations serve to disarm dissent in a way which is itself potentially coercive (the attribution of stupidity/irrationality to those who would take issue; the normalization of Enzensberger's viewpoints).

In some cases, disagreement may indeed be difficult. But Enzensberger's reliance upon this stylistic technique is problematic. For as we know from Shakespeare and elsewhere, it is sometimes 'fools' and 'idiots' who speak sense. Can we really be so confident as to the delineation between 'rational' and 'irrational'; between 'idiots' and 'the enlightened' (*intellectuals*?) And is not such delineation itself problematic not only in terms of the challenging subject matter Enzensberger is explicating, but in terms of the dissolution of boundaries on which, at other times, he wants to insist?

Enzensberger's paradoxical rupturing of dimensions which must be related is reinforced – *indeed, made possible* – by his style of writing. It is a style, I submit, which while in many ways arresting, is nevertheless insensitive to nuance (arresting *because* it is insensitive to nuance?) and unable to account for it. In this way, it also becomes *a technique of evasion;* a means by which actual complexity is deflected and circumvented rather than explored.

To take just one example: Enzensberger asserts that 'theories that ascribe the poverty of the poorest exclusively to external factors offer cheap sustenance to our sense of moral indignation' (*CW*, 35). At one level this is certainly so. But it is arguable that Enzensberger overcompensates in the other direction – a stance which is facilitated by his authoritative mode of argumentation – thereby absolving himself from the need to probe the complex dynamics between 'internal' and 'external' so-called. Thus this stylistic point is intimately related to his tendency to dichotomize the two realms. Enzensberger's assertive style is double-edged in that the very forcefulness of his critique is at the expense of the more probing and fine-grained analysis with which it cannot easily co-exist.

The distinction between 'rational' and 'irrational'

In addition to preserving both a problematical boundary, and the power of the critic over the reader, Enzensberger's attribution of irrationality and/or idiocy to those who would dissent from his formulations has further implications. For notwithstanding his disparaging of the 'irrational', Enzensberger is at different times forced to concede its power and even appeal.

Having spoken of it in scathing terms, he is unable to account for it. Yet like the return of the repressed, the so-called 'irrational' cannot be routed so readily. Thus Enzensberger has to admit that while the extreme territorialism of individuals 'cannot be rationally justified', it 'appears all the more deeply rooted' (*CW*, 105) for that. Similarly, in the context of a discussion of xenophobia, and the 'irrationality' of a controversy surrounding it, Enzensberger notes that 'nowhere does the subject seem easily accessible to reason' (*CW*, 130).

In a recent paper on the subject of nationalism, Walker Connor (1992:48-57) highlights the perennial failure of intellectuals to apprehend its strength, potency and appeal. He attributes this failure to an occupational over-investment in the 'rational', arguing that intellectuals have considered it sufficient to show the illogicality of the claims on which nationalism rests (a mistake, he rightly notes, which nationalist leaders themselves do not make).[11] The point seems equally and tellingly applicable to Enzensberger, who can only admit but not illuminate the vexing allure of the 'irrational'. Moreover, there is again an incipiently coercive edge to Enzensberger's critique in this context, as at times he not only *admits* 'irrationality' (while failing to explore it) but even capitulates to it.[12]

Enzensberger's assurance falters on the problematical (and in his case, disavowed) nexus between 'rationality' and 'irrationality'. The strength of his critique is undercut by the concessions he is forced to make to the power of the 'irrational', even as he is also and elsewhere dismissive of it. The latter intolerance is itself interesting, in that it suggests a reluctance to accept some of the psychic costs of the material with which he is dealing. To accept such costs would be to confront a correspondence which, while implicitly admitted at one level (the 'I am in danger of losing control over the thoughts that come into my head' passage) is clearly resisted in this instance.

It is arguable that attempts at 'understanding', and even explication, entail a degree of personal risk – the risk that the boundaries between lucidity and psychosis may be less clear than we may like to imagine. Lacan (1992:236) is quoted as saying that 'Psychosis is an attempt at rigor. In this sense, I would say that I am psychotic. I am psychotic for the simple reason that I have always tried to be rigorous'. Enzensberger's insensitivity and unreceptivity to the disturbing nexus between 'rationality' and 'irrationality' – between 'lucidity' and 'psychosis' – is a protective mechanism which both contradicts other aspects of his analysis, and limits the depth of his critique. Such insensitivity is also interesting in the light of Elliott's comments on ambivalence (1994:34) and the lack of receptivity to ambiguity which can be *politically* incapacitating.

Problematics of 'prioritization'

The illegitimacy of expectation of 'solutions' to the extremely wide-ranging questions Enzensberger's critique poses needs to be emphasized. But with respect to the perennially challenging (and perhaps impossible to adequately answer) question of 'What is to be Done?', Enzensberger is also problematic. Declaring that it is 'time to bid farewell to...fantasies of omnipotence', Enzensberger maintains that 'in the long run no one – no country and no individual – can avoid coming to terms with the limits of his own responsibility, and setting priorities' (*CW*, 66) .

Leaving aside the implicit tension in his analysis between, on the one hand, the necessary attribution of responsibility, and recognition of its limits on the other, the question of 'priority setting' is problematic in Enzensberger's critique. He rightly, and even movingly, speaks of the 'bitter choices' which confront us, and of 'the agonizing hopelessness involved in every ethic of responsibility today' (*CW*, 67, 68). But I would argue that his own attempts to mediate such complexity are not only inadequate (as perhaps they would have to be given the enormity of contemporary human suffering) but themselves incipiently coercive.

Enzensberger contends (1994:67) that 'to suggest that our scope for action should be both finite and relative is to risk being pilloried as an isolationist'. Yet he goes on to say that 'deep inside *[note the problematic appeal to intuition]* we all know *[note the assumption of the reader's complicity]* that our foremost concerns must be for our children, our neighbours, our immediate surroundings'. Christ himself, he says (*CW*, 67) 'spoke of loving our neighbours, not people miles away'.

I find such sentiments to be disturbing on several grounds, of which the revealing anticipation of the charge of 'isolationism' is but one. Though seemingly innocuous at one level, their more coercive implications are also discernible. For example, such comments are openly dismissive of *the interconnections* between peoples and situations which Enzensberger has not only explicated, but even laboured. How, in reading these contentions, are we to avoid reiteration of an 'us' and 'them' dichotomy that he has elsewhere (and I would argue persuasively) contested?

One could, of course, quibble over interpretations of Christ's reference to 'neighbours' (to the extent that Christ must be invoked at all). But prediction of the charge of 'isolationism' is especially revealing. For in his emphasis on 'our immediate surroundings', and dismissal from consideration of 'people miles away', how does Enzensberger's philosophy differ from that of Neville Chamberlain ('a far away country of which we know nothing') which, crucially, was both rationalization of his own failure to act and contribution to the decidedly coercive outcome? In drawing this analogy, I don't want to pretend that such 'choices' are not complex, or that 'intervention' in such contexts is either easy or itself unproblematic (there is, of course, a vast international relations literature on this topic). Rather, it is Enzensberger's *failure* to make this analogy – as I would have thought he could not help but do – which disturbs me.

Enzensberger asserts that 'the search for the limits of our own responsibility can produce thoroughly positive by-products' (*CW*, 67). But the question arises – *positive for who?* Far from the choices at issue being 'agonizing', Enzensberger's prescriptions (for they amount to prescriptions) seem to take us back to a 'feel good' philosophy in which the need for 'setting priorities' is premised on perennial concern for ourselves:

> We cannot solve the situation in Kashmir; we know little of the struggle between the Sunnis and the Shiites, between the Tamils and the Sinhalese; whatever is to become of Angola must, in the first instance, be decided by the Angolans. And before we put a spoke in the wheels of the warring Bosnians, we ought to mop up the civil war in our own country. Our priority is not Somalia, but Hoyerswerda and Rostock, Mölln and Solingen. That is something we *are* capable of doing, a position we can expect everyone to support. This is what we have to answer for. (*CW*, 69)

I am disturbed by the (surely transparent) implications of this kind of theorizing. Of course 'everywhere we look the war is on our own doorstep' (*CW*, 69). But is this particularly novel? Or cause for surprise? When are things ever 'right' at home? How are we to avoid the impression that Enzensberger's injunction of 'first things first' amounts to a circumscribed credo in which one's own problems are not only artificially detached from those of the rest of the world, but irrevocably held to have first priority? (It is interesting that Enzensberger speaks in the above passage of 'our priority' *singular*, as if we need/can have only one). Presumably Enzensberger would argue that his is the path of 'realism'. But this is a track which, though well trodden in the theory and practice of international relations, is now increasingly recognized to be inadequate. In my reading, Enzensberger's prescriptions amount less to 'priority setting' than to an abrogation of the dilemmas at issue.

A problematic pessimism

Enzensberger's rejection of the more facile forms of optimism is one of the strengths of his critique. Given the enormity of the issues and problems he discusses, the inadequacies of the theories and concepts which purport to describe them, and the many subterfuges by which we cling to comforting illusions, it is difficult, when reading Enzensberger, to summon more hopeful readings with which to combat the bleakness of the scenarios he sketches. And yet, as he has himself argued in a different context (1992:156), 'pessimism cannot be trusted either'. Indeed, not only despite but because of the bleakness of his *Civil War* essays, it is possible to argue that pessimism is itself a luxury that cannot be afforded. To the extent that Enzensberger does not consider this in any detail, his critique in *Civil War* and *Great Migration* again fails to be as persuasive as it could be.

I have suggested that many of the strengths of Enzensberger's critique have their counterpart in weaknesses – indeed, that there is an intimate relationship between the two. This of itself suggests that we should be wary of seduction by the force and facility of his argument, even – and especially – where it may most seem to resonate. Without rehearsing the many – though less immediately apparent – inconsistencies, deflections and shortcomings of his argumentation, the passivity to which it can give rise is itself problematic. Such passivity (which, as noted, Enzensberger himself manifests) is also paradoxical in that a seeming aim of his theses is to disconcert and disturb the reader.

Foucault has remarked (1984:343) that 'If everything is dangerous, then we always have something to do'. To the extent that modes of action remain elusive and unexplicated by Enzensberger, and subsumed by the enormity of the problems he discusses, this constitutes a further and particularly debilitating weakness of his critique. It might be contended that it is precisely *because* of such enormity that remedial action is irrevocably problematic (if not actually precluded) and that Enzensberger is not in any case obliged to suggest 'ways out' of the labyrinth. But in light of the uses to which pessimism can be put, the disturbing features of Enzensberger's critique – and the degree of assertiveness with which they are presented – it can also be argued that the pessimism he evokes is both ethically unacceptable and politically incapacitating.[13]

IV Comments

Said (1994:69) has noted the complexity of 'the public realm in which intellectuals make their representations'. There are many levels at which the critic – even with great care and attentiveness – cannot control and is not accountable for the reception of his or her ideas. Indeed, so risky and uncertain are the effects of conscious interventions into the public sphere (risks of which, as noted previously, Enzensberger is clearly cognizant) many intellectuals prefer to eschew them altogether. Yet as Said also notes (1994:9), 'there is no such thing as a private intellectual, since the moment you set down words and then publish them you have entered the public world'. Intellectual representations (1994:15) put 'the individual on the record and on the line'.

My attempt to dissect the ambivalence Enzensberger's *Civil War* essays provoke in me in no way amounts to a negative critique of the work *per se*. As noted in my opening comments, assumptions that the negative necessarily outweighs the positive in the state we call 'ambivalence' seem to me to themselves need questioning. Yet while there may be approximate symmetry between the aspects of his critique which are compelling, and those which are not (and while, as noted, there are many ways in which the two are intertwined) it is the disturbing features of his analysis that I most want to highlight. This is because the immediate impact of his critique (both intellectual and emotional) can be such that its coercive dimensions risk being subsumed.

Enzensberger is salutary in his critique of theory, ideology and liberalism, his indictment of artists and intellectuals, and his (selective) dissolution of boundaries. But conversely (and correspondingly) he is surely less persuasive in his location of violence, his emphasis on its spontaneous expression, his evasion of politics, denial of innocence, delineation between 'rational' and 'irrational', and problematical style, prioritization and pessimism. Jean-François Lyotard (1993:241) poses the arresting questions: 'What is this discourse? How is it legitimated? Where is it situated? Who authorizes you to speak in this way?' To the extent that the force and impact of Enzensberger's *Civil War* essays may lead us not to apply such questions in his case (which is, at one level, testament to his success as a critic) my reaction to his essays cannot be other than ambivalent.

Bauman (1991) has testified eloquently to the ways in which ambivalence is integral to the contemporary period. His contention

(1991:16) that attempts to dissolve ambivalence 'prove in the end to be counterproductive' seems to me to be amply confirmed in Enzensberger's recent critique. For while forceful and iconoclastic, the *Civil War* essays are complicit in abrogation and inertia; a complicity which, in my reading, radically circumscribes their effectiveness and value.

NOTES

1 For contrasting studies from what is now a burgeoning scholarship, see Crawford Young, ed. (1993) and Benhabib (1992).

2 'Post-modernist' critique is, of course, extremely variegated, and to the extent that it contests the reductionism of labelling, resists conventional definition. See, however, Lyotard (1984), Bertens (1995) and Chambers (1990).

3 Indicative of this state of affairs is that a search in the general catalogue of Macquarie University Library (Sydney) yielded only nine entries under the subject heading 'Civil War', two of which are not directly addressed to the topic. The seven pertinent works are McCoubrey (1995); Weiss, ed. (1995); Moore, ed. (1974); Falk, ed. (1971), Oglesby (1971); Kelly (1969); Modelski (1961).

4 See Bell (1960), Dittberner (1979) and Bracher (1982).

5 Cf. Foucault (in Morris & Patton, 1979:36): 'The first is that, whether one wants it to be or not, it is always in virtual opposition to something like the truth...The second inconvenience is that it refers...to something like a subject. Thirdly, ideology is in a secondary position in relation to something which must function as the infra-structure or economic or material determinant of it. For these three reasons...it is a notion that one cannot use without precautions'.

6 Spivak dissents from what she sees as 'an unfortunate resistance in Foucault's work to "mere" ideological critique', and points to senses in which 'a developed theory of ideology can again be useful' (Spivak in Williams & Chrisman, 1994:68, 81).

7 Here it is also relevant to note that the psychological 'accommodation with violence' he describes (*CW*, 48) in relation to a witness of brutality – from vicarious fascination to a sense of euphoria at limits transgressed – is similar to a reaction described by Gay (1995:12) in relation to the different context of the nineteenth century German duel.

8 For example, he contends that 'the situation overwhelms not just the individuals involved, but existing political systems as well (*CW*, 62)'. Yet as this formulation conveys, he fails to draw the connections between them.

9 See, for example, the opening essay 'The Industrialization of the Mind', which begins (1976:7) 'All of us, no matter how irresolute we are, like to think that we reign supreme in our own consciousness, that we are masters of what our minds accept or reject'.

10 Here it is pertinent to note that Enzensberger twice refers to the LA riots (*CW*, 20, 23) without referring to the obvious catalyst for them (i.e., the 'not guilty' verdict on the police beating of African-American motorist Rodney King). This omission is particularly insidious in that Enzensberger actually *dismisses* the significance of the racial factor (*CW*, 23) by highlighting the extent to which 'victims' of the riots were 'blacks more often than not'.

11 That is to say that there is no such thing as a 'pure' and homogeneous ethnic group: see Connor, 1992:49.

12 Note, for example, the following remark: 'In so far as the origins of the conflicts are at all rationally comprehensible, they cannot be sorted out

by peace missions, because any attempt at mediation assumes that the participants are willing to make peace' (*CW*, 62).

13 Primo Levi (1988:10) has spoken of 'the will and capacity to react' as denoting 'a rudiment of virtue'.

REFERENCES

Barthes, Roland (1977) [1953] *Writing Degree Zero*, translated from the French by Annette Lavers & Colin Smith (New York: Farrar, Straus & Giroux).

Bauman, Zygmunt (1991). *Modernity and Ambivalence* (Cambridge: Polity Press).

Bell, Daniel (1960). *The End of Ideology: On the Exhaustion of Political Ideas in the Fifties* (Illinois: The Free Press of Glencoe).

Benhabib, Seyla (1992). *Situating the Self: Gender, Community and Postmodernism in Contemporary Ethics* (Cambridge: Polity Press).

Bertens, Hans (1995). *The Idea of the Postmodern: A History* (London: Routledge).

Bourdieu, Pierre (1993). *The Field of Cultural Production: Essays on Art and Literature* (Cambridge: Polity Press).

Bracher, Karl Dietrich (1982). *The Age of Ideologies: A History of Political Thought in the Twentieth Century* (London: Weidenfeld and Nicolson).

Chambers, Iain (1990). *Border Dialogues: Journeys in Postmodernism* (London: Routledge).

Connor, Walker (1992). 'The Nation and its Myth', *International Journal of Comparative Sociology* (XXXIII, 1-2, 1992), 48-57.

Deleuze, Gilles & Felix Guattari (1972). *Anti-Oedipus: Capitalism and Schizophrenia* (New York: The Viking Press).

Dittberner, Job L. (1979) [1976] *The End of Ideology and American Social Thought 1930-1960* (UMI Research Press).

Dostoevsky, Fyodor [1880] *The Brothers Karamazov*, trans. from the Russian by Constance Garnett (1968) London: Heinemann.

Elliott, Anthony (1994). 'Living in a State of Torture', review of Kate Millett, *The Politics of Cruelty* (Viking), *The Australian Higher Education Supplement*, 2 November, 34.

Elliott, Anthony (1992). *Social Theory and Psychoanalysis in Transition: Self and Society from Freud to Kristeva* (Oxford: Blackwell).

Enzensberger, Hans Magnus (1994). *Civil War*, trans. from the German by Piers Spence & Martin Chalmers (London: Granta & Penguin).

Enzensberger, Hans Magnus (1992). *Mediocrity and Delusion: Collected Diversions* (London: Verso).

Enzensberger, Hans Magnus (1976). *Raids and Reconstructions: Essays on Politics, Crime and Culture* (London: Pluto Press).

Falk, Richard, ed. (1971). *The International Law of Civil War* (Baltimore: Johns Hopkins Press).

Foucault, Michel (1983). 'Politics and Ethics: An Interview', in Rabinow, Paul (1984). *The Foucault Reader* (New York: Pantheon), 373-380.

Foucault, Michel (1973). 'Power and Norm: Notes', in Morris, Meaghan & Paul Patton, ed. (1979). *Michel Foucault, Power, Truth, Strategy* (Sydney: Feral), 59-66.

Foucault, Michel (1979). 'What Is an Author?', in Rabinow, Paul (1984). *The Foucault Reader* (New York: Pantheon), 101-120.

Gay, Peter (1995). *The Cultivation of Hatred* (London: Fontana).

Gilman, Sander L. *Difference and Pathology: Stereotypes of Sexuality, Race and Madness* (Ithaca: Cornell University Press, 1985).

Kelly, George A. (1969). *Internal War and International Systems: Perspectives on Method* (Cambridge, Mass.: Center for International Affairs, Harvard University).

Lacan, Jacques (1953). 'The function and field of speech and language in psychoanalysis', ch.3 in Lacan (1977). *Ecrits: A Selection*, translated from the French by Alan Sheridan (New York: Norton), 30-113.

LeCron Foster, Mary & Robert Rubinstein, ed. (1988). *The Social Dynamics of Peace and Conflict* (Boulder, Colorado: Westview Press).

Levi, Primo (1988). *Moments of Reprieve*, trans. from the Italian by Ruth Feldman (London: Sphere).

Lyotard, Jean-François (1993). *Libidinal Economy*, trans. from the French by Iain Hamilton Grant (Bloomington: Indiana University Press).

Lyotard, Jean-François (1984). *The Post-modern Condition: a report on knowledge*, translated from the French by Geoff Bennington & Brian Massumi (Manchester: Manchester University Press).

Mc Coubrey, H. (1995). *International Organizations and Civil Wars* (Aldershot: Dartmouth).

Maxwell, Mary (1991). 'Is Cruelty Okay?', in Maxwell, *Moral Inertia: Ideas in Social Action* (Colorado: University Press of Colorado, 1991), 87-113.

Modelski, George A. (1961). *The International Relations of Internal War* (Princeton, New Jersey: Center of International Studies, Woodrow Wilson School of Public and International Affairs).

Moore, John Norton, ed. (1974). *Law and Civil War in the Modern World* (Baltimore: Johns Hopkins Press).

Oglesby, Roscoe Ralph (1971). *Internal War and the Search for Normative Order* (The Hague: Martinus Nijhoff).

Nietzsche, Friedrich [1872] *The Birth of Tragedy* (and *The Genealogy of Morals*), trans. by Francis Golffing (1956), (New York: Doubleday).

Rose, Jacqueline (1989). 'Where Does the Misery Come From?', in Feldstein, Richard & Judith Roof, ed. *Feminism and Psychoanalysis* (Ithaca: Cornell University Press), 25-39.

Said, Edward (1993). *Culture and Imperialism* (New York: Knopf).

Said, Edward (1994). *Representations of the Intellectual: The 1993 Reith Lectures* (London: Vintage).

Sontag, Susan [1967]. 'Against Interpretation', in Sontag, *Against Interpretation* (London: Vintage), 3-14.

Spivak, Gayatri Chakravorty (1988). 'Can the Subaltern Speak?', in Williams, Patrick & Laura Chrisman, ed. (1994) *Colonial Discourse and Post-Colonial Theory: A Reader* (New York: Columbia University Press), 66-111.

Turkle, Sherry (1992). *Psychoanalytic Politics: Jacques Lacan and Freud's French Revolution* (New York: Guilford).

Weiss, Thomas G., ed. (1995). *The United Nations and Civil Wars* (Boulder, Colorado: Lynne Rienner).

Young, Crawford, ed. (1993). *The Rising Tide of Cultural Pluralism: The Nation-State at Bay?* (Wisconsin: University of Wisconsin Press).

Chapter Seven

The 'Balkanised' Subject: Enzensberger, Zizek and the Ecstasy of Violence

Tom Morton

Q. What is the difference between Sarajevo and Auschwitz?
A. In Auschwitz at least they had gas.

This 'Bosnian joke', told to a journalist on assignment in Sarajevo, appeared in a report in *Der Spiegel* about the same time as Enzensberger's essay *Civil War* was published in condensed form in that magazine. Like the essay, the joke draws a connection between the atrocities of the Nazi period in Germany and those occuring in the former Yugoslavia as Enzensberger wrote. Moreover, in its mordant tastelessness, it underlines the particular obscenity of the violence which permeates the everyday reality of the citizens of Sarajevo. The unholy marriage of technological rationality and racist ideology which gave birth to Auschwitz – a place where the human machinery of death operates as smoothly as the opening of a gas tap – is contrasted with a world in which the basic infrastructure of modern urban existence has broken down. Auschwitz belongs to modernity, while Sarajevo, the Olympic city and intellectual metropolis in the heart of Central Europe, plainly does not.

The same contrasts and contradictions run through much of the argument of *Civil War*. Enzensberger's text is unimaginable without the war in former Yugoslavia. Again and again he returns to the bloody events there and the moral questions which they pose; it is this civil war in the heart of Europe which is the paradigm for all the others of which he speaks. Sarajevo, and the murder, rape and torture carried out in the name of ethnic cleansing for which the city itself has become emblematic, exposes an excess of violence at the heart of modernity; indeed, Enzensberger suggests, this excess may itself be a product of modernity.

This paper sets out to read Enzensberger's essay in conjunction with another text which has emerged from within the former Yugoslavia itself, and one which is deeply imbued with the physical and moral effects of the war there, namely, the recent collection of essays from the Slovenian cultural theorist Slavoi Zizek, entitled *The Metastases of Enjoyment*.[1] From very different perspectives, and in very different ways, both Enzensberger and Zizek confront the same questions about the nature of violence, whether on the battlefields of

Bosnia or in the molecular civil wars which Enzensberger sees as endemic to the affluent, developed societies of the European Community or the United States.

This comparison has three aims; to examine the ways in which both Enzensberger and Zizek explore a certain kind of complicity between the spectators and the perpetrators of violence; to explore what this might tell us about the nature of violence itself; and finally to advance a modest hypothesis about the inadequacy of contemporary cultural and political discourse on the subject of violence.

First, though, a brief word in defence of Enzensberger himself seems in order. It is very easy to pick up *Civil War* and come to the conclusion by the time one is half-way through reading it that the publishers have made a bizarre mistake and published under the name Enzensberger a tract by some choleric right-wing cultural pessimist. Once we have reassured ourselves that the essay is indeed the work of Enzensberger, it is even more tempting to take him to task for the way in which he lumps together civil wars and communal violence from the Caucasus to Sri Lanka to the Horn of Africa, without any regard for historical context or cultural difference.

There is however, however, a strong argument in favour of Enzensberger's strategy, namely that it locates all of these conflicts and their causes fairly and squarely in the arena of modernity. It has become a commonplace in the commentaries of the international media that the conflict in Bosnia is the product of ancient ethnic hatreds which were successfully repressed by Tito and Communism, only to burst forth with renewed vigour once the communist lid was removed. This, of course, is nonsense. In the pithy formulation of the Polish intellectual Adam Michnik, 'nationalism is the last gasp of communism, struggling to create a new social basis for dictatorship'. In other words, the current 'ethnic' conflict in former Yugoslavia, though it has roots in certain historical traditions, is very much a creation and invention of the power elites in Serbia – and Croatia. It is an invention enthusiastically and unquestioningly reproduced by most of the world's media. In refusing to repeat this shibboleth, Enzensberger asks us to see the war in Yugoslavia for what it is: a product of modernity, indeed of a specifically European modernity. Or as Zizek puts it:

> In ex-Yugoslavia, we are lost not because of our primitive dreams and myths preventing us from speaking the enlightened language of Europe, but because we pay in flesh the price of being the stuff of *others'* dreams. The fantasy which organized the perception of ex-Yugoslavia is that of Balkan as the Other of the West: the place of savage ethnic conflicts long since overcome by civilised Europe, a place where nothing is forgotten and nothing learned...Far from being the Other of Europe, ex-Yugoslavia was, rather, Europe itself in its Otherness, the screen on to which Europe projected its own repressed reverse. (*ME*, 212)

It's in trying to break down this distinction between the West and its Other, to reveal this particular 'fantasy' for what it is, that both *Civil*

War and *The Metastases of Enjoyment* are most productive and illuminating.

About half way through *Civil War*, Enzensberger quotes at some length from *Among the Thugs*, a book about football hooligans by the American writer Bill Buford. Buford decided that the only way to really understand the destructive behaviour of the hooligans was to become one himself. In the passage quoted by Enzensberger he describes a scene in which six hooligans have got a boy down on the ground and are kicking him. He reflects that he could have stopped the kicking, but chose not to. There is a sensation of time slowing down, of the group of them crossing some kind of threshold; then, he writes,

> There was an immense energy about it; it was impossible not to feel some of the thrill...It was excitement that verged on being something greater, an emotion more transcendent – joy at the very least, but more like ecstasy...Somebody near me said that he was happy, very happy, that he could not ever remember being so happy. (*CW*, 48)

Interestingly, Enzensberger links this passage from *Among the Thugs* with a reference to Yugoslavia. He's reflecting on the infectious nature of civil war, and he quotes onces again:

> 'We don't know what has happened to us'. That is the most common phrase we hear from the survivors of Sarajevo. (*CW*, 47)

We can read this phrase – 'we don't know what has happened to us' – in two ways. At face value, it is a simple declaration: 'we don't understand what has befallen us'. But the juxtaposition with Buford's story lends it a darker meaning: namely that we don't know how it has come about that we have reached the point where we too are capable of acts of senseless violence and brutal retribution, acts of which we wouldn't have believed ourselves capable.

The force of this recognition becomes clearer if we go on to the next section of *Civil War* – which bears the subtitle 'Assumptions of Innocence, Moral Minefields'. Enzensberger recalls his youthful experience of air raids during the Second World War, 'crouching in a cellar, wrapped in a blanket' (*CW*, 49), listening to the bark of flak and the screaming of aerial bombs. With him in the bomb shelters were other 'innocent civilians' – 'the majority of the population', he tells us, 'who never wanted it to happen...These people aren't gunmen or torturers. Their faces aren't scarred by hate for their neighbours. They are grey with exhaustion' (*CW*, 50).

But, Enzensberger reminds us in the next breath, these are the same innocent civilians whose 'eyes lit up every time the Führer spoke...who stood by and watched while the synagogues burned to the ground. Without their enthusiastic support the Nazis could never have come to power' (*CW*, 50). And he goes on:

> Anyone who thinks that this applies only to the Germans is an idiot. Neither the molecular civil war on our own doorstep nor the inferno beyond our national borders can ignite without the 'Piercing energy', the 'joy', the 'ecstasy' Bill Buford speaks of. It always starts with hysterical jubilation, whether it is on the football terraces or on the streets of Rostock or Brixton, Baghdad or Belgrade. (*CW*, 51)

It's precisely this ecstasy, excess, violence out of all proportion to any conceivable cause, which both Enzensberger and Zizek are trying to understand. To this end, Enzensberger stresses the need for a kind of moral 'self-experimentation'; to renounce the privileged position of the spectator of violence, to acknowledge that we too are not only capable of participating in this ecstasy, but in a certain sense do so every time we watch a report on Bosnia on the news.

The difficulty with this position, however, is that in attempting to break down the distinction between spectators and perpetrators, Enzensberger sometimes comes dangerously close to fudging the difference between perpetrators and victims. When he tells us that the 'innocent civilians' who sat with him in the bomb shelter were themselves spectators at the burning of synagogues, his rhetorical purpose is clear. In the civil war, today's victim may be yesterday's perpetrator. But the generalizing tone of Enzensberger's argument veers towards suggesting a kind of moral equivalence between perpetrators and victims; a suggestion which is particularly pernicious if it is applied to the war in Bosnia, as it is all too often by Western diplomats and in the international press.

Yet it is precisely this question of the relationship between victims and perpetrators of violence which Zizek explores in *The Metastases of Enjoyment*. He begins the book with a scene not unlike that described by Buford at the football stadium:

> A famous photo from the time of Nazi anti-Semitic pogroms shows a frightened Jewish boy driven into a corner and surrounded by a group of Germans. This group is extremely interesting in so far as the facial expressions of its members render the entire scale of possible reactions: one of them 'enjoys it' in an immediate, idiotic way; another is clearly scared...the feigned indifference of the third conceals a freshly awakened curiosity; and so on, up to the unique expression of a young man who is obviously embarrassed, even disgusted by the entire affair, unable to yield wholeheartedly to it, yet at the same time fascinated by it, enjoying it with an intensity that surpasses by far the idiocy of immediate pleasure. *He is the most dangerous*; his quavering indecision exactly corresponds to the unique expression of the Rat Man's face noticed by Freud when the Rat Man was relating the story of the rat torture: 'At all the more important moments while he was telling his story his face took on a very strange, composite expression. I could only interpret it as one of horror at pleasure of his own of which he himself was unaware. (*ME*, 1)

Once again, it is a kind of pleasure which for Zizek is the driving energy behind the various forms of violence in late capitalism, whether in Sarajevo or anywhere within what Zizek calls 'the common warfare' (*ME*, 2). This common warfare includes attacks by skinheads and neo-

Nazis, a subject which Enzensberger also takes up; and Zizek, like Enzensberger, is at pains to stress the primarily non-ideological nature of these attacks. The ultimate answer we obtain from the skinhead as to why he beats up foreigners is that it makes him feel good. And where does this pleasure come from? From 'the most elementary imbalance in the relationship between *Ich* and jouissance, the tension between pleasure and the foreign body of jouissance at the very heart of it' (*ME*, 71).

Zizek is arguing here on two levels. Firstly, he follows on from his earlier work in postulating that racism and racist forms of nationalism arise out of a particular kind of fantasy, a fantasy that they – the foreigners, whether within or without – pose a threat to our 'enjoyment', to those particular forms of desire and its gratification which make us who we are. Indeed, by their very existence, by their possession and practice of an enjoyment which is not our own, they must in some sense have stolen a part of ours. Yet – and here is the second level of Zizek's argument – this simple structure is itself deeply ambiguous. In the Lacanian universe, wherever our desire is, the Other is already there; the Other is the 'foreign body of jouissance at the very heart of...our pleasure' (*ME*, 71). When we attempt to destroy the Other, we are attempting to gain access to our own pleasure - and to destroy it at the same time.

What does this rather abstract psychodrama tell us about Sarajevo and Hoyerswerda? In Zizek's view, a similar kind of ambiguity pervaded the ideological structures of Yugoslav communism. On the one hand, State and Party preached the equality of all forms of national 'enjoyment'. But this equality is, according to Zizek, by its very nature inimical to national enjoyment, which 'resists universalization' (*ME*, 71). Not everyone, by definition, can be Australian, Croatian or German. Or to put it another way: any suggestion that other forms of enjoyment can make the same claims to legitimacy as my own, and enjoy the same rights, in a sense calls into question the primacy and uniqueness of my 'national' enjoyment as Australian, Croatian, or German.

Thus, the state ideology of socialist Yugoslavia – which Zizek sometimes chooses to equate with the Law in Lacan's cosmology – sent out two contradictory messages: all forms of national enjoyment are legitimate, yet none which abides by this Law can truly be legitimate in its own terms. All nations were equal – but the essence of the nation was denied. Thus true 'national enjoyment' became associated with what Zizek calls the 'obscene underside' of the Law; with fatal consequences:

> Once the public Law casts off its direct patriarchal dress and presents itself as neutral-egalitarian, the character of its obscene double also undergoes a radical shift: what now erupts in the carnivalesque suspension of the egalitarian public Law is precisely the authoritarian-patriarchal logic that continues to determine our attitudes, although its direct public expression is no longer permitted. 'Carnival' thus becomes

> the outlet for the repressed social *jouissance*: Jew baiting, riots, gang rapes. (*ME*, 56)

The battlefields of Bosnia, in Zizek's terms, represent carnival gone mad, a permanent carnival of obscene revolt against the desideratum of equality, liberty and fraternity. What gives this carnival its own ghastly irony is its pointlessness, in the purely formal sense of the world. The more we try to recover our true, pure enjoyment by destroying the 'Other' who has deprived us of it, the more doomed we are to failure, since the Other is already at the heart of that enjoyment. Moreover, this very intransigence of the Other provokes ever more desperate attempts at eradication. Thus, as Zizek says of the Muslims in Bosnia, 'the more they are slaughtered and starved out, the more powerful is the danger of "Muslim fundamentalism" in Serbian eyes' (*ME*, 78).

One might argue that Zizek's analysis is too specific to the particular conditions pertaining in former Yugoslavia to be of much general use. Yet it seems to me that there are fruitful parallels to be drawn with the situation in contemporary Germany, where, in different ways in East and West, any form of German national self-identification was consigned to the 'obscene underside' of the Law. And in many ways, Zizek raises questions about the true nature and viability of multiculturalism – and its limits. We may not want to go all or even part of the way with Zizek's Lacanian approach; yet even if we don't, it does at very least open up some possibilities for understanding the 'ecstatic' nature of acts of violence. Moreover, Zizek takes us a little further than Enzensberger in suggesting that all of us, as spectators, are guilty of participating in that ecstasy:

> What we have in mind here is rape as 'weapon', used especially by Serbs against Muslims. The form it takes – the raping of a girl...in the presence of her father, forced to witness the affair – is bound to set in motion the vicious cycle of guilt: the father, the representative of the big Other – is exposed in his utter impotence, which makes him guilty in his own eyes as well as in those of his daughter: the daughter is guilty for causing her father's humiliation, and so on. The rape thus entails, beside the girl's physical and psychic suffering, the disintegration of the entire familial socio-symbolic network. (*ME*, 74)

Zizek has a lot more to say about the guilty gaze of the observer, divided between fascination and revulsion, which need not concern us here. There is, however, one further parallel which arises out of the passage just quoted which is worth noting. 'The vicious cycle of guilt' which Zizek describes might apply equally accurately to the West's attitude to Bosnia, which, in the course of the war in ex-Yugoslavia, has increasingly become informed by a tendency to blame the victim. The present peace agreement merely enshrines this tendency in fact. Humiliated by its failure to avert the slaughter of ethnic cleansing, Western Europe in particular has blamed the raped daughter – in this case, multi-ethnic Bosnia – for its own impotence (a humiliation compounded by the fact that only intervention by the United States ultimately forced the signing of the peace agreement). The war in Bosnia, to paraphrase Zizek, has become the necessary 'obscene underside' of European unification and the New World Order.

Zizek's characterization of the 'impotent gaze' of the spectator, and the psychopathology of the relationship between spectator and victim of violence, confronts the same dilemma to which Enzensberger returns in the closing pages of *Civil War*: what he terms 'the agonizing hopelessness involved in every ethic of responsibility today' (*CW*, 68). His argument that we, the citizens of the developed Western world, need to place limits on our responsibility is driven largely by a critique of Western universalist notions of human rights, a critique discussed in a number of other contributions to this volume. Yet it also grows out of a concern about the spectator's reaction to the spectacle of violence in which he or she is totally unable to intervene:

> When the moral demands made on an individual are consistently out of proportion to his scope for action, he will eventually go on strike and deny all responsibility. Here lie the seeds of brutalization, which may escalate to raging aggression. (*CW*, 61)

What Enzensberger describes here is not at all dissimilar to the 'vicious cycle of guilt' induced by the spectator's impotence in Zizek's text. It is this recognition, moreover, which seems to me to point to what is most useful and interesting about *Civil War*, since it is linked to the notions of violence as excess and ecstasy. Enzensberger rigorously rejects existing sociological and philosophical discourses which claim to tell us something about the origins and causes of violence. He pillories both the conservative commentators who invoke an imaginary golden age when 'common decency and discipline were supposedly the order of the day' (*CW*, 32), and their counterparts on the Left whose response to acts of violence is to recite the social worker's catechism of disadvantage:

> Mum didn't want me.
> My teachers were far too authoritarian/liberal;
> Dad came home drunk/never came home at all;
> The bank gave me too much credit/closed my account...
> So there was nothing else for me to do but arson/robbery/murder.
> (*CW*, 33)

Although this may seem little more than a rather crude pastiche of the left/liberal welfarist approach to social conflict and violence, Enzensberger is no less scathing about ostensibly 'scientific' social Darwinist perspectives which see violence as an inescapable product of overpopulation and competition for resources.[2] At one point he invokes the 'Hobbesian ur-myth of the war of everyone against everyone else' (*CW*, 31), but unlike the proponents of these biologistic explanations of violence, Enzensberger does not see the civil war as an irruption of the

Hobbesian state of nature into a weakened social order. Rather, the civil war is in its essence a product of the social order in the conditions of modernity: it is a social, not a natural phenomenon.[3]

It is this dilemma which Enzensberger exhorts us to confront in *Civil War*. What is missing, perhaps, from his account of civil war, is a notion of the symbolic and representational functions of violence in linking the individual's 'ecstatic' experience with broader social meanings. These have been extensively discussed and investigated in contemporary social anthropology, which offers perspectives in some ways complementary to the psychoanalytical framework proposed by Zizek.[4] Yet it is not, I would argue, Enzensberger's primary intention to explain the ecstasy of violence, but rather to expose the poverty of existing explanations. His critique of the redemptive social theology of the Enlightenment, its powerlessness in the face of the ecstatic act of 'collective self-mutilation' (*CW*, 28) is by no means new. However, previous critiques, most notably those of the Frankfurt School, have tended to focus on ideologically motivated mass violence of the Right and Left and the failure of Enlightenment values to withstand such violence. In asking us to consider the meaning of violence which is '*about nothing at all*', Enzensberger invites us to begin struggling towards an ethic of responsibility beyond the totalizing discourses of 'human nature', on the one hand, and human perfectibility on the other. The gaze of the Enlightenment witnessing the civil war, he argues, is forced in so doing to experience its own impotence, with the danger that this experience itself produces 'brutalization' and 'raging aggression', in Enzensberger's terms, a kind of moral self-mutilation which results in the violent rejection of precisely those values which the enlightened subject is powerless to defend. In Zizek's terms, this would amount to the triumph of the 'obscene underside' of Enlightenment, a triumph which, until recently, was rehearsed at a safe distance every evening on television screens in lounge-rooms around the world in the reporting of the war in Bosnia.[5]

Enzensberger's answer to this may strike us as a kind of moral damage-control, an attempt to quarantine the West from the savagery of the war in Bosnia and salvage what can be salvaged from the Enlightenment. Yet I would argue that it is also possible to read *Civil War* as a plea to open up a new kind of ethical discourse about violence, one that attempts to re-connect personal and social responsibility with actions in the world, and allows space for the excessive, ecstatic quality of violence in our conception of the human, without resort to essentialism or redemptionism.

NOTES

1 Slavoi Zizek, *The Metastases of Enjoyment. Six Essays on Woman and Causality*, London, 1994. References to this edition are given in the text as *ME* followed by page number.

2 See *Civil War*, p. 41: 'Biology adds nothing to our understanding of civil war'.

3 An interesting re-reading of Hobbes in the light of contemporary ethnographic research on the role of war in primitive societies can be found in Pierre Clastres, *Archeology of Violence*, trans. Jeanine Herman, Semiotext, N.Y., 1994.

4 See for example Allen Feldman, *Formations of Violence. The Narrative of the Body and Political Terror in Northern Ireland*, Chicago, 1991.

5 Cf Zizek, p. 212: 'How, then, can we not recall, apropos of this European gaze on the Balkans, Hegel's dictum that true evil resides not in the object perceived as bad, but in the innocent gaze which perceives Evil all around? The principal obstacle to peace in ex-Yugoslavia is not "archaic ethnic passions" but the very innocent gaze of Europe fascinated by the spectacle of these passions'.

Chapter Eight

'Something greater, an emotion more transcendent': Violence and the Reconstruction of Group Identity in Enzensberger's *Civil War*

Peter Morgan

I Enzensberger's 'Circle of Responsibility'

After a period of relative obscurity in the early eighties, Hans Magnus Enzensberger shot back into prominence with the essay collection, *Ach Europa*, written over the years between 1982 and 1987. Critics and commentators have noted a fundamental change in Enzensberger's attitudes from the utopian modernism of his Marxist days to a postmodern acceptance of the irrational, the unstructured, the contingent and the improvisatory as the leitmotifs of contemporary life.[1] This postmodernism is taken a step further in *Civil War* *(Aussichten auf den Bürgerkrieg)*, published in 1993.[2] In a world where violence begets violence and reason is powerless against it, Enzensberger appears on the scene as a new Candide with a philosophy of pragmatic self–survival. After the 'end of history', it seems, the project of enlightenment is doomed to failure, and those who still believe in it are either fools or hypocrites. The cognizant intellectual can do no more than draw a circle of personal responsibility around himself. Beyond this circle he cannot and need not go.

Enzensberger has been criticised for rejecting Western universalist enlightenment ideals of individual and social responsibility in favour of newly postmodernist attitudes of contingency. In Germany he has been censured for betraying his left-wing principles in favour of a trendy and marketable postmodernism; and critics outside Germany have registered disapproval of his surrender to the prevailing mood of disillusionment among German intellectuals.

II *Nullpunkt des Denkens*: André Glucksmann's Critique of Enzensberger

André Glucksmann published a response to Enzensberger's essay *Ausblicke auf den Bürgerkrieg* in *Der Spiegel* in 1993.[3] Glucksmann accuses Enzensberger of hypocrisy for resorting to a philosophy of withdrawal at just that point in time when his years of left-wing intellectual advocacy of the oppressed should be matched with practical follow-through:

> As long as racism, fascism and war were occurring in distant places, the streets of the Federal Republic were crawling with fearless and determined fighters...However when millions of refugees are hunted to and fro in the heart of Europe, the streets remain empty! (AG, 248)

In place of a theory of radical action, writes Glucksmann, Enzensberger and the German left-wing intellectuals have re-discovered evil. Now that their utopian philosophies have failed to solve the problems of the world, they are irresistibly drawn toward a pessimistic philosophy of evil as the only possible alternative to the failure of reason. Along with figures such as Botho Strauß and Heiner Müller, Enzensberger has opted for an apocalyptic irrationalism rather than accept a world which no longer conforms to and hence confirms his thinking:

> The world does not confirm my conceptualisations and so it seems without concept. The differentiations which I forced onto the world have turned out to be deceptive and misleading, and so the world itself must be undifferentiated. The same naked, one-dimensional force rules throughout the world because I am incapable of differentiating it. I don't know any more what I should be thinking, and so there is nothing to think anymore. (AG, 249)

Glucksmann criticizes this 'German ideology' of the intellectuals as a form of escape, a means of avoiding the hard work of philosophy and of geopolitical analysis:

> Just because you recognize that there is no final solution to the existence of evil, that does not mean that you cannot curb the multiplication and explosive proliferation of the consequences of evil, or even stop them altogether. (AG, 248)

And he considers Enzensberger's philosophy of ever-smaller circles of personal responsibility to be conceptually inadequate in an increasingly post-national world. Using Enzensberger's own example of the AIDS epidemic he writes:

> I am amused by the idea that the happy citizens of Munich or Vaison-la-Romaine are not affected by what happens in Moscow, Belgrade or Chernobyl. Especially in an era in which ecological, ideological and military forms of pollution extend over national borders as never before. Each for himself and the epidemics for all? (AG, 249)

Glucksmann's critique of Enzensberger has been reiterated in reviews since the appearance of the full-length essay, *Aussichten auf den Bürgerkrieg*, shortly after the *Spiegel* article in 1993. There is little doubt that Enzensberger is exploring ideas usually associated with the so-called 'New Right' in German intellectual circles, or that this marks a clear turn away from earlier stances.

This chapter will focus on a particular aspect of Enzensberger's argument, namely on how it reflects changes in the self-understanding of the German intellectual in a time of paradigm change and critical self-reflection. From this perspective *Civil War* is less interesting as an essay on modern group violence than as a self-articulation of the German intellectual. This reading will yield an argument which is at odds with Enzensberger's image as a left-wing maverick. On the contrary, it presents us with a figure seeking re-integration into a form of civil community. As the traveller in *Europe, Europe,* Enzensberger obsessively sought out the margins and peripheries as an implicit critique of the centripetal tendencies of the centre (i.e., of Brussels and of European politics). In *Civil War* in a very different way he can be seen to be seeking a reintegration into a national community. The aim of this reading is not so much to focus on the irrationalist thesis of *Civil War*, but rather to explain why it is that Enzensberger along with other leading West German intellectuals, has proven so accessible to such irrationalist intellectual positions at the end of the post-war era.

III Enzensberger's Metonymic Argument

In an interview published in *New Left Review* in 1989, Enzensberger remarked of the form of the German essay:

> If you choose a linear argument and form of writing, then you are liable to eliminate the things that don't fit, and your writing becomes poorer because the linearity ties you down.[4]

It would be difficult to present *Civil War* as an exercise in linear argument. However, as Enzensberger points out, his aim is to experiment with where writing leads him, not to present a closed thesis. This point is important, because it focuses our attention on the personal aspect of the essay. In *Civil War* Enzensberger posits a persona or narrative consciousness, as well as an abstract thesis. He thereby brings attention onto the figure of the public intellectual in his essay on collective conflict. Although clearly structured in twelve sections, the essay oscillates in tone and form between a personal tirade and a philosophical treatise, and at important points the argument is explicitly based in the author's personal experience.

Enzensberger refers to the origins of European history in Thucydides' *History of the Peloponnesian War* in order to justify his opening assertion that civil war is 'the primary form of all collective conflict' (*CW*, 11). Civil war predates the 'cultivated war' of the nation-state era and has resurfaced as the typical form of conflict in an increasingly 'post-national' era, that is, an era in which the power-monopoly of nation-states is breaking down. With the end of the east-west divide and the final victory of capitalism, ideological and national pretexts for war have become obsolete, since the advanced capitalist nations have realized that 'war does not pay'.

This revised perception of collective conflict has gained a new relevance after the end of the post-war era, Enzensberger argues, in that the decline of the nation-state as the primary structure for modernization and capitalist development has laid bare similarities between the contemporary and the pre-modern situations. In what he calls the 'civil wars' of the present we are witnessing a resurgence of primal forms of group conflict which were masked during the era of the nation states (c. 1650 to 1990) by the ideologies of capitalism, imperialism and colonialism. The Thirty Years War is for him the archetypal civil war, demonstrating Hobbes's dictum of the 'bellum omnium contra omnes', after which for several centuries violence and aggression were channelled into the building and expanding of the nation-states.

Moreover the civil wars which have sprung up throughout the 'Third World' since 1989 are complemented by the rise in urban violence in the developed nations. In the violence of British football hooligans and skinheads, south-eastern European ethnic groups, Rostock neo-Nazis and Berlin *autonomous youths*, Enzensberger sees the same phenomenon: ideology-free destructiveness in the form of developed or incipient (or as he terms it, 'molecular') civil war. The resurgence of molecular civil war is attributed to the breakdown of patriarchal structures. The aggressive drives of young men have been freed from the traditional structures of control and coercion and now partake in an unstructured and self-destructive cycle of violence. The ideological façade is gone, leaving the armed mob with no goal other than destruction. The common denominator is the dissolution of the link between ideology and violence: 'in today's civil wars there is no longer any need to legitimize your actions' (*CW*, 20).

Civil war, then, is the result of fundamental, aggressive drives in human beings – or at least males – which become destructive if they are not channelled into socially useful spheres, such as the protection of the nation-state, imperialist and colonial wars, or curbed by means of social rituals. This destructiveness is 'inexplicable'. It is biologically given, not learned. Enzensberger still operates within an anti-capitalist framework. Postmodern civil war is the last stage of capitalism, since ever larger groups (undeveloped countries, urban sub-proletariats) drop out of the capitalist cycle of exploitation and production of wealth because they are not worth exploiting. These groups thereby lose the last vestiges of a structure of control and fall into the cycle of self-destructive behaviour that anticipates full-blown civil war. However, Enzensberger criticises Marxist and other left-wing modernization theories for failing to explain why victims of oppression turn on each other rather than on their oppressors. This pattern unites the neo-Nazis and skinheads of Rostock and Mölln with the blacks in the ghettos of Los Angeles and the warring factions in Bosnia.

Civil war in its incipient or its developed form, then, is endemic in human society. On the basis of this recognition Enzensberger completes the passage from economics and history as the determinants of human behaviour to biology and anthropology, a transition that links him to the so-called 'new right' among German intellectuals. He cites theorists of cultural pessimism from de Maistre to the late Freud and Hannah Arendt in order to expand the concept of civil war to include not only violent group conflict and individual aggressive drives, but self-destructive violence as well.

Enzensberger's primary metaphor for civil war is the AIDS virus, taken from the realm of biology. He carefully avoids naming it for rhetorical reasons, since he knows that it has become a standard metaphor for civil breakdown in reactionary social commentary, especially among those whose view of the world is based on repression rather than reason.[5] Civil war is, he writes, a 'political retrovirus' (*CW*, 30) continually mutating into different forms during its long latency period, which can become epidemic even pandemic. Defence against it is impossible.

By section six, 'Evidence and Self-Experimentation', Enzensberger has collected under the rubric 'civil war' everything from aggressive drives and self-destructive urges to pre-modern group conflict, nation-state warfare, and post-national urban and ethnic violence. However, as André Glucksmann comments, the geo-political work of examining and differentiating the elements of this so-called 'civil war' has not been carried out. Enzensberger neither validates his re-definition of civil war, nor provides any new insights into the nature of group conflict. He has merely discovered something hardly new, namely that violence – and with it, evil – exists:

> With a shout of triumph Hans Magnus Enzensberger has rediscovered the truth. Violence and barbarism are increasing. Eureka! What a discovery! War really exists...and along with it cruelty and all sorts of dreadful things. Many thanks for this information. (AG, 248)

Peter Schneider, the writer and left-wing intellectual of the 'student generation' has, since the late eighties, criticized the blinkered and taboo-bound thinking of his erstwhile comrades. In a recent essay on the German left-wing intellectuals' fascination with the question of evil, the so-called *Wiederkehr des Bösen*, he writes:

> The helplessness, the pseudo-intellectual waffle, the idiocy of civil society reveals itself in seeking explanations for something that cannot be explained, that does not need explanation and that is in fact the moving force of cultural endeavour: the fact that all of us have the raw potential for aggression, which is capable of anything, and which is only kept under control by an unlikely and extremely fragile achievement called culture or civilization.[6]

Both Glucksmann and Schneider point out that there is nothing new in Enzensberger's 'rediscovery of evil'. Neither of them, however, asks the question why Enzensberger has fallen victim to this type of thinking.

It is, I believe, unimportant to Enzensberger whether civil war originates in the individual or his environment. He uses two contradictory metaphors or images for the origins of aggression. The AIDS metaphor is one of disease, contagion, and latency. The other image is internal, coming from the sphere of physiology and behaviourist psychology: chemical messages to the brain initiate automatic responses of aggression and destructivity. These responses are physiological and do not pass through a process of conscious reflection. The important thing for him is not to identify origins, but to link the accelerating process of civil degeneration he sees in the world around him to the potential for aggression in the individual.

By defining civil war in terms of innate aggression, Enzensberger links its elements metonymically, taking the part for the whole. The point of the essay lies in the renaming of the known. He takes parts of different processes – war, group conflict, individual aggression – in order to construct a single line of determination from the individual to the group, regardless of history. The equation runs as follows: individual aggression *equals* group conflict *equals* war *equals* evil. The metonymy is more than a merely rhetorical device. It creates an argument by reducing all aggression to a common denominator called 'civil war'. 'Civil war' thus becomes Enzensberger's metonymic term for evil: it is the unenlightened, the irrational, the violent, the self-destructive. He thereby participates in the creation of a universal counter-myth to the enlightenment, and places himself in the company of his new masters, de Maistre, Nietzsche, the late Freud, Bataille, Jünger and others.

More importantly, though, Enzensberger's myth of evil reconstitutes the link between the individual and the group. Evil is no longer capitalism, or even Nazism or fascism. There is no longer a clear line of division between good and bad, which can be defined in terms of political and other criteria. Evil is inherent in human nature and is to be found everywhere.

Thus Enzensberger arrives at the inexplicable origins of 'civil war' in evil. The historical, economic, political and social determinants of civil violence are unimportant in the face of its universality. 'Civil war' is a form of 'social autism', which arises not from the interdependencies of history and the individual, but from the destructiveness at the core of individual being. Socio-economic and historical structures are important only in as much as they give legitimation to destructiveness. Violence no longer occurs in the name of ideologies, and hence is no longer controllable. It emanates from the core of the individual. Enzensberger has successfully completed the turn from an open, socio-economic and historical model of individual identity to a closed, deterministic, biological and anthropological model.

IV Enzensberger's Reconstitution of Self in *Civil War*

Enzensberger's argument is structured in terms of a descent through sections one to six from the universal to the individual, mirrored in sections seven to twelve by the ascent towards a pragmatic philosophy of reduced community and limited responsibility, ending with his revision of the myth of Sisyphos as a trope of human survival. While the tirade form disguises the logical structure of Enzensberger's argument, the two sections of the work mirror each other in terms of rhetorical strategies and argument and counter-argument. He makes an important transition at the centre of his essay (between sections six and seven) from objective reflections on individual violence to subjective and personal memories. In the remainder of this essay I will focus on what I believe to be the deeper intent of *Civil War*, namely Enzensberger's attempt to come to terms with the effects of the past on himself, and to reconstitute a sense of group-identity (*Wir-Gefühl*) on the basis of the metonymic argument that evil resides in all of us and cannot be externalized onto environmental factors. This, not the rediscovery of evil, it seems to me, is the significant part of *Civil War*. Enzensberger's essay thus becomes a symptom of the malaise of the left-wing German intellectual at the end of the post-war era, or as Peter Schneider puts it, *am Ende der Gewißheit*, rather than a credible exercise in social anthropology.

Enzensberger makes the transition from the general to the personal at the point where he has isolated the common denominator of civil war as the individual's enjoyment of violence. He makes use of material from the American journalist Bill Buford, who produced a protocol of his experiences among English skinhead gangs under the title *Among the Thugs* in 1991. Buford's book was well received in certain German intellectual circles during the early nineties in the context of the debates about the end of the post-war era, the *Wiederkehr des Bösen* and the relativisation of evil. These issues had been reopened by Jürgen Habermas during the *Historikerstreit* in the mid-to-late 1980s. Material from Buford's book, *Among the Thugs*, was quoted in an influential article by Rüdiger Safranski which appeared in the *Frankfurter Allgemeine Zeitung* in late December 1992 on the de-civilizing effects of modern society and the descent into barbarism as a result of the relativisation of values.[7] As parts of *Aussichten auf den Bürgerkrieg* appeared in *Der Spiegel* in mid-1993, it is unlikely that Enzensberger was unaware of Safranski's article when writing *Civil War*. For Safranski, the importance of Buford's book lies in its documentation of the fundamental power of evil in human nature, and its explanation of *Zivilisationsbruch* as the 'return of evil'.

In a passage quoted by Enzensberger, Bill Buford describes his feelings after participating passively in a mob attack by English hooligans on a young boy at a soccer riot in Italy:

> With that first exchange, some kind of threshold had been crossed, some notional boundary: on one side of that boundary had been a sense of limits, an ordinary understanding – even among this lot – of what you didn't do; we were now someplace where there would be few limits, where the sense that there were things you didn't do had ceased to exist...It was an excitement that verged on being something greater, an emotion more transcendent – joy at the very least, but more like ecstasy. There was an immense energy about it; it was impossible not to feel some of the thrill. Somebody near me said that he was happy, very happy, that he could not ever remember being so happy. (*CW*, 48)

Buford's theme here is the crossing of boundaries as a result of a primal experience (violence) and the sense of personal release that it generates. He calls it a 'notional' boundary. I would rather call it a visceral and emotional boundary between civilization and barbarism. For Enzensberger this passage functions as a bridge to personal reminiscence. His interest lies in the breaking of the taboo on group violence, the euphoria, and the sense of a community regained, for which recognition of violence is the initiation ritual. This latter point is important. The metonymic argument in *Civil War* is primarily about the re-attachment of individual and society. Buford's euphoric experience of violence is expressed in terms of the 'oceanic feeling' of oneness with the group. Likewise Enzensberger's armed mobs are disempowered individuals who re-achieve a sense of community in the experience of a primal state of group violence.

Buford describes the fascination of the descent into violence,

> when the web tears, the fabric falls apart, the house burns. It is always about this line, this border: I am fascinated, elated by what I find on the other side. It arouses me; I know of no stronger feeling. Here, on the edge of an experience, which is anathema to society and civilization, one finds heightened experience. What sort of experiences are these? Pain. Fire. Certain drugs. To find oneself in a crowd. And, even stronger, to find oneself in a crowd which commits an act of violence. What we find there is nothingness.[8]

After quoting Buford Enzensberger passes from reported to personal experience. He begins his next chapter with a curious formulation: 'Just the mention of civil war sooner or later turns into a kind of self-experimentation' (*CW*, 49). Remembering his own childhood and early adolescence during the Nazi period and the Second World War, he writes:

> I have been infected. I feel the rage, the fear and the hate building up inside me. I am deeply involved in my subject. My brain is flooded with chemical messengers I know nothing about. I am in danger of losing control of the thoughts that come into my head. (*CW*, 49)

It seems in this case that the latency period for the 'political retrovirus' is almost fifty years. The battle against the aggressive impulses which his experiences have engendered in him becomes a battle against himself, in which 'he' – i.e., his civilized consciousness – is bound to lose. In remembering the scenes of terror of his childhood he reminds himself that it was the 'innocent civilians' cowering in fear who had brought this on themselves. He now recognizes, however, that the euphoria and the devotion to Hitler were merely the culturally specific symptoms of something broader, namely the desire for ecstasy which involves transgression and violence, which he now calls 'civil war'.

And now he, the writer, in his 'brooding silence' on these issues, feels the rising tide of anger, resentment and bitterness at those responsible for Hitler, the destruction of Germany and the discrediting of 'Germanness'. The battle with himself, the 'self-experimentation', which he describes here is a strongly worded personal reflection on Buford's description of the crossing of the threshold between civilised and barbaric actions. Enzensberger feels himself in danger of crossing this threshold in response to his own memories of childhood and the war. These memories arouse 'rage, fear and hatred' against the Germans of his parents' generation. He writes:

> It is impossible to have a linear discussion on this theme. Merely stating your own position fans the flames of conflict. There is no Archimedean point. I have stepped into an intellectual and moral minefield...I don't see eye to eye with anybody, not even with myself. (*CW*, 49)

Enzensberger's description here of the battle against himself and of the split between identification with and rejection of his nation echoes that of his contemporary, Martin Walser. Both writers are here broaching the question of the intellectual's personal relationship to the past, a theme which has been suffused with taboos, guilt and resentment for their generation and those following them:

> When the conversation turns to Germany, you know from experience that it is not going to turn out well. Even if I discuss Germany with myself – whether in writing or in dialogue with myself – it always turns out badly. I get into conflict with myself and with everyone else. The end-result is a sense of unconsolable misery. [9]

Enzensberger's thesis of civil war has its roots in his own sense of anger and resentment at his parents' generation. However there is a certain contradictoriness in his argumentation. On the one hand he attributes these feelings to the German past which 'infected' him. But on the other hand he can only accept feelings of aggression, or 'civil war', within himself by universalizing them. Having recognized the aggressive impulses in himself, he seems constrained to interpret these impulses as something universal, because otherwise they would be an indication of his Germanness. He attributes his thinking about violence, barbarism and a breakdown of civilization to his own experiences as a child during the bombing raids of the Second World War. But he then passes directly to a universal argument linking Nazis with football hooligans, rioting blacks in Los Angeles, Serbian soldiers and the civilians of Saddam Hussein's Baghdad:

> Anyone who thinks that this applies only to the Germans is an idiot. Neither the molecular civil war on our own doorstep nor the inferno beyond our national borders can ignite without the 'piercing energy', the 'joy', the 'ecstasy' Bill Buford speaks of. (*CW*, 50-51)

It is this conjunction of the personal and the universal that I wish to explore more closely at this point. This section, the core of the work, reveals the motive behind Enzensberger's metonymic argument. It allows him to put his feelings of aggrievance and his hostilities, bitterness and resentments into a universal context in which all violence is understood under one rubric, and history, politics, society and culture pale into insignificance. It seems to me that this extraordinary rejection of the historiography of the past half century, aimed at ascertaining the specificities which allowed a nation to plumb the depths of barbarism in the Holocaust, needs explanation.

Enzensberger makes use of an image which occurs often in German writing since the *Wende* of 1989: *ins Bodenlose fallen*. The word 'bodenlos' recurs in images of loss of the ground beneath one's feet, losing control, falling through a net, or sinking into a maelstrom or an abyss: falling into a bottomless pit. Enzensberger quotes Buford's sense of release at falling through the net of civilization, and he is reminded of his own loss of certainties in the memory of his childhood and the hostility towards the Germans of the Nazi generations. In his recent collection of poems, *Der fliegende Robert*, he describes this sense that his value-system is spiralling out of control:

> Manches entgeht mir,
> ich schlüpfe durch, es entzieht sich,
> ist weg. Schon bin ich aus der Fassung
> gebracht, kann mir kein Herz mehr,
> keinen klaren Gedanken, lass,
> was nicht zu fassen ist, fallen,
> falle, lasse mich fallen, alles,
> was der Fall ist, lasse ich,
> ein Faß ohne Boden, auf sich beruhn.[10]

The experience of loss of certainty is frightening. But the sensation of falling from the position of moral certitude also entails the sensations that Buford recognizes: release from the strains and constraints of civilization. 'Merely stating your own position fans the flames of conflict' (*CW*, 49). Even words here become the gateway to civil war. For they unleash the passions which are suppressed and denied expression. The strain which Enzensberger has placed himself under is clear. The quotation from Buford expresses the fascinated envy of the left-wing intellectual vis-à-vis evil, *Zivilisationsbruch*, and the perpetrator of unlicensed violence, the taboo-breaker.

Suddenly the deeper intent of *Civil War* comes into focus: in the pessimism of his thesis, Enzensberger, like Martin Walser and others, can find an end to the downward spiral into loss of certainty that has come about at the end of the post-war era. The pessimistic universalism satisfies the longing for resolution of the isolation and detachment of the post-war intellectual. The moral insecurity and the repressed desire for rapprochement with the national community find expression and resolution in the image of 'losing control'. If the isolated and suffering intellectual is to regain a sense of community, it must be by recognizing the same original evil in everyone. Therein lies the logic of Enzensberger's metonymic argument. It draws a single line of causation from individual aggression to the Holocaust and thereby saves the link to humanity that he needs in order to save himself. A tone of apocalyptic disappointment replaces that of overwrought expectation as the descent into pessimism provides answers where the optimism of the post-war era has failed. Hans Magnus Enzensberger discovers and acknowledges that he too, like his forebears and with the rest of humanity, is capable of evil.

V Over-Determination by the Past

'Anyone who thinks that this applies only to the Germans is an idiot', he writes of the Germans' descent into barbarism. But the people who most typically apply this type of thinking about the uniqueness of evil to the Germans are Germans such as Enzensberger himself. His own generation, and the post-war generation (the Sixty-Eighters) who followed him, were typically the most zealous critics of Germany – to the point where categories such as inverted racism and self-hatred must be considered. The rejection of the German past by the members of these generations has been extreme. It manifested itself in the bitterness at the parents' generations, in the rejection of Germany and 'Germanness', in the ridding of themselves of anything felt to be German and hence 'infected' with Nazism, and in shame at feelings of 'Germanness' in the eyes of a hyper-critical world. For the left-wing intellectuals, the spokespersons of this generation, being German was suspect or even anathema, and the recognition of their own Germanness was repressed in a variety of ways. The main way for the intellectuals was to identify in terms of the universal ideology of Marxism/socialism. Socialism meant first and foremost an explicitly anti-national dogma, not merely a set of socio-economic policies. Socialism, too, was making one Germany 'pay' for the crimes of Nazism, while the other Germany appeared to be rewarded by Western capitalism during the post-war era.

However, as the post-war era came to a close in the late eighties, the mechanisms of repression of the link between past and present for the post-war generations became more and more fragile. Marxism had failed as a humanist-enlightenment practice, they themselves were ageing and becoming aware of patterns of self-identification other than those of their youth, and in their travels in the West and elsewhere, they encountered newly valorized concepts of ethnicity and national identity. All of these factors posited patterns of identification which were threatening for a generation which had predicated its identity on the idea of a 'zero hour': *Stunde Null*.

During the post-war era (from the 1960s until the 1980s) this generation had 'quarantined' itself from its parents, families and from the national culture in order to cut off any possibility of 'infection' by 'Germanness', of passage of the virus of Nazism from past to present. By taking strong ideological stances in favour of Marxism and socialism during the sixties and seventies and in favour of various other movements in the eighties – environmentalism, pacifism, anti-racism, the Intifada and various 'third-world' political movements, etc. – this generation quarantined itself on the side of the right and the good, against the past and against Nazism and everything that Germany had come to represent. The intention was meant well but it also imposed impossible strains, strains which expressed themselves in political extremism, in the ambiguity of causes such as the support for the Palestinians, and in the over-sensitivity and the hysteria of the left-wing intelligentsia on so many trivial as well as important issues. In the late eighties the process of 'normalization' of Germany became unavoidable – to the unease of the left-wing intellectuals. The Nazi generation were dying out, the Sixty-Eighters were in or approaching their fifties, and their children and grandchildren did not share their preoccupation with the past. The old slogan of 'beware the beginnings' (*Wehret den Anfängen!*) had lost its power. They recognized that Nazism was rapidly becoming history. They would soon be the last generation to have any memories – even childhood ones – of Nazism, the War or the immediate aftermath of the German tragedy. It is not surprising in this context that the *Historikerstreit* was such an impassioned affair. It was a rear-guard action to retain the memory of Nazism as a unique historical event, and to stop it becoming a part of history, a symbol of their own passing.

The role of the post-war left-wing intellectuals as the super-ego of the nation became strained by the movement of history. The position of extreme tension which they had taken up vis-à-vis the nation was taking its toll. In *Civil War* we can observe the effects of this strain. Enzensberger's 'civil war' is the culmination of his resentment of and bitterness at a world which has failed to meet his moral requirements. The left-wing utopias of group identity had begun to crumble earlier for him than for others of his generation, but they did at least offer the promise of an alternative to 'Germanness' as the basis of group identity. *Civil War* still reverberates with anti-capitalist passages echoing Enzensberger's earlier unorthodox Marxism. But now, after the collapse of the east-west divide and the failure of his stylization of the marginal and the peripheral in the works of the mid- to late eighties (*Mittelmaß und Wahn* and *Ach Europa!*) as the answer to growing uncertainty, Enzensberger's Marxism is exhausted. In *Civil War* he reconstructs group identity on a new, irrationalist and pessimistic basis. However it is not the recognition of 'civil war', 'evil' or 'aggression' which is the problem here. It is the motives behind their rediscovery. Enzensberger's apocalyptic pessimism is the counter-image of his earlier utopian hopes. And the universality of the argument is the counter-image of the specificity of his and his generation's national obsession. The problem in both cases is the over-determination by the German past.

The end of the post-war era, symbolized in the fall of the Wall dividing Germany from itself, meant the end of the conflict which ensured the peculiar existence of the left-wing intellectual. With the normalization of relationships of individual and society in Germany, the post-war intellectuals have lost their positions of moral certainty and authority. They are no longer able to predicate good and evil in terms of ideological positions without reference to the personal sphere. Enzensberger has, as André Glucksmann observed, discovered human nature. But he has done so in order to discover himself, in order to release himself from the quarantined loneliness of the left-wing German intellectual after the end of the post-war era.

We are now in a position to complete Enzensberger's series of equivalences: war *equals* group conflict *equals* aggression *equals* evil *equals* Germany/Nazism. The final component in the series is the return of the repressed identity of Germanness. It completes a vicious cycle of self-hatred and repression, a pessimistic and disillusioned identity in which violence and aggression are paramount. The evil of Nazism has returned as universal civil war in Enzensberger's apocalypse. This explains the rejection of any form of socio-historical relativisation of violent group conflict in the work. Enzensberger has come to terms with the repressed implications of his German identity by projecting himself onto the world. The group identity of violence discovered in *Civil War* is a manifestation of the return of repressed national identity in the post-war German intellectual. By recognizing the core of evil in everyone, Enzensberger gains access to a new sense of community and to a new set of potentially nationalist values.

The approach of a period of normality in Germany at the end of the century has elicited from Enzensberger and others of his generation a philosophy of civil war and human evil, rather than of civil society and of human good. Enzensberger's new-old philosophy of evil is determined by the failure to come to terms with his personal and national past. The shortcomings of *Civil War* are a measure of his inability to liberate himself from an obsolete and regressive relationship to Germany. *Civil War* belongs with *Anschwellender Bocksgesang* and the novels and essays of Bodo Kirchhoff, Martin Walser and others as another instalment in the sad confessions of the German left-wing intelligentsia at the end of the post-war era.

Read in the light of his encumbered relationship to the German past, Enzensberger's plea for a revised sense of national community seems suspect. At the point of Germany's emergence from the post-war era Enzensberger champions a new provincialism in which German intellectuals would be able to regain their moral security in defining German problems and German responsibilities. *Civil War* is the manifesto of a new political *Innerlichkeit* appearing at a time when world politics demands precisely its opposite – a strengthening of Europe and the United Nations and a clear sense of resolve in controlling, not capitulating to, human aggression.

NOTES

I should like to express my gratitude to the Alexander-von-Humboldt Foundation whose support has enabled me to complete the research for this article.

1 See Rolf Warnecke, 'Kurswechselparade eines Intellektuellen – Konsequent inkonsequent: Hans Magnus Enzensberger', in *Vom gegenwärtigen Zustand der deutschen Literatur*, ed. Heinz Ludwig Arnold (*Text + Kritik*, vol. 113, January 1992), Munich, 1992, pp. 97-104; Paul Michael Lützeler, '"Ein Böhme, ein Vagant": Hans Magnus Enzensbergers *Ach Europa!*', in *Spätmoderne und Postmoderne: Beiträge zur deutschsprachigen Gegenwartsliteratur*, ed. P.M. Lützeler, Frankfurt/Main, 1992, pp. 52-66.

2 Enzensberger published a short article in *Der Spiegel* in which the main themes of *Aussichten auf den Bürgerkrieg* were aired: 'Ausblicke auf den Bürgerkrieg', *Der Spiegel*, 25/1993, pp. 170-175.

3 André Glucksmann, 'Ein neuer Vogel Strauß', *Der Spiegel*, 37/1993, pp. 247-249. References in the text hereafter given in brackets as AG followed by page number.

4 Martin Chalmers and Robert Lumley, 'Enzensberger's Europe', *New Left Review*, 178 (1989), p. 88.

5 Cf. Susan Sontag, *Aids and its Metaphors*, New York, 1989; Sander L. Gilman, *Disease and Representation: Images of Illness from Madness to AIDS*, Ithaca, 1988.

6 Peter Schneider, 'Vom dünnen Firnis der Zivilisation', in *Vom Ende der Gewißheit*, Berlin, 1994, p. 38: 'Die Ratlosigkeit, die pseudointelligente Geschwätzigkeit, die Idiotie der zivilen Gesellschaft zeigen sich gerade darin, daß sie nach Erklärungen für etwas sucht, was nicht erklärt werden kann, keiner Erklärung bedarf und das eigentliche Movens der kulturellen Anstrengung ist: die Tatsache, daß es ein rohes, zu allem fähiges Aggressionspotential zwischen Menschen gibt, das nur durch eine eher unwahrscheinliche und äußerst fragile Leistung, die gemeinhin Kultur oder Zivilisation genannt wird, in Schranken gehalten wird'.

7 Bill Buford, *Among the Thugs*, London, 1991 (translated into German under the title *Geil auf Gewalt*, Munich, 1992). Rüdiger Safranski, 'Über die Wiederkehr des Bösen: eine Weihnachtsbetrachtung', *Frankfurter Allgemeine Zeitung*, 24 December 1992; reprinted as 'Destruktion und Lust: Über die Wiederkehr des Bösen', in *Die selbstbewußte Nation: 'Anschwellender Bocksgesang' und weitere Beiträge zu einer deutschen Debatte*, eds. Heimo Schwilk and Ulrich Schacht, Berlin, 1994.

8 Buford, *Among the Thugs*, p. 195. This passage is quoted in Safranski, 'Destruktion und Lust', in *Die selbstbewußte Nation: 'Anschwellender Bocksgesang' und weitere Beiträge zu einer deutschen Debatte*, p. 240.

9 Martin Walser, *Über Deutschland Reden*, Frankfurt/Main, 1989, p. 79.

10 Hans Magnus Enzensberger, *Der fliegende Robert: Gedichte, Szenen, Essays*, Frankfurt/Main, 1989, p. 15.

Chapter Nine

Universalism in One Country? Hans Magnus Enzensberger and the Reaction of German Intellectuals to the Return of War in Europe

Richard Herzinger

The return of war in Europe has fundamentally shaken the self-perception of intellectuals, not only in Germany, but throughout Western Europe. The incessant ethnic war of annihilation and expulsion in former Yugoslavia, which the Western strategy of appeasement – trapped in the logic of the old policy of détente – is unable to bring to a halt, has reduced theories of posthistoire, the 'end of the subject', the 'disappearance of reality' and the 'redundance of politics' to absurdity. Moreover, it has also shattered the pacifist illusions of the German peace movement along with the hopes expressed by social democratic and liberal optimists of an epoch of unendangered prosperity and peaceful co-operation in an undivided Europe which flourished for a brief time after 1989.

The Western debacle in Bosnia is the consequence of bad politics; more precisely, it is the consequence of the complete lack of a resolute and unified policy on the part of the West in relation to the new totalitarian challenge which has descended upon Europe with the excesses of ethnic nationalism. The Bosnian catastrophe has laid bare a deep crisis in the liberal democratic civilisation of the West. The lack of readiness in the West to rigorously defend its values and ideals on its own doorstep – if necessary, militarily – proves that the content and spirit of these values in the West itself are no longer adequately understood nor held in high enough esteem. Bosnia is not simply a distant flashpoint; it is the appalling manifestation of a possible future for the whole of Europe. The sanctioning of a nationalistic social order in former Yugoslavia, an order based on ethnic extermination, unavoidably constitutes a powerful impetus for nationalist cultural tendencies and for the 're-ethnicization' of Western Europe itself. Indeed, the European New Right is already formulating the ideological program required for this process.[1]

The Bosnian catastrophe can no longer be explained with the apparatus of the leftist theoretical tradition, or rather, can no longer be explained away. There is no anonymous 'modernisation process', no autonomous march of 'instrumental reason' which bears responsibility for this development; the blame for these events cannot be laid at the door of 'capitalism', 'imperialism' or indeed of some blindly destructive force of the 'world market'. The guilty and those who either directly or indirectly share responsibility have names and addresses; the Bosnian massacre makes drastically clear that political action and political decisions on the part of concrete subjects have in no sense become superfluous or irrelevant.

And yet precisely at this juncture, when the defence of the essential values of the open society of the West emerges as the decisive task of the moment, the intellectual class finds itself in a state of far-reaching theoretical and moral paralysis. In the eyes of many intellectuals, the failure of their own utopian conceptual frameworks has discredited public engagement as such. The ideology-critical deconstruction of the values of Western liberalism and their denunciation from a cultural relativist standpoint as being an instrument of colonial repression has produced an effect whereby the notion of universals, such as the concept of human rights, having a place in reality is frequently disputed. However, what poststructuralist, discourse-analytical and systems-theoretical approaches cannot explain is the fact that respect for these universals is now proving to be the undeniable precondition for a minimum level of civilized behaviour within society – a fact which Enzensberger himself stressed in *The Great Migration*. On the other hand, those moralists who, in the epoch of the nuclear arms race, would appeal whenever possible to the conscience of humanity, are now, in regard to Bosnia, above all noticeable for their silence. German intellectuals are tending to spare themselves a precise opinion on the events in Bosnia and the future of the process of European unification, or are ignoring these problems completely. In so far as they have anything to say at all about Bosnia, their concerns are less for the daily victims of the ethnic cleansers than for the potential civilian victims of possible military operations by the UN and NATO and for the spread of the Balkan conflict which could conceivably result from a military intervention. Such abstentionism and isolationism is alternatively rationalized by conjuring up apocalyptic visions of catastrophe or by referring, with an air of sober 'realism', to pressing problems in one's own country.

Hans Magnus Enzensberger's much discussed essay on *Civil War* combines both variants of this flight from the political in exemplary fashion. At the same time, apparently guided by the impetus to ruthlessly expose reality and the strategies which suppress the recognition of its true character, the essay seems to be addressed to those who do not want to see this reality. Although it reproduces and reinforces opinions which for the most part are widely held by members of the German intellectual (and general) public, the essay presents itself as a provocation intent on breaking taboos. Enzensberger claims that we now find ourselves in the midst of a 'civil war' which is escalating on a worldwide scale, one which the West can neither understand nor check. This civil war, according to Enzensberger, has already reached the metropolitan centres of the Western industrial countries, expressing itself in an increasing and uncontrollable use of violence by all against all. However, Enzensberger draws a surprising conclusion from this alarming finding: it is necessary – and it is possible – to 'drain' or to 'dry up' [*austrocknen*] the 'molecular civil war' in one's own land. The contrary notion of a pacification of the whole planet with the help of international institutions is, according to Enzensberger, the expression of an illusionary universalism which in reality represents nothing other than the secularized concept of the Christian mission. Universalistic morality is thus seen by the author as the 'last refuge of Eurocentrism' (*CW*, 59).

Enzensberger simultaneously delivers a global scenario of catastrophe and a justification for calling off for the moment any consideration of appropriate international countermeasures. At the same time it is noticeable that, although the essay offers numerous concrete observations of disturbing signs of a spread of excessive violence and thereby gives the impression of a diagnosis based on conclusive empirical material, its basic theses in fact stem from extremely abstract, a priori premises.

Enzensberger presents war as an anthropological constant, the driving forces and mechanisms of which have still not been penetrated. He enquires after the atavistic images of the enemy upon which the hatred which ultimately vents itself in warlike aggression is ignited. Enzensberger writes:

> There is an unexplained linkage between hating one's neighbour and hating a stranger. The original target of our hatred was probably always our neighbour; only with the formation of larger communities was the stranger on the other side of the border declared an enemy. (*CW*, 12-13)

This highly speculative premise serves as a fulcrum for Enzenberger's argument in two respects. In the first place, its function is to back up his thesis that we have entered a new world-historical period in which traditional warring between states has been replaced by completely uncontrollable civil wars spreading on a global scale. Secondly, it serves, in an – as it were – mirror image inversion, as grounds for his rejection of universalism and his call for an ethics orientated towards the 'nearest' rather than the 'furthest'.

Enzensberger argues that the warlike massacres throughout the world which he draws together under the concept of civil war represent a form of relapse back into a pre-civilized state of humanity. The '"cultivated" war [*der 'gehegte' Staatenkrieg*] waged between nations and against external enemies is...a relatively recent development' (*CW*, 11), he writes, one which first reached a completely rationalized stage in the nineteenth century. The 'state war' thus appears as a phenomenon of a civilized transition period, which is now being brought to an end by the resurgence of atavistic patterns. And these patterns, according to Enzensberger, imply that the war against 'the strangers beyond the border' belongs to a later, more refined cultural stage whereas the butchering of one's immediate neighbour, by contrast, is the original form of warlike aggression. It should be added that Enzensberger here takes an opposite turn to that followed by typically conservative arguments. According to the conservative world-view, the natural object of love is first the family, followed by the neighbour and only then by the stranger. Enzensberger reverses this argument in so far as he seems to claim that it is the neighbour who is the natural object of initial hatred.

Enzensberger's speculations on the sudden eruption of atavistic patterns of behaviour through the thin crust of civilization provide him with a cultural-philosophical foundation for his own core thesis: namely, that the contemporary world cannot be explained with the apparatus of thought which we have at our disposal, an apparatus committed to the conception of the world of the Enlightenment and of Rationalism. Moreover, according to this thesis, our knowledge of the causes and interrelations of the processes with which we are confronted is not enough to enable us to master them. 'It's not just that the mad reality eludes formal legal definition' (*CW*, 12), writes Enzensberger:

> Even the strategies of the military high commands fail in the face of the new world order [*Neue Weltunordnung*!] which trades under the name of civil war. The unprecedented comes into sudden and explosive contact with the atavistic. Old anthropological questions come to the fore. (*CW*, 12)

In order to paint this picture of an elemental eruption of uncontrollable forces, Enzensberger places all forms of non-state excesses of violence in principle on the same level and subsumes them under the category of the 'molecular' and the 'macroscopic civil war'. This civil war, he claims, is raging not only in Africa and in the former Yugoslavia: 'it has long since moved into the metropolis...The combatants are no longer justs terrorists and secret police, Mafiosi and skinheads, drug dealers and death squads, neo-Nazis and cowboy security guards' but 'even ordinary members of the public are transformed overnight into hooligans, arsonists, rioters and serial killers'. To be sure, there is still in the industrial countries 'an overwhelming majority' who 'prefer peace'. However, as the example of Los Angeles shows, the 'molecular civil war can escalate at any time to epidemic proportions' (*CW*, 19-20).

Of course, the qualitative difference between the violence of South American death squads and that of members of private security services patrolling public utilities such as the underground railways, must have struck even Enzensberger as must the lack of comparability between ghetto unrest in American capitals and the policy of systematic ethnic annihilation and expulsion practiced by the Serbs in Bosnia. Nevertheless, Enzensberger has to suggest that all these forms of violence spring from one and the same cause and are all facets of one and the same phenomenon in order to lend plausibility to his claim that even political movements today misuse ideologies merely as a pretext for giving in to a blind urge to destroy. Even Islamic fundamentalism, he argues, is not in fact pursuing any political or ideological goals, but is on the contrary an example of the progressive 'autism' and 'atrophy of conviction' which can be observed among perpetrators of violence the world over: 'The various sects, factions and militias are at each others' throats. What we see is not conviction, but its facsimile' (*CW*, 23).

In Enzensberger's view, precisely the same applies to right-wing radicalism in Germany. For the neo-Nazi youth, he writes, ideology is 'no more than a charade': 'He knows nothing about national socialism. He's not interested in history. The swastika and Hitler salutes are optional extras' (*CW*, 24). Obviously Enzensberger has never devoted much attention to the real neo-Nazis or to the New Right. The ideological agendas and well-planned strategies of fundamentalist organizations in Algeria, Egypt and Palestine have also quite plainly eluded him as has the fact that, rather than indiscriminately murdering people, the Serbian militias carry out their massacres as part of a rigorous implementation of their nationalist campaign of conquest. Totalitarian political ideologies have always been characterized by a considerable share of irrational destructive energy; but the assertion that this irrational share has now suddenly become absolute is quite simply pure invention.

Enzensberger claims that the combatants in the global civil war have become slaves to a blind desire for destruction and self-destruction, the secret driving power of which is represented by the wish to remove oneself from the world: ethnic wars of extermination and fundamentalist terror as the expression of an ultimate discontent within the culture, as the most extreme form of a collective death instinct. On the basis of such a mystificatory diagnosis, Enzensberger attempts to fundamentally call into question the premises of universalistic ethics. Whoever demands that all citizens of the West should feel themselves responsible for all the victims of the blind exercise of violence everywhere in the world expects too much of people and provokes precisely the opposite reaction. Already 'the sheer weight of information with which we are bombarded', argues Enzensberger, 'makes any kind of intelligent analysis impossible' (*CW*, 60). Here he falls back on a classical argument of conservative anthropology and the sociology of culture, according to which the modern society of mass communication represents an excessive demand on the human being. The individual is understood here as capable of developing ethical standards only in relation to his or her immediate or nearest sphere of experience. However, in the information society, information from everywhere, even from the most distant corners of the globe is mediated only via 'secondary' experiences. Such information can only be absorbed by the individual in a limited manner. Should the individual be forced to assimilate too much secondary information, the preparedness to develop ethical forms of behaviour in relation to foreign phenomena abruptly changes into aggression and rejection.[2]

This conservative argument fundamentally contests the possibility of realizing a universalistic ethics and of translating it into practical action. Enzensberger, too, postulates that universalism 'recognizes no difference between near and far':

> The obligation it places on all of us is, in principle, unlimited. Here the declaration reveals its theological origins which have survived all attempts at secularization. We should all be responsible for everyone else. (*CW*, 58)

This claim, so Enzensberger, presupposes 'omnipresence' and even 'omnipotence' and therefore comprises the demand to become like God. 'But since our scope for action is finite', argues Enzensberger, 'the gap between the claim and the reality opens ever wider. Soon you cross over into objective hypocrisy and, in the end, universalism reveals itself as a moral trap' (*CW*, 58).

Undoubtedly Enzensberger is right to draw attention to the hypocrisy which governments throughout the world and some moralizers indulge in when dealing with human rights. And he justifiably criticises the large discrepancy which is evident between ethical precepts and the practical actions which follow from them and which frequently results in a lack of credibility in regard to Western resolve. But Enzensberger is mistaken when he claims that universalism is unable to distinguish between ideal and reality, and that it is incapable of establishing priorities in regard to the defence of human rights. Universalism simply does not demand 'unlimited deployment, everywhere and at every time' (*CW*, 65). Postulating the claim that particular universals are relevant to all people and to all times does not in any sense mean that this postulate can be asserted everywhere and every time to the same extent. The fact that this is not possible, however, does not mean that the moral premises of universalism themselves are rendered invalid. Whoever makes this claim must either speak from a position of ethical relativism or turn their back on the problems beyond their own borders and seal themselves off from the outside world. Had the adherents of the Enlightenment during the eighteenth century followed such a logic, we would today hardly be in a position to even reflect on the defence of human rights. Already then there were more than adequate grounds to despair of the capacity for human atrocity. The rights we enjoy today we owe not least to the fact that those supporting the Enlightenment did not do precisely this.

The nationalistic conclusion, which is being called for by the New Right, is one which Enzensberger, however, expressly does not want to accept. He is also a long way from accepting cultural relativistic justifications for human rights violations. His own suggestion amounts rather to the practice of what might be termed 'universalism in one's own country': this is where the civil war at home should and could be ended. As far as other civil wars throughout the world are concerned, on the other hand, there is no other option, according to Enzensberger, than simply to leave them to 'exhaust' themselves. He writes:

> Before we put a spoke in the wheels of the warring Bosnians, we ought to mop up [*austrocknen*] the civil war in our own country. Our priority is not Somalia, but Hoyerswerda and Rostock, Mölln and Solingen. (*CW*, 69)

However, apart from the fact that Enzensberger does not explain how the 'mopping up', or the 'drying up' in the original German, of the civil war in one's own country is to proceed, given that the violence which has been liberated is supposedly uncontrollable and motivated by nothing other than a yearning for self-destruction, and apart from the fact that the formulation, 'the warring Bosnians', testifies to an almost provocative ignorance in regard to the actual relationship between perpetrator and victim within that country – the proposal Enzensberger presents in the tones of the realist is no less unworldly than the cosmopolitan idealism which he so harshly criticizes. How can the war being waged by the neo-Nazis against the open society be brought to an end when in Germany's immediate neighbourhood culturally nationalistic regimes of terror are triumphing? And in the name of what values is the struggle against the perpetrators of violence to be waged if not in the name of the very universalistic values which Enzensberger holds to be the products of a secularized theology and, as a consequence, to be irreconcilable with reality?

Far from providing a realistic assessment of the present state of the world, Enzensberger's position cultivates the state of panic which has spread in the light of the apparently insoluble problems in Europe and the world. Moreover, he articulates the aversion of former leftist intellectuals to a confrontation with the complex causes of a confused and crisis-ridden international political situation.

But how has it come about that Enzensberger of all people, whose positions have until recently always been among the most advanced of those formulated by German intellectuals, has now taken on the function of front rider in the retreat and harbinger of the capitulation of thought? The answer lies in the fact that Enzensberger's thought and intellectual stance still moves *ex negativo* within the conceptual boundaries of the old Left. Enzensberger wants to provoke this section of the intellectual and political spectrum, to confront its dogmatism and sentimentality. As a means of counteracting their utopianism, he insists on a radical scepticism which not only – as already in the case of the liberal, Karl Popper, fifty years ago – disputes every notion of a higher meaning and any principle of good within the process of history, but also – unlike Popper – denies any possibility of positively influencing the course of history in a conscious manner.

In an article for *Kursbuch* in 1978, Enzensberger already made those on the Left intractably clinging to a belief in 'History' take note of the fact

> that there is no world spirit; that we do not know the laws of history...that social and natural evolution know no subject and that they are therefore unpredictable; that we therefore, when we engage in political action, never attain that which we set out to attain, but instead something quite different...and that it is precisely here that the reason for the crisis of all positive utopias can be found.[3]

At that time these insights had a liberating and forward-looking effect in contrast to the historicistic dogmatism of the Left. By 1990, on account of the events dominating world politics, of the unexpected collapse of communism, Enzensberger could well feel that his assessment had been roundly endorsed; and he repeated, in another context, his theses of 1978. In another essay, also in *Kursbuch,* he explained that the most recent developments in Europe were proof of the fundamental impotence of politics and politicians:

> The foolish impression which governments are making in the light of the most recent European developments, their helpless crowing, is...no accidental embarrassment...it follows from the impossibility in principle of foreseeing the societal process, of subjecting it to a general calculation and mastering it from above.[4]

In 1990 Enzensberger, influenced by the euphoria of liberation in 1989, rather more optimistically awaited this farewell to politics. The politicians, he proclaimed, would have to come to terms with the 'banal fact that democracy is an open, productive, risky process, which organizes itself and which eludes, if not their influence, then their control'.[5]

If Enzensberger still believed at this point – in almost anarchist undertones – that the democratic society of citizens was a self-regulating body which could manage without any political leadership at all, then this conviction suddenly metamorphosed in 1993 into a harsh historical and cultural pessimism, after his own positive expectations had proved illusionary. Whereas his thesis of the fundamental uncontrollability of social and historical processes had led him in 1978 to renounce any prophetic role, his clinging to this basic conception subsequently in fact enabled him in 1990, and then above all in 1993, to step into the role of soothsayer of the dawning of a new age: in 1990 the herald of an epoch of a self-organizing democracy, in 1993 the prophet of the apparently immanent decline of civilization in an unbridled, irrational war of all against all.

The actual target group of Enzensberger's polemic in *Civil War* is the Left. Its members are accused by Enzensberger, justifiably to a large extent, of over-estimating their own abilities and of harbouring an idealistically distorted image of the world. Yet his rejection of any possibility of planned action on the part of political subjects actually reproduces the notoriously troubled relationship of the German Left to concrete, pragmatic politics. Because it is precisely a pragmatic politics that is needed today more urgently than ever, Enzensberger's trademark critical gesture, which once so agreeably stood out against the sterility of the Left's belief in salvation and self-pity, can no longer provide a forward-looking impulse. Instead it assumes the form of a conservatively tinged, anti-political attentism.

Already in 1964, following Enzensberger's claim that, in the age of nuclear weapons, politics and criminality had become identical,[6] Hannah Arendt accused him of 'escapism'. Enzensberger's generalizations, so Arendt, amounted to the elimination of all moral differences. 'Where all are guilty', so Arendt, 'noone is guilty. It is precisely the specific and the particular that is again drowned in the sauce of generalization.'[7] This diagnosis also applies to the essential formulations presented in *Civil War*.

NOTES

1 See Mark Terkessidis, *Kulturkampf. Volk, Nation, der Westen und die Neue Rechte*, Cologne, 1995. See also Richard Herzinger and Hannes Stein, *EndzeitPropheten oder Die Offensive der Antiwestler. Fundamentalismus, Antiamerikanismus, Neue Rechte*, Reinbek bei Hamburg, 1995.

2 This position is formulated in exemplary fashion by the conservative sociologist of culture and anthropologist Arnold Gehlen. See Arnold Gehlen, *Moral und Hypermoral*, 4th ed., Wiesbaden, 1981.

3 Hans Magnus Enzensberger, 'Zwei Randbemerkungen zum Weltuntergang', *Kursbuch*, 52, May 1978, pp. 1-8, here p. 7.

4 Hans Magnus Enzensberger, 'Gangarten. Ein Nachtrag zur Utopie', *Kursbuch*, 100, June 1990, pp. 1-10, here pp. 2-3.

5 Enzensberger, 'Gangarten', p. 10.

6 See Hans Magnus Enzensberger, *Politik und Verbrechen. Neun Beiträge*, Frankfurt/Main, 1964.

7 Hannah Arendt/Hans Magnus Enzensberger, 'Ein Briefwechsel', in Reinhold Grimm (ed.), *Hans Magnus Enzensberger*, Frankfurt/Main, 1984, pp. 82-89, here p. 83.

Chapter Ten

Hans Magnus Enzensberger Takes the Stand on *Civil War*: A Talk Show Scenario

Rainer Stollmann

I Gulf War

Talk Show Host (TSH): Herr Enzensberger, I should like to thank you for this talk.

Hans Magnus Enzensberger (HME): Why, are we done already?

TSH: No, but since you are usually rather reluctant to grant interviews...

HME: What do you mean? Here I am, ready for any kind of mischief.

TSH: True, but, after your essay on the Gulf War a lot of papers wanted to have a statement from you...

HME: Yes.

TSH: ...which you declined to provide...

HME: I could just about imagine what would happen if I compared Hitler to Saddam Hussein in *Der Spiegel*. Thus there was no need to intervene again. You throw a small pebble into the pond of the public sphere and then you watch how the circles spread outwards.

TSH: You do not regret identifying Hussein with Hitler? These two photos, Hitler with a child, Hussein with a child....?

HME: I don't want to hide behind the excuse that it was the editors who chose the photos. With democratic politicians one might expect a degree of sensitivity for the obscenity of this motif. Dictators on the other hand seem to have a strong need for the decorative display of childlike innocence. No, there is nothing I need to take back. At the necessary moment I said words that were meant to clarify the fronts; and I think that's what happened.

TSH: Oskar Negt compared you and Biermann to the poets of the war euphoria in 1914.

HME: But the enthusiastic tirades of hate in 1914 were written in verse, the majority of them anyway. There were no reflective essays. More importantly, the poets of 1914 were speaking to an agitated mob, in order to incite it even further. I spoke to the despondent and timorous left-liberal readers who were running the risk of falling into the trap of their own holy antifascism, with its correlating pacifism or, at least, strong antimilitarism – while at the same time German neo-Nazis were offering their services to Iraq as volunteers. It is obvious that my situation in February 1991 was quite different compared to that of German intellectuals in August 1914. And incidentally, in 1914 German writers and German professors were blowing into the same horn; now, Professors Habermas and Negt wrote analytical articles against the war (each one of them shaking their head very mildly about what Biermann and I had said). This is real progress, a great achievement in terms of disunity and the potential for differentiation, a milestone for German intellectuals!

TSH: The late dramatist Heiner Müller commented on your article that the times must be bad for thinking if an intelligent head such as yours could produce such rubbish.

HME: Did he say 'rubbish'?

TSH: Perhaps not exactly the word.

HME: Of course Müller was right in saying that not every epoch is equally favourable for thinking. Such a height of autonomous critical thinking as in France in the eighteenth century or, if you prefer, in Germany at the time of our classical authors, has not been reached again until today. Our thinking is only a weak reflection of that. But should I shut up because of that? I must be allowed to let my modest intellectual light shine at least occasionally. I assume what my colleague Müller said was that the time for art has arrived when the time for thinking has passed – but I cannot have a sonnet published as an essay in *Spiegel*, and no other poetic form either could have created this public debate.

TSH: What did the essay achieve?

HME: Well, you would have noted the considerable rustling in the forest of the media which one can take as an indicator for a real debate. Even the party convention of the Greens in December 1995 could not agree on an abstract pacifism with regard to the question of whether or not to send German troops to the Balkan.

TSH: Do you consider your article was responsible for that?

HME: Among other things. The article of course was followed by two further essays. And there were other contributions as well. But I think I can expect a degree of openness at least among some of the Greens, i.e., that they read what I write. Incidentally: in my opinion the Greens ought to have voted against the deployment of troops, for tactical reasons.

TSH: I beg your pardon?

HME: Too much unity is undemocratic. Strength lies in disunity: it would have been enough if the motion in favour of deployment had been carried with a slim majority. The SPD also should have voted against it. Such a vote would have represented my own personal *Bundestag*. I am not one hundred per cent in favour of sending German troops to Yugoslavia! Fifty-two per cent at most. Surely this expresses not only my own uncertainty. Of course the soldiers will have to serve with one hundred per cent of their person, but they too will have doubts. I would have preferred to have seen this doubt documented in Parliament, rather than a display of pseudo-sentiment, of 'Unquestioned Loyalty' towards NATO and *Humanity*. The apparent unity only covers up the bureaucratic interests of the military and its allied industrial interests: the deployment will easily generate an extra five percent for the defence budget the next time around. I'm sure most people, myself included, don't want this to happen! We need to be thrifty, as everyone knows!

TSH: Perhaps we can turn to a different topic, namely 'molecular civil war'...

HME: That's not really a different topic. That's what's happening in former Yugoslavia.

TSH: But the Gulf War is a different story.

HME: Only in as much as it was a war between states: in this sense it was of course not a civil war. But if you look at the degenerate soldiery in former Yugoslavia: they too tried very hard to hide their massacres, butchery and plunderings, i.e., terror against civilians, behind the cover of a traditional state war, or even more hypocritically, they tried to pass it off under the banner of a cultural clash between different ethnic groups. They did this, it needs to be said, with the eager support of the Europeans, with the Federal Republic up front. The hasty recognition of these stunted states – which will not be viable in the long run – has contributed to bring about the dilemma in which the Western states now find themselves.

TSH: But a peace treaty has just been signed in Dayton.

HME: It is winter.

TSH: You mean, the war will break out again in summer?

HME: Let's wait and hope for the opposite.

II The War of Images

TSH: Herr Enzensberger, among researchers of war, and in the United Nations as well, the following definion of war is current: 'War is every military operation in which a member of the system of states current at the time is involved and in which a threshold of one thousand victims of combatants is reached or surpassed'.

HME: Definitions of this kind are something for bureaucrats who want to administer war. This definition excludes civil war, it does not count civilian victims, as in massacres. I rather prefer Clausewitz: 'War is an act of violence to force the enemy to surrender to our will'. This definition, complemented by others of Clausewitz, such as 'War is an extended duel', provides a useful analytical concept to describe all kinds of wars, e.g., war between the sexes, trade war, ideological war, advertising or election campaigns. How can one define war, that is to mark it off against something else, when in reality nearly all human relations are shot through with war? Molecular civil war is a product of the disintegration of civilisation where it is previously present as structural violence; in the process of the erosion of civil society, it condenses to manifest violence.

TSH: But expressions like trade war or war between the sexes are surely only metaphors.

HME: Well, the word 'war' itself is also a metaphor if it is used to describe, without differentiation, such totally different things as what happened in Troy three thousand years ago, or in Carthage, the conquest of Gaul, the Thirty Years War, Napoleon, 1870-71, or the so-called First and Second World Wars. If you were to take the definition of Clausewitz serious and compare it to what happened between 1939 and 1945, very little would be left that one could describe as war. When the German bombers bombarded Coventry, or when the air force of General Harris pulverised Dresden, the victims were not given the opportunity to surrender. Where is the war here in the sense of an 'extended duel' or as a clash between two wills? This is not at all anymore about the will of the real inhabitants of the cities who are sitting in their air raid shelters praying that the bombs may miss their houses. Their will is not a factor here; if they had the choice they would have preferred to surrender to the will of the bombers, rather than die. But they are being burnt as deputies, as part of the hostile 'whole', in the deceptive hope that the 'whole of the enemy' will be so shocked by this that their morale will be broken: 'moral bombing', that's what it was called at the time.

TSH: The aerial bombings were supposed to destroy the will to fight of the enemy nation?

HME: Precisely. The fate of the people of Dresden or Cologne was meant as a signal to the Germans what would happen to them if they did not capitulate. What happened to them will happen to you – that was the message of the terror bombings. The will, the morale of the rest of the nation was to be destroyed by the devastation of allotments of the national territory. But then – strictly speaking – it is not the carpet bombing or the fire storm that is war but rather the image, the pictures of the destroyed cities. The real weapon, the means of war, is the effect, the message transmitted by these pictures, mental images and rumours. This is what I call metaphorical war, war of the images. To a large extent this is what war in the twentieth century is about. Verdun already was a metaphor. Frederick the Great would have been horrified by the complete lack of strategic or tactical reason in that battle. The commanding German general, Falkenhayn, used terms such as 'blood pump' and 'chopping-board'.

TSH: Are you seriously saying that the wars waged in our war-mongering century have been essentially metaphorical?

HME: Yes, indeed. This is not true only for our century. Probably all wars are to a very large extent metaphorical processes, that is to say not essentially – as Clausewitz has it – 'extended duels', clashes of two wills. Napoleon's soldiers said of the campaigns in Spain and Russia where they were worn down by guerillas: This is no war. The guerilla mixes up war and civilian life, he does not want to be recognized as a soldier. 'No German city is worth the bones of a British soldier', was the reason given by Harris for the aerial bombings. He wanted to avoid heavy casualties after the landing of troops on the ground. As you know this did not happen, it was an illusion. And I cannot see, to come back to this point, how one can realistically understand this wild, bloody but also unreal, metaphorical business if one proceeds as Singer and Small do. By cutting out parts of the picture, for instance civil war, the whole picture does not become more real.

TSH: But Dresden and Cologne were destroyed in reality and not only in the cinema.

HME: It wasn't about Cologne or Dresden. It was not about Hiroshima, either. Maybe Germany did surrender just in time, otherwise the atom bomb would have been dropped on Berlin. Hiroshima was chosen because it is situated in a valley, in the hope that the effects of radiation could be studied better under favourable climatic conditions. No armament industries were destroyed, no transport links, no single concrete target as an important moment of the will of the enemy was hit. A metaphor is a shortened form of comparison: what happened to Cologne, to Hiroshima, to Coventry will happen to you. That is the message, and the real weapon is the picture of the destruction: it is metaphorical, even if real people die, empirically. What we have come to call war is an objectified, objectivistic fiction.

TSH: Could you please explain what 'objectivistic fiction' is?

HME: Something that is real, that exists empirically and in fact, such as weapon systems, buildings, areas declared off limit, factories, machines, etc., but that is nevertheless pure imagination, that is essentially without foundation in reality. Everything is built up and put together according to unreal ideas that do not function. Take a stunt man in a 'desaster movie', for example: the man has an accident and dies. He is now 'really' dead but the context in which his death occurred was thought up by Hollywood, it is pure fiction. Don't you sometimes also have the impression that human history, Alexander the Great, the witch trials, the inquisition, Napoleon's conquests, racism, nationalism, that all this has more to do with wildly realised phantasies than with the hope that being determines consciousness? The gigantic expenditures for the German navy before World War I, a policy that contributed greatly to the outbreak of war: they were all in vain. This fleet spent most of the time in port until it was sunk in 1918 at the end of the war. What can you say against the sentence: the German imperial navy was pure imagination?

TSH: But other things came to be deployed...

HME: What I mean is the same as Mao Zedong when he speaks of the atom bomb as a 'paper tiger'. The atom bomb was deployed and nevertheless is a paper tiger. Don't forget that Mao Zedong was a highly successful soldier; he knew what he was talking about. The things that the military are dealing with in the twentieth century are essentially not weapons but monstrosities. The atom bomb does not, as a weapon, end the war but it demonstrates that war has become an absurdity. The technological progress has taken away the possibility for human beings to wage war. This is true not only for nuclear war but for industrial war generally. Thus we are using a rather old-fashioned word metaphorically for a new process which so far, and maybe in principle, escapes conceptualisation.

TSH: War as kind a broom, of the sorcerer's assistant, that is out of control?

HME: In the Gulf war, the American military deployed the weapons of the twenty-first century. They computerised their weapons, used satellites as navigation aids for individual soldiers, video cameras in their missiles, etc. They did this in order to control their own weapons of the twentieth century (rockets, tanks, planes). And so they beat the enemy, an army out of the nineteenth century.

TSH: And they were successful.

HME: Well, yes.

TSH: Well, weren't they?

HME: Nobody could predict that it would take them six weeks to succeed.

TSH: So, what?

HME: According to US sources, the war cost between one half and a billion dollars a day. Germany paid for fourteen days. Imagine the war had lasted twelve or eighteen weeks.

TSH: It would have been expensive.

HME: It would have ruined the budgets of the states of the Western world! What would have been the significance of a military victory then? The triumph of the American generals is basically due to the short duration of the war – and that could not be guaranteed and, more importantly, cannot be guaranteed for any future war. Most German believed in August 1914 that the war would be over in four weeks.

III The Molecular Civil Warrior

TSH: In 1966, in your debate with Peter Weiss on the possibility of international solidarity, you wrote: 'The difference between what happens in Kreuzberg and what happens in Calcutta is supposed to be glossed over with the five words: "It is essentially the same"'.

HME: So?

TSH: Today, twenty-seven years later, this is exactly the message of your essay on *Civil War*: 'Every carriage on the underground can become a miniature Bosnia'. Doesn't that mean: Chechnyia, Bosnia, Columbia and the 'autonomous' mafia of Kreuzberg are essentially the same? One wonders: why is true for the molecular civil war what is utterly untrue for international solidarity – which you described at the time, rather unkindly, as a 'comfortable religion'. Maybe your idea of the ubiquitous civil war is also a comfortable religion, albeit a negative one.

HME: I don't think I need to become entrapped in my own, earlier quotation. We are talking about two completely different things, fundamentally opposed to each other: one is politics, the other is anti-politics. The first one aims at autonomy, the second one aims at heteronomy, i.e., violence. Processes of political concretisation and production always lead to diversity, to the recognition and consciousness of differences. Real processes of abstraction escalate in violence, and that is indeed the same everywhere. What seems new to me is that the political retrovirus, the transformation of politics into crime, happens spontaneously, on the lowest molecular level of society, while previously I thought that the world of the bureaucratic machineries was the ideal breeding ground for this transformation.

TSH: In *Civil War* you quote from the book by Bill Buford on English hooligans:

> In the following scene, the accomodation with violence reaches its climax. 'There were now six of them, and they all started kicking the boy on the ground. The boy covered his face. I was surprised that I could tell, from the sound, when someone's shoe missed, or when it struck the fingers and not the forehead or the nose. I was transfixed. I suppose, thinking about this incident now, I was close enough to have stopped the kicking...But I didn't. I don't think the thought occurred to me. It was as if time had dramatically slowed down, and each second had a definite beginning and end, like a sequence of images on a roll of film, and I was mesmerised by each image I saw.

The author calls this 'ecstasy', and the last sentence of the passage reads: 'Somebody near me said that he was happy, very happy, that he could not ever remember being so happy' (*CW*, 48).

HME: 'All pleasure wants eternity': time is stopped here, as it were; for a moment eternity is produced.

TSH: Like in a slow motion sequence in a desaster movie...

HME: ...a process which apparently is not just a technological-ideological invention of the consciousness industry but rather a factual possibility of sensual perception; it reflects a condition of the senses. Of course, this can be easily understood in bio-chemical terms, as the artificially triggered production of an overdose of endorphines, the hormones of happiness. Probably this can be trained systematically. Street battles in the wake of football matches which escalate with proper timing in conjunction with alcohol abuse: finally, they build up to the delirious moment of an excessive, bloody brawl at the edge of death for which these 'soul-animals' or 'soul-things' of the twentieth century seem to live.

TSH: Previously, in connection with the Red Army Faction and Ernst Jünger, you spoke about 'the emptiness at the centre of terror'. Here the terrorist does not feel empty but happy.

HME: It's the same. Deliriousness is exactly the absence of consciousness. Emptiness means that terror does not need the legitimation of content; it does not need communication, consciousness, purpose, aims. It is its own purpose. The quotation by Buford provides a good illustration for that. We, as civilised people, do not know the happiness of the mob. We find it difficult to see joy and violence together. We do not like to accept that 'the pursuit of happiness' can take on such a ghostly form. Believe me: the molecular civil war is the rule of the pleasure principle.

TSH: Is the pleasure principle something criminal?

HME: It is reckless and without deference, therefore criminal.

TSH: But you don't write this in your book.

HME: I'm telling you now.

TSH: Freud speaks of the 'battle at the borders' of the *I*, of the 'war between consciousness and unconsciousness'.

HME: He does so in the context of a debate on melancholia, something refined and decadent. That's not what we are talking about here. Freud has to do with the very civilised forms of an inner war of the nineteenth century. This interior life has characteristic structures which have become so rigid that they can even wage 'war' against each other. If you asked me to describe the interior of a molecular civil warrior, I would choose the image of a desert or of a devastated landscape of ruins in which such precious things as Self, Consciousness or the Unconscious exist only vaguely, in rudimentary form, and thus are incapable of engaging in such a definite relationship as a war with each other. What is the intoxicating rush of blood, the ecstatic delirium of violence? Consciousness? The expression of the Unconscious? Both do not seem to apply because we are talking here about less qualified conditions of biological life. The *I* of the molecular civil warrior is fragmented, incomplete; there has not been an experience or a history of conflict between pleasure and reality principle, at least not to any significant extent. The principle of self-preservation, which the Critical Theorists believe is the foundation of Enlightenment, has remained a bungling torso, a shoddy piece of work. Take for example a band of Serbian soldiers who occupy a hospital in Sarajevo. In order to make it clear to the nurses that it is pointless to resist rape, their leader pulls a knife and cuts across the palm of his hand so that the blood drips to the floor. Rather than threatening the women with his knife, he shows – in a fast and graphic demonstration – that he does not submit to the reality principle of self-preservation, and that he is therefore a more dangerous enemy.

TSH: You speak in *Civil War* about the erosion of patriarchy and about associations of men who show a new kind of manliness, no longer tamed by patriarchy, which can no longer distinguish between courage and cowardice.

HME: Is it courage if I maim myself? It certainly does not seem to be cowardice either. If one observes these civil warriors, like the six German skinheads who beat an African man to a pulp, one cannot but feel that they completely lack any consciousness of the concept of cowardice. It seems to me that we are dealing here with a product of civilisation that is only half or quarter finished and to which the concepts of Freud, which he derived from a perfectly developed bourgeoisie, do not apply. To me, the molecular civil war appears as a kind of pleasure principle that is mechanised, or machine-like, and therefore dead but permanently in motion. One cannot deny the ritualistic aspect, the repetition. The hooligan needs to be drunk every Saturday, and it makes no difference whether he is in Birmingham, Rome or Barcelona: the experience is always the same. This goes for the graffiti sprayers as well: I refer to the rather more harmless, silly form of civil war. Just look at our cities, especially the older residential areas: What kind of pleasure is it to smear paint on house walls night after night? If you walk through our inner cities, or through university corridors for that matter, you cannot but escape the impression that certain contingents of young people have remained fixated at the anal stage of development.

TSH: It was the students of the New Left who started this with their political slogans.

HME: Thirty years ago! Marx writes in *The Civil War in France* : 'It is the customary fate of new social creations to be taken for a parallel expression of older and even out-lived forms of social life with which they carry some resemblance'. Part of my motivation to write *Civil War* was my growing alienation in view of this strange, objective irony which sees in the very different, destructive processes of today, which are directed against every kind of community, the supposed appendices of '68. The so-called 'autonomous' youths in Germany, or the graffiti sprayers, are in reality criminal gangs, just like the pseudo-political gangs in the Third World.

TSH: Commandante Marcos in Mexico?

HME: Possibly an exception, possibly something new.

TSH: The liberation movement in Eritrea?

HME: An exception.

TSH: Mao Zedong had called upon the traditional bandits and secret societies of China to join him on the 'long march'. The French Revolution was often in danger of plummeting to the deepest abyss of murderous violence, denunciations, plunderings, etc. We know similar occurrences from other revolts, for example during the Munich Soviet Republic of 1919. Do you forget that the wall adjacent to crime was often rather thin on the emancipatory side of politics?

HME: I do not forget the political side of things which could have perhaps neutralised criminality; for the moment, it is history that is doing the forgetting.

IV Science, Theory, Essay

TSH: What would you say to the criticism that your essay on *Civil War* is the product of a bad-tempered old man who quarrels – admittedly in an intelligent way – with the world and with young people in particular.

HME: First of all I would consider this an injurious slander based on nothing but the abstraction of my age. Secondly : why should a more advanced age be more disadvantageous to one's own thinking than a lesser age? Thirdly: I would find such a blind faith in psychology very boring.

TSH: Some students who had read your book were enraged that you 'throw everything into the one pot' and that you 'prove nothing'.

HME: They should go and read the blue volumes of Marx and Engels. There they can find everything neatly sorted and proven.

TSH: You brought out two volumes of *Conversations with Marx and Engels* yourself, in 1973. Why the irony now?

HME: I am not being ironic. I am completely serious. It would do any student of today no harm at all if he – sorry: s/he – were to 'study the classics'. Yes, I really think that's what they ought to do. Perhaps, then, after a few years, they might be enticed to pick up an unscientific, undifferentiated little text of mine.

TSH: You quote, from the *Süddeutsche Zeitung*, a French social worker: 'They have destroyed everything: letter-boxes, doors, stairways. The health centre, where their younger brothers and sisters receive free medical care, has been demolished and looted...When they are given a new football-pitch, they saw down the goalposts.' Then you continue: 'A reporter tells how he witnessed an armed band smashing up a hospital in Mogadishu' (*CW*, 28, 29). At different places around the globe senseless acts of destruction are carried out. Your conclusion is that we witness the dawn of a new era whose contours are gained methodologically by a kind of intuition of paradoxy. But maybe the French social worker is only a little unexperienced; perhaps he must learn to be patient, to persevere. Instead he capitulates. Perhaps sawing off of the goalposts has something to do with inter-group rivalry among the young people. I wonder what a quotation such as this *can* prove.

HME: What do you mean with 'intuition of paradoxy'?

TSH: Firstly: with Adorno and Horkheimer we have described the enlightenment as 'self-preservation through self-surrender'. You carry this paradox a little further so that something new appears: existence or presence in the process of destruction or self-destruction. Secondly: In other essays you have speculated about the transformation of politics to crime. Now, at a time of an obvious weakness of grassroot groups, you apply the same idea, paradoxically, to the grassroots movements whose apparent perspective you had previously adopted for your analyses: here as well the greater part of politics is supposed to have been transformed to crime. A differentiated perspective which would have taken into account the different historical origins of different sources of violence might not have produced the smooth and polished picture of a new epoch of civil war. You are being carried away by the elegance of your associations: to the detriment of your analysis?

HME: You overestimate me. You overestimate what theory can achieve, particularly at the end of the twentieth century. The misery of classical theory was its greatness. This made possible that it was turned into a *Weltanschauung*, a substitute religion: Marxism, psychoanalysis (even though in this case it turned out more a business than a religion). We must avoid the great theories. I produce insights, 'political crumbs', no *Weltanschauung*. My book is called *Aussichten auf den Bürgerkrieg* ('Prospects of Civil War') and not 'The New Era of Global Civil War'. Such titles you are more likely to find among the academic literature.

TSH: What about *The Great Migration*?

HME: *Touché*. But seriously: I know that my thinking is, and must be, more fragmented than that of the nineteenth century. I avoid a scientific aura because I think we live in an age of scientific scholasticism. The scientific thinking of today in its dominant tendency stands in the same relation to the eighteenth or nineteenth century as the theology of the late middle ages stood to the early Fathers of the Church. What you criticize in my essay is what I would call 'free thinking'. Today, one is no longer familiar with it as one once was, at the time of its origins in the eighteenth century. And as to your remark concerning aestheticism – not quite fresh, by the way – I should like to remind you that the principle of 'first things first' provides, at least I hope so, a quite practical, useful pointer towards a political orientation. All the statements of television newsreaders who editorialize about the great issues of world politics, including the commentaries of tv journalists on the war in former Yugoslavia, are much more 'aesthetic': they are usually nothing but the sentimental proclamation of despair.

TSH: Adorno said: 'Thinking is unscientific'.

HME: There you have it! Obviously I am not the first and certainly not the only one who has noticed that. The point is to see connections. I have done nothing but to describe as precisely as I could what appeared to me was a new connection. Contrary to opinions voiced elsewhere I continue to value and to read Marx. However, one has to confront the problem that the great achievement of his work also provides the legitimation for the *Gulag*. Without the seductive truth of materialism, Stalinism could never have survived for so long. I think this is really tragic. But we cannot simply continue like before; we have to try to protect our thinking against being abused in this way. Benjamin, Adorno and Horkheimer are writing quite different, more 'unscientific' compared to Marx. Today there is no such great theory anymore as in the nineteenth century, and this is not only because of the experience of epigones but also because of this horrible, terroristic transformation of scientific theory into practice. The idea to start again at the beginning, with an essay for example, appears quite plausible to me.

TSH: But your images and sentences sometimes do not sound modest and fragmented at all; they sound very much like *Weltanschauung*. For example in the last chapter of *Civil War* where the true heroes of the civil war speak who begin with the work of repair after the destruction: 'They even know that the murderers will be back, in a week or in a decade. Civil war doesn't last forever, but it constantly threatens to start again'. And then you recall Sisyphus, as the symbol of the true hero of everyday life, who is actually a very intelligent 'trickster'. Your book concludes: 'Later, as a punishment for his human understanding, he was condemned to push a heavy boulder up the side of a hill for the rest of time. The name of this stone is peace' (*CW*, 71). Please tell us if one can read this as something other than a piece of *Weltanschauung*, as an expression of firm belief in the eternal cycle of war and peace?

HME: Well, I believe one can read it differently. The friendly, well-meaning, even naive mode of reception you are proposing here is quite illusory. Human communication is not as simple as that. We are living in a world in which it has become impossible, at least for myself, to formulate a sentence like 'We must fight for peace', or other sentences that are similarly positive. There are whole series of books which are nothing but variations on such an attitude. I believe they are quite ineffective. If you now take the picture of Sisyphus which most readers have in their mind, then you notice how war will erupt all of its own due to historical gravity, just like the boulder is rolling down the hill due to physical gravity. This is what Sisyphus is working against. One also notices that war and peace cannot be separated; they are out of the same material. These are two moments of recognition for which this image seems to provide an appropriate vessel. The mythical element – this is your critical comment – is already broken in the figure of Sisyphus himself. He tied up death and for that he was punished by the gods. Sisyphus belongs to that interesting line of demi-gods and destroyers of myth, like Oedipus, Heracles, or Ulysses, who did not put up with the *mythos*. The contradiction in this 'broken' image is that it does not conjure up the *mythos* but that it does not deny it either. That's what makes it interesting. It is perhaps only a somewhat more complex, more dynamic notion of politics than the one offered by Max Weber: 'patient drilling of thick boards of timber'.

TSH: Sisyphus is a politician?

HME: He acts politically. If this kind of political practice were to exist in institutionalised form, performed by professional politicians, in larger, recognizeable quantity and not only in the form of individual failure – last great example: Gorbachov – then it would not be necessary to resort to Greek mythology.

TSH: We wish you a good flight for the rest of your journey, Herr Enzensberger.

HME: Many thanks.

SOURCES

Hans Magnus Enzensberger, 'Hitlers Widergänger', *Der Spiegel*, 6, 1991; Oskar Negt, 'Das moralische Dilemma des Golf-Krieges', *Frankfurter Rundschau*, 23.2.1991; Jürgen Habermas, 'Wider die Logik des Krieges', *Die Zeit*, 15.2.1991; Wolf Biermann, 'Kriegshetze – Friedenshetze', *Die Zeit*, 1.2.1991; Heiner Müller, Interview with Alexander Kluge in 'News & Stories', SAT 1, 26.4.1993; J. David Singer, Melvin Small, *The Wages of War 1916-1965. A Statistical Handbook*, New

York, 1972; Carl von Clausewitz, *Vom Kriege* (first chapter); Hans Magnus Enzensberger, 'Peter Weiss und andere', *Kursbuch*, 6, 1966; Jane Kramer, 'Krach in Kreuzberg', in *Sonderbare Europäer. Gesichter und Geschichten*, Frankfurt/Main, 1993, pp. 165-222 (first published in *The New Yorker*, 1988); Bill Buford, *Among the Thugs*, London, 1991; Sigmund Freud, *Briefe an Fließ*; Max Horkheimer, Theodor W. Adorno, *Dialektik der Aufklärung*, Frankfurt/Main, 1985; the story of the Serbian marauder and rapist is told in an as yet unreleased documentary film by Helke Sander about the camps in Serbia; Karl Marx, *The Civil War in France*, in *MEW* 17, p. 340; the quotation from Adorno in *Minima Moralia*, Frankfurt/Main, p. 161.

(Translated by Gerhard Fischer).

III

Great Migration and the Politics of Identity

Chapter Eleven

Enzensberger and the Politics of Identity

Bernd Fischer

In *Great Migration* Enzensberger criticizes multiculturalism as follows:

> The multicultural society remains a confusing slogan as long as the difficulties which it throws up, and fails to clarify, remain taboo. The wearisome dispute will never be resolved if no one knows, or wants to know, what culture means – 'Everything that humans do and do not do' seems the most precise definition. For this reason alone, the debate is condemned to reproduce the contradiction between deliberate underestimation and denunciation, idyll and panic. (*CW*, 134-5)

The US debate on multiculturalism and cultural identity has circumvented this most crucial problem to its theoretical validity by implicitly and for all practical purposes equating culture with ethnicity and, furthermore, by defining ethnicity along the lines of some rather crude racial categories. The debate on cultural diversity and identity was for many years dominated by literary critics whose political roots could be found somewhere on the Left. On the one hand the debate provided new conceptualizations for the ageing and faltering idea of a pluralist society and, on the other hand, it provided an ideological justification for traditionally leftist political programs like political recognition, affirmative action, minority rights, subsidization of sub-cultural enterprises, etc. It did not take long, however, before ideas of a separatist African-American nation or of Native American nations (for instance, designed around casinos on tribal lands) and an infinite number of smaller independence movements began to show a structural resemblance to classical nationalisms that were and are equally based on imaginations of ethnicity, race, religion, history, etc.[1] The classical meaning of culture was thus slowly contaminated and ultimately inversed from cultivated or cultured to natural; that is, to the idea of supposedly natural belongings to historical or imagined communities[2] characterized by ethnic, religious, or ideological sameness. Consequently, ideas that claimed to be in favor of rejuvenating the old Enlightenment project of an open and pluralist society actually tended to preach the opposite: the compartmentalization of constitutional democracies into ideologically closed, monolithic, and emotionally charged identity camps. Paradoxically, all this was and is possible at a time when central nationalist categories like history, cultural conformity, ethnicity, and race have been seriously undermined by recent scientific evidence in genetics, ethnography, archeology, regional history, etc.[3] Henry Louis Gates puts his finger on this paradox, when he reminds us of the ethnologist Jean-Loup Amselles' objection to the politization of ethnicity.

> [Amselles] contends that the very notion of discrete ethnicities is an artifact of his discipline. Warning against what he dubs ethnic or cultural fundamentalism, Amselles maintains that the notion of a multicultural society, 'far from being an instrument of tolerance and of liberation of minorities, as its partisans affirm, manifests, to the contrary, all the hallmarks of ethnological reason, and that is why it has been taken up in France by the New Right'...'Cultures aren't situated one by the other like Leibniz's windowless monades,' he argues. Rather, 'the very definition of a given culture is in fact the result of intercultural relations of forces.[4]

Gates draws the following important conclusion:

> While the discourses of identity politics and of liberation are often conflated, they may be in mortal combat on a more fundamental level. Identity politics, in its purest form, must be concerned with the survival of an identity. By contrast, the utopian agenda of liberation pursues what it takes to be the objective interests of its subjects, but it may be little concerned with its cultural continuity or integrity. More than that, the discourse of liberation often looks forward to the birth of a transformed subject, the creation of a new identity, which is, by definition, the surcease of the old.[5]

In my view, there is an important lesson to be learned from the North American debate: namely that multiculturalism cannot succeed as a theoretical model for a pluralist and open society, if it refuses to inherit the old Enlightenment and yet modernist concept of the multicultural individual, the cosmopolitan citizen, and with it an understanding of culture that retains notions of cultivation, of intercultural communication, of integration and acculturation, of a dynamic and open-ended history that is characterized by creativity and change – progress, if you wish.

From the eighteenth century to the present such a multi- or inter-cultural individual has mainly been conceived of within the political framework of constitutionalism, i.e., within a state whose idea of nationhood is defined by citizenship and not by heritage, ethnicity, culture, etc. Serving as a building block and stepping stone for an ultimate world republic (Kant), the constitutional republic is one of the central political projects of the Enlightenment and of what I would call Western Modernism as opposed to its Central and Eastern European counterpart – which, in one way or another, refers back to German Idealism, most significantly to Fichte's philosophy from about 1800 to 1809 (*Der geschloßne Handelsstaat, Die Grundzüge des gegenwärtigen Zeitalters, Reden an die deutsche Nation)*. Within the framework of the civic society, interculturalism (along the lines of some universalist concepts like human rights and democratic representation) describes the process of civilization – which, in this sense, is indeed in 'mortal combat' with the politics of cultural identity.

A word of caution might, however, be in order. We are, of course, not dealing with absolute opposites when we employ our structurally shaky and theoretically questionable concepts of ethnicity, culture, and acculturation – a complication which might, in part, be responsible for the political confusion and ideological potential of the multicultural debate. Ethnicity and acculturation are neither independent entities nor oppositional concepts; they are at best regulative ideas. Every socio-genesis we know of takes place in a space that is not fully marked by either one of these two poles, in spite of their implicit ideological claims to totality. From a historical point of view, ethnicity and acculturation are closely intertwined. Not only does the one not exist without the other, more often than not, they describe the very same phenomenon or process. Historically speaking, ethnicity comes about by way of acculturation, i.e., acculturation can be defined as the forming of ethnicity.

Within the German discourse, Enzenberger's two essays, *Great Migration* and *Civil War* compile a number of innovative observations and underrepresented discussions. Of particular importance are his observations on xenophobia as fear of poverty (*CW*, 37) and a form of self-hate (*CW*, 120-21), migrations as economic equalizers (*CW*, 122), his analysis of right-wing radical violence (*CW*, 139-44) and of the changed conditions and meanings of migrations and civil wars in high modernity (*CW*, 115-16), and his discussions of multiculturalism (*CW*, 134-36) and ethnicity (*CW*, 103-08). Only the last three issues will be discussed here.

At the same time, Enzensberger's trademark, his negative or pessimistic pathos, produces some paradoxes of its own. Most importantly, it condemns what his analysis actually defends: modernism. In both essays we are dealing with an exaggerated stylistic habitus that is quite capable of opposing what its own text seems to suggest. In this particular case, Enzensberger's rhetorics operate (as is somewhat typical for most of Germany's political voices) with notions of nationhood which are, in the same breath, questioned by the informational value of his essays. In spite of all the evidence he has collected to prove the contrary, Enzensberger's assumptions of identity implicitly continue to employ cultural and/or ethnic definitions and underestimates the integrationist value and potential of constitutionalism and contractionism and their innate relationship to identity concepts of self and individualism.

For instance, Enzensberger simply errs when he speculates that ethnicities and tribes, unlike nations, came or come about naturally and that tribes have no need for ideologies, rituals, and symbols.

> Clan and tribal groups have existed since the earth was inhabited by human beings; nations have existed for only 200 years or so. It is not difficult to see the difference. Ethnic groups come into being semi-spontaneously, 'of their own accord'; nations are consciously created, and are often artificial entities, which cannot get by without a specific ideology. This ideological foundation, together with its rituals and

> emblems (flags, anthems), originated in the nineteenth century. From Europe and North America, it has spread over the whole world. (*CW*, 107).

This statement of conventional wisdom needs fundamental qualifications. For today we know once again – this knowledge had been around for centuries before it was subdued by the mythologies and inventions of ethnology and national historiography – that, like many other political formations, so-called tribes are also the result of territorial and civil wars, migrations, and intercultural alliances with specific ideologies and political programs.[6]

To be sure, it would not be fair to accuse Enzensberger of sweeping, essentialist notions of nationality, culture, or mentality. Many of his critical ideas seem to be grounded in a conception of change, of dynamic socio-political and cultural interdependencies. However, whenever it seems rhetorically convenient for the benefit of bending the discussion into a political message of despair, Enzensberger too takes the construction of differences – the categorical roster of historical and socio-political discourse, of cultural and socio-psychological metaphysics, i.e., the politics of identity – as expressions of historical substance. While his post-Marxist, materialistic understanding of history is markedly less streamlined towards the idea of a fixed telos, he does not fully escape the tradition of German metaphysics of history with regard to the other end of processuality: the question of origin and nature. At times, he falls back to notions of an albeit anti-teleological, yet naturalist historicism, which – in the German context – was most prominently developed by Herder. The possibility of a teleological view on history is rejected by both; however, for Enzensberger (unlike Herder), the open-endedness of history begins to vanish with it as well. This new historicist gaze is, in a more radical sense, compelled to look backwards, to seek order and meaning in socio-cultural constructions of the past – for it can no longer be certain of a future to come. This postmodern historicism, if you like, once again tends to forget that the past too has nothing to offer but artificial, ideologically charged constructions of differences – that the past too has no privileged road to nature. The backward gaze holds as 'nature' whatever feels natural within the framework of a momentary and politically actualized construction of history.

This is what Enzensberger's clinging to notions of 'natural' ethnicities and tribes, also known as 'primitive civilizations' illustrates. What the oxymoronic quality of the latter term or, for that matter, of the term 'natural cultures' so openly gives away, has obviously been forgotten once again. While our conventional and romanticized wisdom still likes to call such communities tribes or native societies, defined by a homogenic culture and race, upon closer scrutiny they are found to be quite diverse and complex political organizations brought about by the contingencies of war, by coalitions and cultural melting, by ethnic cleansing and intercultural cooperation, by political contracts and geographical necessities.

Ethnicity is a constantly changing process, one of acculturation. Nothing remains fixed, often not even in the lifetime of one generation. Civic societies too are necessarily characterized by both, political acculturation and cultural diversity (class, sociolect, dialect, custom, mentality, region, etc.). The only permanence of ethnicity is its consistent fluctuation. The ideology of ethnicity, on the other hand, lies in its claim to be or become the opposite of the never-ending interplay of acculturation and differentiation that it is. Enzensberger cites a number of observations that support this thesis. 'The normal state of the atmosphere is turbulence. The same is true of the settlement of the earth by human beings' (*CW*, 103). 'Stationary populations form again and again over the millennia. On the whole, however, they remain the exception...A considerable proportion of humanity has always been in motion, migrating or in flight for the most diverse reasons, in violent or peaceful manner' (*CW*, 104).

> Germany is a country that owes its present population to huge movements of migration. Since earliest times there has been a constant exchange of population groups for the most diverse reasons. As a consequence of their geographical position alone, the Germans, like the Austrians, are a very mixed people. That blood- and race-ideologies became politically dominant here, of all places, can be understood as a form of compensation. The Aryan was never anything more than a risible construct...A cursory glance at a historical atlas is enough to show that the idea of a compact German population is unfounded. Its function can only be to prop up, by means of fiction, an especially fragile national identity. (*CW*, 128)

This potential awareness of the unfeasibility of an ethnic German identity is, however, being put aside by Enzensberger, when he addresses the status of Western modernism and its politics of identity that favor citizenship over ethnicity, culture, and tradition. In the end we are still dealing here with a typically German obsession: the continual search for alternatives to the legacy of Western modernism and its political models.[7]

The differences between competing concepts of nationhood that are significant for our discussion regard their intellectual outlook. Most importantly, the constitutional nation views itself, in a more radical sense, as a political and intellectual project, as a revolutionary idea pursuing a political formation that has not existed before, but should; for it seems reasonable (within the framework of what one might call humanism). The identity project of this type of nation (in theory) relies on the integrational force and potential of its constitution. German politicians and postmodern theorists alike fail to understand that political integration – i.e., a politically defined identity – is not a mere side effect of constitutionalism, but rather one of its most essential concerns. Therefore and strictly speaking, the constitutional project cannot be reconciled with the notion of displacement that has recently gained much notoriety, if not ideological primacy in postmodern thought. According to Enlightenment theories of constitutionalism the place of humans depends to a lesser extent on where they come from than on where they ought to go in order to become individual selves and sovereigns of their political affairs. In this context displacement is seen as emancipatory: it describes the individual's escape from a state of existence and mind that seemed only natural (for instance, the family, region, culture, class, etc., into which one is born by mere chance), but now appears as political or cultural and, therefore, can be analyzed and criticized as *self*-inhibiting. In other words, foreignness is one prerequisite of political and cultural enlightenment. To a certain degree, one has to become foreign to one's own origin, heritage, familial culture, etc., in order to enter the open-ended project of becoming an individual self, for whom little can remain unquestioned and untested. This is, by the way, not only true for the Enlightenment, but indeed for all spiritual and intellectual movements that build upon the centrality of the individual self, including Christianity and other religions.

Enzensberger's post-Marxist scepticism of teleological claims to politics and history compels him to reject political analyses that rest on notions of a mere incompleteness of modern civic societies (i.e., Habermas). Indeed, power relations, as well as the statistics of the world's economy of consumption and ecology, seem to illustrate the end of modernity. At the same time, the promise of the multicultural individual of the eighteenth century, who could be regional and cosmopolitan at once, has obviously not yet been fulfilled. There are plenty of groups in our cosmopolitan centers and elsewhere who have all the right in the world to feel victimized and colonized, who are stuck in this other kind of foreignness of exclusion, superfluousness, and, worst of all, a constant state of insult. As Enzensberger points out, increasingly their voice is being heard as one of hate and destruction of society and self. In an ironic play of history, this amounts for Enzensberger to the end of Eurocentrism, for there is no longer any realism in attempting to spread European concepts of universalism around the globe. What remains for Europe is to take care of its own house, to restore and develop the civic society in its own streets. One might ask, however, if this 'political priority' (*CW*, 66) is not in a very real and extreme way eurocentric itself. The dilemma of this particular version of 'Europe for the Europeans', of a universalism that refrains from becoming universal, has historically been addressed within the context of anticolonialism (for instance by Herder). Today, however, it would not be enough to refrain from illusions of cultural and moral superiority, it would require us to erect fences and walls to keep those other cultures and humans out (a dilemma that Herder could not foresee).

Within his ideological framework of anti-universalism, Enzensberger once again cannot help but to distort the historical role of nationalism.

> By focusing only on the emotive chauvinism that characterized old-style European nationalism it is easy to overlook the constructive contribution it made. After all, it helped bring about the drafting of constitutions, the abolition of serfdom, the emancipation of the Jews, the establisment of the rule of law and the enfranchisement of the general population. (*CW*, 22)

This familiar statement of conventional wisdom also needs major qualifications and differentiations. For what is, in part, true for the American and French nationalisms of eighteenth-century constitutionalism is not true for the German nationalism of unification in the nineteenth and twentieth centuries. Civic societies (nations of politically represented citizens) are the product of Western Enlightenment thought and constitutional revolutions, and not of any kind of nationalism that attempted to emulate the successes of Western modernism by other means, like the identity politics of fictitious ethnicity or mythological historicity. In Germany the civic society was decreed by the victorious Western powers of 1806, 1918, and 1945 and adopted by reformers of the time.

Still, these misconceptions of the history of Western Enlightenment and Modernism, which are, in my view, as dangerous as they are common, cannot disqualify Enzensberger's central analysis of the current European crisis. Quoting Hannah Arendt, he convincingly stresses the loss of self and with it the loss of individual morals as the most crucial ingredient of self-destructive mass hysteria, may it be the small band of skinheads terrorizing a subway car or the Bosnian Serbs (*CW*, 26-27). What he refuses to see is that this self amounts to nothing less than the project of the Enlightenment and that it lies at the very core of modern constitutionalism and contractionism.

Considering all this, it cannot come as a surprise that, although quite polemical, Enzensberger's critique of universalism remains vague and contradictory.

> But the rhetoric of universalism is a specific trait of Western societies. They expect their decrees to apply to everyone, indiscriminately and without exception. Their universalism recognizes no difference between near and far; it is absolute and abstract. The obligation it places on all of us is, in principle, unlimited. Here the declaration reveals its theological origins which have survived all attempts at secularization...Soon you cross over into objective hypocrisy and, in the end, the universalism reveals itself as a moral trap. (CW, 58)

In the Enlightenment tradition, human rights are indeed 'unlimited' in both meanings of the word. They are an infinite project that cannot be abandoned, whenever the difficulties increase and seem insurmountable. For sure, the singular citizen in front of his/her television set is indeed overwhelmed by all the small and big civil wars of our time, by genocides, and even by the countless incidents of xenophobic violence. But does that mean that he/she can only be responsible for his/her own backyard, for his/her own children, community, or country? While there are certainly different levels of responsibility and priority, as Enzensberger stresses (*CW*, 66-69), this conclusion cannot stand. First of all, when Enzensberger employs a cynical play on words and states that 'morality is the last refuge of Eurocentrism' (*CW*, 59), he ought to add that individual ethics are also the primary goal and core of the fragile concept of the civic society, of the *Rechtsstaat* that he, on the other hand, feels compelled to defend. The conclusion that I would draw from Enzensberger's analysis is opposite to his own: The moral pressure on the citizens of Western democracies can only be relieved by and channeled into international institutions for the defense of fundamental universal principles. Any other conclusion, I would call 'objective hypocricy' and a cynical one at that. I realize, of course, that many of our international institutions like the United Nations or the International Court have in their current forms proved to be quite inept to take on such a role. But that can hardly be an excuse to abandon all attempts of internationalism, before we have even begun to work through its political implications. Let me repeat this appeal with a recent comment by Jürgen Habermas on the Bosnian crisis:

> If, in spite of the unspeakable suffering, we, nevertheless, talk of principles, we have to talk about nationalism and internationalism. Can we allow that the UN's human rights politics, which are still in their initial stages, will be discredited for decades, may be for an incalculable time, by ethnic delusions? Further more, should those triumph who also in our country flirt with the so-called ethno-pluralism and who take ethnic identities for the true reality?[8]

While the individual citizen and single countries cannot be held accountable for ending the civil wars of this world, they can be held responsible for committing a part of their wealth and expertise to global institutions which attempt to find solutions to unlawful power struggles, to end incidences of genocide by military force, to tumble terrorist regimes by international blockades (a means Enzensberger himself seems to favor; cf. *CW*, 63), and to put sufficient force behind the existing global consensus on elementary human rights so that potential violators have to think twice. In one sentence, moral obligations on an international level must also be institutionalized, rather than cynically perpetuated in a postmodern existentialism that thrives on nihilistic notions of despair and the pleasures of unbearable insolvabilities of modernist fallacies or impasses.

At the end of *Civil War* Enzensberger himself returns indirectly to the Enlightenment project of the civic society, when he praises the unsung heroes of our times: those who never give up, who always rebuild. 'The persistence of these people is close to miraculous. They know they cannot put the world to rights. Only a corner of it – a roof, a wound. They even know that the murderers will be back, in a week or in a decade' (*CW*, 71). Enzensberger employs the Sisyphos myth to explore the existentialist mystery of these stubbornly dedicated rebuilders of civility. In a political sense, the building of civic societies is, however, more than a means of survival or even meaningful existence, it is or ought to be the Western contribution to a common goal which was most aptly described by Herder as humanism.

NOTES

1 Some better known recent examples are the politics of Louis Farrakhan, leader of the Nation of Islam, the warfare of different factions of the 200-member tribe of the Lake County Pomo Indians over the management of the Pomo Palace Casino, and, of course, the numerous right-wing movements like the Aryan Nation, etc.
2 The term was coined by Max Weber and is discussed extensively in Benedict Anderson's *Imagined Communities: Reflections on the Origin and Spread of Nationalism*, London, 1983.
3 Cf. Werner Sollors, ed. *The Invention of Ethnicity*, New York, Oxford, 1989; Luigi Luca Cavalli-Sforza, 'Alle aus demselben Holz', *Die Zeit*, 7/1992, pp. 17-20; Mark B. Shchukin, *Rome and the Barbarians in Central and Eastern Europe: 1st Century B.C. – 1st Century A.D.*, Oxford, 1989.
4 Henry Louis Gates, 'Beyond the Culture Wars: Identities in Dialogue', *Profession* (1993), pp. 6-11, here p. 8.
5 Gates, 'Beyond the Culture Wars: Identities in Dialogue', p. 8.
6 One might think, for instance, of the history of North-American populations like the Creek, a so-called tribe with vastly different cultures, several language groups and many languages and dialects, class warfare, fundamentalist and terrorist movements, generational and religious divisions etc. Cf. B. F., 'Beobachtungen zum historischen Gehalt von Charles Sealsfields Indianer-Romanen', *Neue Sealsfield-Studien: Amerika und Europa in der Biedermeierzeit*, ed. Franz Schüppen, Stuttgart, 1995, pp. 175-93. The same, of course, holds true for the Germanic tribes that were encountered by the Roman Empire and described by Tacitus and other Roman historians.
7 For a more extensive discussion cf. B. F., *Das Eigene und Eigentliche: Klopstock, Herder, Fichte, Kleist. Episoden aus der Konstruktionsgeschichte nationaler Intentionalitäten*, Berlin, 1995.
8 'Wenn wir schon, trotz des unsäglichen Leidens, von Prinzipien reden, müssen wir über Nationalismus und Internationalismus reden. Soll die Menschenrechtspolitik der Uno, die ganz in den Anfängen steht, vom ethnischen Wahn auf Jahrzehnte, vielleicht auf unabsehbare Zeit diskreditiert werden? Sollen gar die triumphieren, die auch bei uns mit dem sogenannten Ethnopluralismus flirten und völkische Identitäten für die eigentliche Realität halten?' Interview in *Der Spiegel* 32 (1995), p. 34.

Chapter Twelve

From Emigration Country without Emigration Law to Immigration Country without Immigration Law: German Paradoxes in the Nineteenth and Twentieth Centuries

Klaus J. Bade

I

There is a long history of emigration in Germany. This tradition has never been interrupted but has today receded into the background because of the much larger influx of people coming into Germany at the present. In the emigration movements out of the areas of German language or culture, the continental migration to Eastern and South-eastern Europe was predominant until the early nineteenth century. In a sense, this early history of emigration from 'Germany' has now returned to public consciousness with the 're-migration' (*Rückwanderung*) to Germany of the descendants of the original migrants, the so-called *Aussiedler*. It was only in the 1830s that the continental migration stream eastward was overtaken by the trans-atlantic mass emigration which led millions of Germans overseas, mostly (up to 90%) to the United States. Between 1816 and 1914 approximately 5.5 million German emigrants settled in the United States, followed by another 1.5 million since the first World War. The most important 'push' factor, in terms of economic and demographic history, was the disproportionate growth of population and employment during the crisis of transition from agrarian to industrial society. The most diverse hopes and expectations came together in the 'American dream' shared by German emigrants. Their motifs for emigrating were based on religious-ideological or social-utopian concepts or, in the case of the revolutionary emigrants of 1848/49, they were political refugees. But clearly the dominant factors were economic and social motifs and goals. In the jargon of the late twentieth century, most Germans who participated in the nineteenth century mass exodus to the New World were 'economic refugees' in the best sense of the word.

In the 1840s, there was an extensive public and political debate on questions relating to emigration. It found its climax in the preparation of an Emigration Law passed by the Frankfurt National Assembly in 1849. The legislation provided for a central Emigration

Office to be established as Ministry of the Reich. Its central ideas were unlimited freedom of emigration, protection of German emigrants and travellers abroad, the licensing of immigration agents and supervision of immigrant ships. When the revolution failed, the emigration legislation and and the emigration office remained a dream. A second climax of the emigration debate came in the early 1880s, in the context of the debate on German colonial policies. Again demands for state legislation of emigration and an emigration policy were raised. However, the transatlantic mass exodus was largely left to run its own course.

Of course, a 'German' emigration law could not have been on the agenda before 1871. However, there was a 'Federal Commissioner' (*Bundeskommissar*, later *Reichskommissar*) for Emigration, appointed in 1869 after sensational reports of scandalous conditions on board of ships taking German emigrants to North America. He was responsible for the protection of emigrants, the supervision of immigrant ships in the ports of Hamburg and Bremen; he had to report on conditions, investigate grievances and co-operate with local authorities to take remedial measures. Governmental activity was otherwise restricted to matters of domestic policies in the individual German states, notably with regard to the work of foreign immigration agents and to prevent the emigration of persons required for military service.

The imperial constitution of 1871 clearly established the Reich's competence in questions of emigration. However, during the era of Bismarck's chancellorship, there was no chance of any emigration legislation or an emigration office to be established. Bismarck and other powerful, agrarian-conservative circles were of the opinion that legislative measures to deal with emigration would only lead to an increase in emigration due to state recognition of the issue. This was seen as highly undesirable because the main supply of emigrants during the 1880s came form the predominantly agrarian North East of the Reich which suffered from chronic labour shortages. Only a quarter of a century after its foundation, the Reich made first use of the competence in emigration matters which it had been given in 1871: the first imperial law regulating emigration came into effect in 1897. By that time, however, the mass exodus of nineteenth century emigrants had already become a thing of the past. It was only in the early years of the Weimar Republic that an 'Imperial Office for German Emigration, Re-migration and Immigration (Imperial Migration Office)' was founded in anticipation of large migration movements in the wake of the war. However, they did not eventuate, and thus the Office – which existed, caught unhappily between two ministries, from 1919 to 1924 – was reduced in size and cut down to a '*Reichsstelle* for Emigration' in 1924.

II

The continental migration into Germany was met from the beginning by an energetic involvement on the part of the authorities; the state responded with clearly defensive intent. Policies originated in Prussia, as the largest groups of continental immigrants arrived via the Eastern borders. Since the late nineteenth century, migration movements across German borders were characterized by a considerable overlap of continental immigration and transatlantic emigration. During the economic boom of the two decades before the First World War, a shortage of labour had replaced the traditional surplus which had previously been the decisive 'push' factor in the economic and demographic history of overseas emigration.

Thus, during the 1890s, the continental influx of foreign workers to Germany and to Prussia, in particular, assumed the character of a mass migration movement. While there had been 1.8 million German emigrants between 1880 and 1893, the number of 'foreign migratory workers' (*ausländische Wanderarbeiter*) in 1913 was officially estimated at 1.2 million. Most migrant workers came from Eastern Europe, especially Poles from the area of Russian Central Poland, as well as Poles and Ruthenians from Austrian Galicia, and from Italy.

In the debate on the 'migrant workers question' in Prussia of the 1880s and early 1890s, economic and political interests collided: politicians were concerned about a potential destabilization in areas of Eastern Prussia with predominantly Polish character where the revolutionary dream of a national renaissance of the Polish state was not to be suppressed, while employers were keenly interested in hiring 'cheap and willing' workers from across the border. The Prussian 'defensive policy' was motivated by a concern about a 'Polonization of the East' through immigration from Eastern Europe.

A compromise in the conflict between economic and political interests was found in the attempt to control the stream of incoming Polish labour by way of enforced rotation to achieve a transnational seasonal migration pattern. A supply of labour coming from Eastern Europe was welcomed in Spring. Before Christmas the migrants were expected to leave Prussian territory again, on pain of deportation. Agricultural employers had few difficulties with this arrangement. Employers in trade and industry fought for exemption permits that allowed the employment of Polish migrants during the winter months as well, but mostly with little success.

In Germany, the question of how the state could or should deal with transnational migration is thus characterized by clearly contradictory tendencies and intentions. The goal was protection for German overseas emigration and protection against continental immigration to Germany. The reason for this paradoxical state of affairs has to do with the German development, as described by R. Brubaker, from a national-cultural to an ethno-cultural and ethno-national concept of identity which was accompanied by a strengthening of the tradition of *ius sanguine*. The principle of ethnic descent as an integral component of citizenship legislation and the concept of nationality was codified in the 'Imperial Citizenship Law' of 1913. Despite many changes and amendments, this law has defined the principles and perimeters of state action until this very day. It has obstructed the introduction of the more generous territorial principle (*ius soli*). The German states had come to an agreement on the general validity of the principle of ethnic descent in citizenship legislation already in the early nineteenth century, i.e., in the era of pre-national Germany. The ethno-nationalist intentions became part of this concept of citizenship only gradually but more forcefully since the late nineteenth century.

Even so, the concept of an independent 'German' citizenship did not exist in the Reich before 1913, except in association with a federal state. The Nationality Law of the North German Federation of 1869, which had been adopted in the constitution of the Reich, provided that the association with the German nation could only be established via an association with a federal state. There was thus no concept of 'national descent'. You would have been, for example, a citizen of the Kingdom of Prussia, of the Bavarian Kingdom, or the Grand Dukedom of Baden – and only by way of this citizenship of the federal state you would have been a member of the German nation state. This was changed only with the Imperial Citizenship Law of 1913.

The law codified the principle of ethnic descent; it gave priority to the concepts of nation and 'people' (*Volk*), putting them before those of law and republic, as a stern counter projection to the territorial principle with its implied references to popular sovereignty and human rights, and thus to the democratic principle in a republican sense. The law of 1913 aimed at providing the possibility for Germans living abroad and for emigrants of original German descent to inherit and to regain German citizenship; on the other hand, it limited the acquisition of German citizenship by foreigners of non-German ethnic descent to exceptional cases only.

The Imperial Citizenship Law of 1913 is a typical product of the period of Wilhelminian imperialism before the First World War. It reflects the concept of *Volk* and the ethno-nationalist ideas of its time of origin. It was also an expression of the ethno-ideological politics aimed at the 'preservation of *Germanness* (*Deutschtum*) abroad' and of a defensive 'bulwark mentality', which itself was no less based on ethno-nationalist sentiment, in response to a feared 'flood out of the East'. In the background of all of this was the old fear of new mass migration movements, of new *Völkerwanderungen*, fuelled by the enormous demographic pressure originating in Eastern Europe.

Two contemporary East-West migration movements across the German borders provided a contemporary background for this experience. The first was the 'transit migration' of millions of Poles and Jews from the Russian Empire via German ports to the United States. Despite rigorous controls, approximately 78,000 of these 'Eastern Jews' (*Ostjuden*) remained in Germany between 1880 and 1914; here they constituted no less than 12% of the Jewish minority. The other example was the transnational labour migration into Germany, mainly across the Eastern borders of Prussia but also from Southern Europe. The numbers fluctuated annually but reached more than a million in the years preceding the First World War.

In springtime, thousands of workers congregated every day at the border crossings where they could apply for the 'legitimation cards' required for employment in Prussia and some other German states. They arrived at the border led by hired guides, labour agents, representatives of local agricultural estates and foremen of factories, or on their own. The processing of applications for work permits for 'foreign migrant workers' was the responsibility of the semi-governmental 'German Workers Centre' (*Deutsche Arbeiterzentrale*). After a cursory check for infectious diseases, the migrant workers were housed temporarily in huge camps at their own expense. They were then hired out to interested German employers following a set course of negotiations – which resulted not uncommonly in reduced wages – unless the migrants had already signed a contract. Such experiences, added to the traditional background of anti-Semitic and anti-Polish resentment, were largely responsible for creating the horror images of undesirable immigrants flooding across the Eastern borders. Such prejudices also appeared in the debate on the Imperial Citizenship Law in the German Reichstag of 1912/13; they found expression in the most diverse scenarios of threat and impending catastrophe.

Germany's dual position as country of origin of transatlantic emigrants and as the destination country of continental labour immigrants resulted in a singular ambivalence. This could be seen most clearly during the Weimar Republic. As an emigration country, Germany opposed protectionist measures to restrict immigration which were increasingly adopted by countries around the world, notably the United States. As a country of 'labour import', however, Germany itself had to defend a restrictive limitation of continental immigration; the protectionist aims of the German measures were clearly comparable to the American immigration policy.

During the period of National Socialism, the issue of 'Germanness' and emigration was re-defined to create policies to increase Nazi influence among the German communities abroad (*Auslandsdeutschtum*) and to motivate German emigrants or emigrants of German descent to return 'home' (*heim ins Reich*). Inside Germany itself, the persecution and legal discrimination of persons and of minority groups because of racial, political and religious-ideological reasons often led to victims fleeing abroad or being pressured to emigrate. In the period leading up to the Holocaust, the Nazis pursued a systematic policy of humiliation and persecution of Jews who were progressively stripped of their rights and possessions, a policy which must also be seen in the context of 'Germanness' and citizenship. With regard to continental migration, a new phase again was reached during the Second World War: the temporary employment of imported labour migrants under the foreigner legislation during the Wilhelmine Empire, the Weimar Republic and the time of NS-Germany of the pre-war era, was now followed during the war by the importation of slave labour, so-called *Fremdarbeiter* ('foreign workers'), who were forcibly deported mainly from Eastern Europe. They were completely without rights.

III

The contradictory attitude in dealing with problems of transnational migration, which had appeared during the Wilhelmine Empire and the Weimar Republic, was continued even after the period of National Socialism: an ambivalent tension between protecting emigrants from Germany and rejecting immigrants to Germany remained the characteristic feature of the German position. The traditional policy of protection of emigrants provides a clear example of such continuity: the 'Reichsstelle' for emigration affairs which existed from 1924 to 1944 was re-established with the same personnel in 1950 as a *Bundesstelle*; in 1952 it changed its name to 'Federal Office (*Bundesamt*) for Emigration'. The legislative continuity is also clearly evident: the line from Weimar to the Federal Republic links the 'Regulation against Abuses in Emigration' of 1924 to the Law for the Protection of Emigrants passed in 1975. In 1959/60, the Federal Office for Emigration was integrated into the Federal Administration Office (FAO; *Bundesverwaltungsamt*). Among its central duties are problems regarding transnational migration. The office, however, concentrates almost exclusively on emigration matters rather than on immigration. A clause in paragraph two of the legislation establishing the FAO simply states that the office can take over the same functions in the area of immigration as in the area of emigration. This clause, however, has never been used, and it has remained virtually unknown. Furthermore, the Basic Law (Art. 73, Para. 3) explicitly grants the federal government the power of legislation with regard to immigration matters. This means that the constitution pre-supposes that the regulation of immigration is a task to be administered by a central state authority. The Basic Law thus makes immigration laws possible; indeed, the demand that the administration is to be become active in such matters is already written into the constitution. Yet no immigration legislation exists. There is only a slowly growing acceptance to merely consider thinking about such legislation, even though a constitutional change or amendment would not be necessary. As we have seen, the refusal to undertake this task is rooted in tradition.

The FAO deals with immigration matters only in the context of the migration and integration of persons recognized as *Aussiedler*. These 'returning settlers' are, however, not considered immigrants under the prevailing interpretation of the law: they are returning emigrants of ethnic German origin who can claim German citizenship and all associated rights on arrival. The legal basis for this policy was last confirmed in the so-called *Kriegsfolgenbereinigungsgesetz* ('Law to Rectify Consequences of the War'). This law speaks of a 'pressure of expulsion', re-phrased in an amendment in 1993 as 'war consequence', with regard to the ethnic German minorities in Eastern Europe, and in those Far Eastern regions to which the descendants of ethnic German emigrants were deported in the wake of the destruction of the Volga Republic. German ethnic descent and a 'commitment to Germanness' (*Bekenntnis zum Deutschtum*) are prerequisites for the official recognition as *Aussiedler*.

In this area, too, there is a clear continuity from the Citizenship Law of 1913 via the Basic Law (Article 116) to the War Consequences Law of 1993. Descendants of emigrants who had left 'Germany', in some cases centuries earlier, were always given the possibility of re-emigrating. The tradition of *ius sanguinis* as part of German ethno-cultural and ethno-national identity permitted the possibility of re-migrating over generations. The War Consequences Law and the *ius sanguinis* tradition thus codify a practice which essentially amounts to an informal immigration policy based on ethnic criteria. In the areas of origin of the returning *Aussiedler* this policy functions as a kind of peaceful German contribution to 'ethnic cleansing' (R. Olt). A similar continuity, on the other hand, is present in the rejectionist position towards any kind of immigration law and regular immigration policies. A change of this position would clearly require replacing the principle of of *ius sanguinis* with the more liberal *ius soli* principle. However, there has been no change towards questions of emigration and immigration, despite the fact that the balance between the two has dramatically changed in favour of the latter in the decades since the Second World War.

IV

Three processes of integration can be distinguished in Germany since 1945:

1. The integration of refugees and displaced persons in East and West Germany; in the West, they defined themselves programmatically as *Heimatvertriebene* ('deportees') and were organized in powerful associations, constituting a lobby group with considerable political clout; in East Germany, they were euphemistically described as *Umsiedler* ('re-settlers') in consideration of the sensibilities of the neighbouring countries of Eastern Europe.

2. The integration of the non-German labour force, beginning in the mid-1950s with the recruitment of foreign workers to the debate on the question of *Gastarbeiter* ('guest workers') in the

1960s and early 1970s and to the existing 'real' immigration problem since the turn of the decade of the 1970s and 1980s.

3. Finally, the new problem of integration in the context of the united Germany since the early 1990s.

Many post-war refugees and displaced persons did not yet feel 'at home' in their new situation when the German-Italian treaty of 1955 marked the beginning of an organized import of foreign labour into Germany. This was also the beginning of the pre-history of the second important post-war integration process. The building of the Berlin Wall in 1961 accelerated West Germany's unintentional development towards an immigration country: after the influx of Germans from the German Democratic Republic had stopped, the hiring of workers from abroad was increased. There was no comprehensive or long-term concept either to deal with the social problems brought about by this migration or to provide for the permanent integration of the imported labour force. *Ausländerpolitik* ('policies relating to foreigners') remained an issue of labour market policies for decades, complemented by a precarious mixture of tentative offers of 'temporary social integration' and efforts aimed at increasing a 'readiness to return'.

The period of the 'guest workers' in West Germany ended with the hiring stop of 1973. It had a boomerang effect: while it decreased the number of foreign workers for a short period, it also stopped the transnational fluctuation of 'guest workers' and further intensified the tendency towards permanent stay and family reunions. While periods of residency grew longer, the intention to remain permanently also increased, thus leading to a gradual change in the status of guest worker to that of an immigrant. Labour migrants with restricted residence permits became informal immigrants with legally secure permanent resident status.

Already in the early 1980s, a large proportion of the foreign minority that had grown out of the original 'guest worker' population were living as permanent residents in the Federal Republic, but in a paradoxical situation: they were immigrants in a country without immigration. This fact was officially 'denied' and considered taboo or non-existant by the administration and within the political decision making process. As a logical consequence, concepts for immigration and integration policies were not developed.

On a much smaller scale, foreign workers were also imported into the German Democratic Republic on the basis of bi-lateral state agreements. Officially, the employment of foreign workers was not acknowledged but rather played down as temporary training or education. Just like the 'guest workers' in the FRG, the 'foreign workers' in the GDR were mostly employed in jobs least desired by Germans and under the toughest conditions; for instance, three quarters were involved in shift work. The foreign workers who had been brought to the GDR on the basis of temporary contracts were subject to an authoritarian, administrative 'care' (*Betreuung*); on the whole this meant state imposed segregation rather than social integration. They were usually accomodated in communal housing estates. The distance and the social vacuum created by the segregation of the foreigners resulted in latent xenophobic tensions which openly erupted after the end of the enforced totalitarian discipline.

The process of unification of the two German states brought together Germans who had become strangers to each other due to a multitude of differences in political-ideological and biographical-historical experiences. Unresolved problems, on both sides, in the relationship to foreigners thus contributed to the difficulties of the unification process. The tensions which had been built up in East and West led to the xenophobic explosions of the early 1990s. The names of German towns where incidents of violence and terror against foreigners occurred have since become known in headlines around the world. In the East, these names include Hoyerswerda (17-22 September 1991) where asylum seekers were expelled from their accomodations, attacked and injured by stone-throwing mobs and finally transported to safety in buses. In Rostock (23-27 August 1992) asylum seekers were attacked and besieged for days, their apartments were set on fire while crowds of bystanders stood watching and cheering. In the West there was Hünxe (3 October 1991) where two refugee children were seriously injured in a fire bomb attack. There was also Mölln (23 November 1992) and Solingen (29 May 1993) where members of Turkish families, who had either been living in Germany for many years or who had been born and grown up here, were burned to death in their houses or survived fire bomb attacks with serious injuries. In the night of 25 March 1994, a synagogue was burned in Lübeck, the first such incident in Germany since the Nazi-pogroms of November 1938.

The murders in Solingen were followed by days of rioting, both there and in other West German cities, indicating an increasing readiness on the part of the addressees of the anti-foreigner violence to respond in self-defence but also aggressively, notably among the young 'German Turks'. There is a growing danger of ethno-social tension. In addition, there are other areas of potential conflict deriving from problems in the countries of origin of foreigners living in the Federal Republic, as shown for example in the actvities of the Kurdish Workers Party (PKK) which led to the organisation being banned by the German authorities. Other Kurdish organisations were also banned. New problems arose because the line between political and ethno-cultural activities of minority organisations is not always easily drawn in a legal context. An unmistakable example of this was offered by the violent and bloody demonstrations of Kurds in March of 1994: they were occasioned, ethno-culturally, by the celebration of the Kurdish new year in Germany; politically, however, the demonstrations were motivated by the struggle of the PKK against the repression of the Kurdish minority in Turkey.

V

Many of the explanations of xenophobia and violence against ethnic minorities in the unified Germany dealt with the essential issues at stake here only in a marginal way: immigration, integration, questions of minority rights and their social-political management. This is all the more remarkable as one important cause for the hostility towards foreigners is to be found in the long tradition of political disorientation of the population with regard to social problems and tasks in the area of migration and integration. The political disorientation has its reason in a defensive policy that refuses to recognize an irrefutable fact, namely that for over a decade now the Federal Republic has become an immigration country of a new type – not in terms of a legal definition but in social and cultural reality. However, the simple statement of all official pronouncements on the matter reads: 'The Federal Republic is not a country of immigration'. This is the smallest common denominator of federal government policy; it has not changed for decades. Bonn continues to respond to questions of immigration not with immigration legislation and immigration policy, but with legislation and policy relating to 'foreigners'. As an answer to one of the most urgent social-political problems of our time and of the future, this policy is only partially inadequate; partially, it is simply wrong.

The continuing opposition in the Federal Republic against immigration legislation and policy is quite comparable to that of Bismarck and his conservative-agrarian allies in the Wilhelmine Empire who opted against legislative solutions of the emigration problem. The result then was that, historically, the first Imperial Emigration Law of 1897 came too late to be effective. For millions of German emigrants it meant a lack of protection on their journeys overseas with sometimes grave consequences. As I warned in the early 1980s already:

> A delay in the introduction of immigration legislation could lead to serious social problems for the receiving country, apart from the fateful personal consequences associated with failed immigration processes...de-facto immigrants who are living in Germany will remain 'outside the law' as immigrants as long as they will not be able to orient their life perspectives within the framework of an immigration law. The wide-spread belief that immigration legislation means an uncontrolled acceptance of immigrants is simply based on error. If there should be a lesson derived from the history of emigration and immigration, it would be this: immigration policy is not simply a means of assistance to people wishing to immigrate. It is also a regulative instrument of political management for the receiving country to protect itself.[1]

Such warnings and similar statements by like-minded scholars and scientists, by the churches and the unions, by politicians or social workers involved with foreigners living in Germany, remained spectacularly ineffective and without response. They simply bounced off a wall of official denial. The 1980s, even though they were eventful years, remained a lost decade in Germany as far as the question of immigration and integration is concerned. The political and social scenario seems to have become progressively more ghostly: the politicians at the top deny and declare as non-existant what at the grassroots level of daily experience is recognized as an increasingly multi-ethnic and multicultural reality – the paradoxical situation of immigrants in a country that declares officially that it is not a country of immigration.

The reverse side of this denial is a lack of political concepts and answers. The growing pressure of the problem was thus not only an issue because of the growing hysteria in the wake of the influx of asylum seekers in the late 1980s and early 1990s. The pressure was fed out of deeper and older mistakes in migration politics; the asylum debate only functioned as a diversionary battle. Below, at the grassroots level, there was a growing fear of 'strangers' or 'foreigners'; at the top, among the politicians, there was a growing fear of a voter backlash. The combination of popular fears and the lack of answers and concepts contributed decisively to the crisis of political legitimation of which commentators had spoken for many years, albeit in vain. For a short while, the crisis even seemed to turn into a crisis of the parliamentary-democratic system itself. Chancellor Kohl spoke of a 'state emergency' in the Fall of 1992. Others were reminded of the carrousel of crisis of public conflict, decline of state power and rejection of parliamentary democracy during the Weimar Republic.

Xenophobia, an increase in hostility towards foreigners and a growing acceptance of violence since the beginning of the unification process in Germany are not simply 'necessary consequences of immigration and integration but avoidable consequences of a lack of political management'; they are, in the final analysis, 'an aggressive response to the lack of concepts in immigration policy': thus reads one conclusion in the *Manifesto of the Sixty*, presented by sixty scholars from the humanities and social sciences on the question of 'Germany and Immigration'.[2]

VI

Migration policy must be understood as social policy in the widest sense of the word; it requires comprehensive and integrated concepts. Questions regarding migration and associated problems of integration and the role of minorities are today no longer marginal issues. They are centrally important tasks of social policy and will be even more so in the future. A migration policy can only be successful if it is supported by a broad, fundamental consensus. In a liberal democracy it cannot be implemented against the wishes of a local majority if dangerous consequences are to be avoided – to the disadvantage of the immigrant minorities but also to the disadvantage of the political system as a whole. Therefore, such a policy needs to be promoted and advertised. The problem in Germany is a lack of political will rather than a lack of know-how, as the successful campaign to promote the *Aussiedlerpolitik* has shown (even if it occasionally generated counter-productive, divisive formulas such as the unsettling slogan 'Returning Settlers [*Aussiedler*] aren't Foreigners', with its unintended suggestion of an implied hostility towards other 'foreigners').

After the hysterical discussions and xenophobic excesses, we have experienced a kind of breathing-space since 1994. This is due partially to the end of the devastating struggle concerning the constitutional change of the right to political asylum, and it is because of the dominance of other topics of public debate in 1993/94, such as the economic crisis and unemployment. But it is also due to the decision of the political parties to remain silent about migration matters and immigration policy during the campaign of the 'election year' of 1994. This silence was motivated by the fear that a new discussion of these matters would lead to renewed escalation of hostility towards non-Germans. Instead of the sometimes hysterical asylum debate of the 1980s and early 1990s we now have the strategic withdrawal by media and politicians. The explosive topics of immigration, integration and minority rights are being left alone: a change from alarmist concern to disinterest. At the end of the day, however, the paradoxical situation of 'immigrants in a country without immigration' remains; we are still confronted by open questions with only very tentative steps towards a solution and towards political management in the future (e.g., the 'nationality status of children': *Kinderstaatszugehörigkeit*, 1994). There is also a vague hope that, in time, the problem might disappear of its own. However, an attitude of 'wait and see' in immigration questions can be a considerable risk, as earlier experiences show. The price for the suppression of pent-up social problems is fear and aggressiveness which in turn will need to be addressed with new security measures – a vicious circle of defensive refusals to recognize problems and the delayed implementation of substitute solutions vis-à-vis pressing social tasks that simply cannot be overlooked. An active immigration policy with regard to integration and minority rights supported by transparent concepts would be the best contribution to reduce xenophobic projections and hostility.

What is needed are integrated concepts to meet the social challenges of integration domestically. Such concepts would begin with a reform of the Imperial Citizenship Law of 1913. They would include a right to naturalization for the second and third generation of immigrants, the generous acceptance of dual nationality for those minorities who up to this day have been barely tolerated, as well as anti-discrimination laws and efforts to increase equal opportunities by way of compensatory preferential measures in favour of discriminated minorities. What is needed at the European level are integrated concepts to regulate the pressure of immigrants from outside – less in the sense of a defensive security policy ('Fortress Europe') but rather as a set of clear, transparent and humane 'traffic rules' to regulate and to manage future migration to Germany and Europe.

At stake are not only our own interests. We must distinguish between two areas of migration, despite all overlaps in a complex reality: refugees and asylum seekers on the one hand, labour migrants and immigrants on the other. With regard to refugees and asylum seekers, the policy criteria must be the protection of individuals combined with measures to combat the causes of refugee movements in their countries of origin. With regard to labour migration and immigration, legislation and policy must address the mechanism of regulating access in the context of a carefully considered self-interest of the receiving country. Both areas need to be co-ordinated as part of an overall concept and strategy; they should not be traded off or played out one against the other. If this is done under consideration of the interests of the countries of emigration, then a bridge will be built to a migration-oriented development policy or, respectively, a development-oriented migration policy. Such a bridge could not be built without providing for an 'international cost transfer' (*internationaler Lastenausgleich*, F. Nuscheler) if the impending global disaster, which is rapidly increasing migration movements worldwide, is to be arrested. Such a policy development would indeed be a contribution to the idea of 'sustainable growth' as a basic concept, today unfortunately no more than an empty catch-word, which suggests that economic, ecological and social intervention and management should aim at creating a world that is inhabitable but not at the cost of the survival of future generations.

NOTES

1 Klaus J. Bade, *Vom Auswanderungsland zum Einwanderungsland*, Berlin, 1983, pp. 122-123.

2 *Das Manifest der 60*, Munich, 1994, pp. 19, 20.

REFERENCES

Klaus J. Bade (ed.), *Auswanderer – Wanderarbeiter – Gastarbeiter: Bevölkerung, Arbeitsmarkt und Wanderung in Deutschland seit der Mitte des 19. Jahrhunderts*, 2 vols., Ostfildern, (2nd. ed.) 1986.

Klaus J. Bade (ed.), *Deutsche im Ausland – Fremde in Deutschland: Migration in Geschichte und Gegenwart*, Munich, 1992.

Klaus J. Bade, *Homo Migrans: Wanderungen aus und nach Deutschland. Erfahrungen und Fragen*, Essen, 1994.

Klaus J. Bade (ed.), *Das Manifest der 60: Deutschland und die Einwanderung*, Munich, 1994.

Klaus J. Bade, *Ausländer – Aussiedler – Asyl: Eine Bestandsaufnahme*, Munich, 1994.

Rogers Brubaker, *Citizenship and Nationhood in France and Germany*, Cambridge, Mass., 1992.

Lutz Hoffmann, *Das deutsche Volk und seine Feinde. Die völkische Droge – Aktualität und Entstehungsgeschichte*, Cologne, 1994.

Franz Nuscheler, *Internationale Migration, Flucht und Asyl*, Opladen, 1995.

Dieter Oberndörfer, *Der Wahn des Nationalen. Die Alternative der offenen Republik*, Freiburg/Breisgau, 1993.

Reinhard Olt, 'Zwischen Selbstpreisgabe und Hoffnung. Die Lage nationaler Minderheiten in Osteuropa', *Frankfurter Allgemeine Zeitung*, 28 February 1994.

Alexander Steineck, *Ökonomische Anforderungen an eine europäische Zuwanderungspolitik*, Baden-Baden, 1994.

Werner Weidenfeld (ed.), *Das europäisache Einwanderungskonzept*, Gütersloh, 1994.

(Translated by Gerhard Fischer)

Chapter Thirteen

A German Dilemma: Ethnic Identity and the Debate on Citizenship

Stephen Castles

I Citizenship, Foreigners, Unification

In the first half of 1995, the two partners in the ruling coalition in Germany, the FDP and the CDU, were involved in an argument about a new notion of citizenship, known as *Kinderstaatszugehörigkeit* (child citizenship). According to this peculiar notion, a new category of quasi-citizenship was to be created, which would give children born to foreign parents legally resident in Germany for a certain period the right to choose either to be German or to retain their parents' citizenship at the age of 18. This construction would offer neither a guarantee of naturalisation nor protection from deportation to the young people. In the meantime, the Coalition appears to have dropped the plan for *Kinderstaatszugehörigkeit*, partly because it was all too clearly a merely symbolic gesture but also because it would require changes to a whole range of laws and international agreements (*Frankfurter Rundschau*, 20 June 1995).

This blatantly tokenistic plan is just the most recent in a long line of attempts (starting with the Kühn Report of 1979, see Castles, 1984; 1987) to resolve a basic dilemma of contemporary Germany: how to regulate the legal status of the immigrant population which has emerged from the mass migrations of recent decades. Today there are seven million foreign residents. Most came as so-called *Gastabeiter* (guestworkers) or their dependants between 1956 and the 1970s, while more recent settlers came as asylum-seekers. With reunification in 1990, the issue became exacerbated by fears of uncontrollable influxes of people from the East and the South. Growing racism and extreme-right mobilisation led to severe racist violence, including attacks on asylum-seeker hostels, arson against Turkish families and violence against foreign-looking people in the streets.

Racist violence is probably no greater in Germany than in France, Britain or other European countries (Björgo and Witte, 1993), yet in view of Germany's history of extermination of minorities it has attracted great attention both internally and internationally. Mainstream German society has been at pains to distance itself from the neo-Nazis and skinheads: the demonstrations and *Lichterketten* (candlelight processions) of the Left received at least verbal support from conservative leaders. However, many CDU/CSU politicians claimed that it was uncontrolled entry of asylum-seekers that caused racism – a classic blame-the-victim approach. The German Left seeks political integration of foreign residents through radical reform of exclusionary citizenship laws. Denial of citizenship is seen as a major cause of political, socio-economic and cultural marginalisation. Moreover, labelling immigrants as outsiders with inferior rights makes them obvious targets for racist violence. Thus the Green Party, most of the SPD, the trade unions and the major churches now call for easing of naturalisation rules for the first generation immigrants, a right to citizenship for subsequent generations and the acceptance of dual citizenship. This position is increasingly supported by some parts of the moderate Right, as will be discussed below.

But if reunification has made citizenship for immigrants an urgent issue, it has simultaneously made this demand harder to achieve. This is because reunification has brought about an important shift in the collective self-concept held by many Germans. It has revived an old and bitter debate about the notion of the German nation and people. The dilemma of ethnic identity put forward in the title of this article primarily concerns not immigrants but Germans. The article will examine current discussions on citizenship and national identity in Germany, and look at the contributions of theorists like Dieter Oberndörfer and Jürgen Habermas. It will be argued that the rather fatalistic ideas on inter-group conflict put forward by Hans Magnus Enzensberger in *Die Große Wanderung* (1992) are of little help in resolving the dilemma.

II The Notion of the German People

When we think of the modern nation-state, we tend to think in the first place of the political nation – as it emerged above all through the French and American Revolutions. Recent historical-theoretical approaches, such as the work of Ernest Gellner (1983) and Benedict Anderson (1983), argue that the modern nation-state is the result of modernisation and rationalisation. It is closely linked to the emergence of capitalism and industrialisation, and the resulting pressures for economic, political and cultural integration and homogenisation. The nation-state is the appropriate political form for the emancipation of the bourgeoisie and for its rise to political domination.

The rise of the nation-state meant replacing a rule based on the 'god-given' privileges of monarchy and aristocracy with rational government based on the democratically-expressed will of the people. This made it necessary to clearly define 'the people', in order to regulate access to the rights of citizenship, above all the right of political participation. The Republican Model embodied in the French revolutionary constitution provided an inclusive definition of the *citoyen*, which gave full rights to anyone resident on French soil who accepted the Declaration of the Rights of Man. Race, ethnicity and national origins were irrelevant. Citizenship was decoupled from nationality. Thus the archetypical nation-state was based on a progressive form of nationalism, which was linked to the notion of rule by the people (democracy) and the Rights of Man. Rousseau's idea of the General Will could easily co-exist with individual rights, but not with group rights based on race or ethnicity.[1]

But Germany never fitted the political model of the nation-state. Unity as a nation came much later than in countries like France, Britain or the Netherlands. Germany was a politically and economically backward patchwork of principalities and mini-states with absolutist rulers until the end of the eighteenth century. Nation-state formation did not come through internal impulses for modernisation and democratisation, but as a reaction to conquest by an external enemy: the Napoleonic armies at the beginning of the 19th century. Thus as Habermas points out, national consciousness was not based on democratic civil liberties and popular sovereignty, but on 'the romantically inspired middle-class notion of a *Kulturnation*, a nation defined by its culture' (Habermas, 1994: 146). Thus 'national consciousness in Germany could be linked with the pathos of the uniqueness of its culture and ancestry – a particularism that has enduringly stamped the Germans' self-understanding' (Habermas, 1994: 146).

This German *Sonderbewußtsein* (sense of specialness) was to play a decisive historical role. In his study on recent trends in German nationalism, Lutz Hoffmann (1994: 108-30) stresses the anti-democratic notion of the German people which was popularised by romanticism. As the prevailing set of philosophical and literary ideals, romanticism understood itself as a protest against the Enlightenment and rationality. Feeling was seen as superior to reason. Romanticism portrayed individuals not as autonomous, but as part of an organic whole; freedom meant not individual rights but acceptance of one's role in the greater organism. The state was the embodiment of this superior meaning, which could only be interpreted by great leaders. Democracy had no place in the model, for historical or mythical legitimation was more important than immediate majority consent. The 'people' was a central category of romanticism – not as a collective of democratic subjects, but as a natural, primordial whole, with its roots in racial history.

The essence of the German people could not easily be defined, for the population of Germany was in fact the result of centuries of migrations and interminglings. Thus the only way of defining the German people was in contradistinction to a succession of internal or external enemies, including:

- The French during the *Befreiungskriege* (wars of liberation) against Napoleon, and throughout the nineteenth century;

- Jews, Gypsies and other 'non-Germanic' minorities during the period of unification of the *Reich* in the late nineteenth century;
- the French, British and Russians during the period of struggle for colonies leading up to the First World War;
- the foreign powers responsible for the *Versaillesdiktat* after 1918;
- Jews, communists and other internal minorities after the First World War and above all in the Nazi period.

The *Feindbild* (concept of the enemy) was central to German nationalism, which took on a particularly aggressive form through its repeated assertions that the German people was constantly subject to attack by dangerous enemies from within and without. This was clearly linked to the lateness of German nation-state formation and industrialisation compared with its western neighbours. German capital was late in the struggle for colonies and overseas markets, and tried to compensate for this through the use of state power and military might. The romantic *Sonderbewußtsein* was both a reaction to Germany's historical situation and a justification for the authoritarian and aggressive state which arose from this situation.

The defeat of the Nazi regime brought fundamental change after 1945. Germany was divided and occupied. Many Germans were affected by collective shame over the Holocaust, the brutality of Hitler's rule over conquered nations and Germany's role as an international pariah. Three main sources of identity were to emerge in the following years. The first was a new *Feindbild* through membership in one or other of the Cold War power blocks. In the Federal Republic of Germany (FRG), anticommunism became a powerful force for political integration. A similar function was served by anticapitalism and 'antirevanchism' in the German Democratic Republic (GDR).

A second source of identity in post-1945 Germany was to be found in the economic sphere. As the *Wirtschaftswunder* (economic miracle) unfolded in the 1950s and 1960s, economic growth, technological innovation and high living standards provided a new focus for national pride. This applied particularly in the FRG, although the propaganda apparatus of the GDR was also quite successful in convincing East Germans that they were better off than the rest of the Soviet Bloc – at least until the 1970s.

Thirdly, by the 1980s, the FRG seemed to be moving towards a civic culture and democratic political identity closer to the French model. This was the result of the success of the FRG's constitution, the *Grundgesetz* (Basic Law), as a basis for a democratic state, the emergence of democratic social and political movements, and the development of a fairly strong democratic public sphere. Habermas (1994: 128-35) argued that a form of *Verfassungspatriotismus* (constitutional patriotism) was developing, which might have provided the basis for a new form of national identity and citizenship.

These new sources of identity were shattered by the unexpected end of the Cold War and the precipitate reunification. The Cold War perceptions of external enemies were no longer relevant. Economic prosperity appeared threatened by German reunification: East German industry and employment collapsed, while the West Germans feared that the costs of economic integration would lead to high taxes, unemployment and declining real wages. The emerging *Verfassungspatriotismus* was swamped by a new nationalism. The prevailing slogan shifted quickly from the democratic *Wir sind das Volk* (we are the people) of the East German 'Monday Demonstrations' of 1989, to the nationalistic *Wir sind ein Volk* (we are one people) of the CDU-led mass rallies of 1990. Hoffmann (1994) argues that the mobilisation of nationalist feelings in the reunification processes was a deliberate political strategy, designed to maintain control by existing conservative leaderships. Again, as so often in German history, the reunification of 1990 can be seen as a revolution from above, rather than the result of democratic processes from below. There are trends towards a regeneration of the old *Sonderbewußtsein* in a new form, based on Germany's economic and political strength in the centre of a restructured Europe.

One facet of the new German nationalism has been an explosion of racist violence against immigrants, refugees and asylum-seekers. Non-European appearance and Muslim dress have become triggers for violence, although aggression against older minorities – Jews and Gypsies – is also widespread. Before discussing the character of racism in Germany today, it is therefore necessary to examine the way in which Germany has become a multi-ethnic society.

III Multi-ethnic Germany

Fifty years ago, the Nazis tried to homogenise the 'German people' by destroying its historical minorities. Just a generation after this, Germany acquired new minorities in an entirely unplanned way. Now Germany is in the paradoxical situation of being officially regarded as not being a country of immigration, and yet having had some of the largest inflows of any country since 1945: nearly 20 million people in all, including no less than 1.5 million per year in 1991 and 1992. This has brought about major changes to society and culture. There are two main categories of immigrants:

1. 'Ethnic Germans', who migrated from the East immediately after 1945 (some 8 million) and then again since 1989 (about 2 million). These *Volksdeutsche* or *Aussiedler* have an immediate right to citizenship, even though their forebears may have left Germany to settle in the Volga valley or in Romanian *Siebenbürgen* centuries ago. Indeed many of the recent arrivals speak no German at all or archaic dialects incomprehensible to modern Germans. Their culture and values are in many cases worlds apart from those of the contemporary Federal Republic,

and their social integration presents considerable difficulties. So why are the *Aussiedler* seen as Germans who have an immediate right to passports and all the privileges of being citizens of one of Europe's richest countries? Because of the principle of *ius sanguinis* (law of the blood, or citizenship by descent) which is the basis of German nationality. A person is German if he or she has German blood. Since German blood is chemically no different from any other, the proof is a social one: the *Volksdeutsche* must be able to show cultural belonging through use of the German language and belonging to a German community – as demonstrated for instance through parish birth and marriage records. This perpetuates the principle of the *Kulturnation*.

2. Foreign residents, who are in Germany mainly because of mass labour recruitment between 1955 and 1973. The Government brought in 'guestworkers', mainly from Southern Europe and Turkey, who were meant to work in Germany for a few years and then go home. The Government stopped recruitment at the time of the 'Oil Crisis' in 1973, hoping that surplus foreign workers would leave. In fact, many stayed on, and family reunion continued. By the late 1970s it was clear that permanent settlement was taking place (Castles, 1984; Castles and Miller, 1993). Since the mid-1980s, increasing numbers of temporary workers from Poland and other Eastern European countries have been employed in building, domestic work and other informal sector jobs – a resumption of historical patterns going back to the 19th century. In addition, there have been substantial inflows of asylum seekers, with an upward curve from 100,000 in 1986 to 438,000 in 1992 (OECD, 1994: 78). Many came from Africa and Asia, but the main growth since 1989 has been in East-West movements.

There are about seven million foreign residents in Germany today. The main groups in 1993 were Turks (1.9 million), former Yugoslavs (930,000), Italians (563,000), Greeks (352,000) and Poles (260,000; OECD, 1995: Table B1). The myth of temporary sojourn still shapes the legal status of foreigners, except those from European Union (EU) countries, who enjoy social and economic parity with German citizens. Non-EU residents are denied many rights, particularly concerning political participation. The *ius sanguinis* principle makes it extremely hard for foreigners to become citizens. Apart from a qualifying period of generally ten years, there are high fees and restrictive rules concerning employment situation, financial security and police records. In 1993, there were just 37,042 naturalisations (0.5 per cent of the foreign population) (OECD, 1995). On that basis it would take 200 years for all foreign residents to become citizens. The *ius sanguinis* principle also means that children born to immigrant parents in Germany have no automatic right to citizenship. In other words, young people who have been born in Germany and know no other country can, under certain circumstances, be deported. This hardly leads to clear future perspectives or political integration.

The political exclusion of foreign residents is frequently linked to socio-economic marginalisation. Most were recruited as manual workers and have had few chances of upward mobility. Concentration in poor housing areas with few amenities is frequent. Inadequate educational opportunities and discrimination in training and employment has carried this disadvantaged position over to much of the second generation. Such marginality and exclusion has fed into the stereotypes of difference and inferiority fostered by extreme-right racist groups, especially since 1989. One result is growing racist violence against both long-standing foreign residents and new asylum-seekers. Another consequence has been growing mobilisation of immigrant youth – especially Turks – to fight racism and discrimination. Since mainstream political expression is largely denied, mobilisation is largely around cultural and religious symbols – further strengthening fears of 'otherness' and fundamentalism.

IV The Specificity of German Racism

In the early 1990s, most Germans reacted with shock to the pogrom-like onslaughts on asylum-seekers and Gypsies, and to the escalation of racist violence against immigrants. A strong anti-racist movement emerged. One of its central demands was the granting of citizenship to long-term foreign residents. Citizenship was seen as a way of overcoming marginalisation and hence combating racism. Is this a realistic recipe for anti-racism? To answer that question it is necessary to understand the specific character of German racism. Racism and racist violence are severe in Britain, France, Belgium and the USA too, but, for historical reasons, German racism is often seen as having special character. Is this really the case?

German social science has been slow to provide an adequate analysis of racism. Until the 1980s, the main tendency was denial of racism. Social scientists were fixated on Nazi racism (in particular anti-semitism) and refused to analyse the phenomenon for immigrants, asylum-seekers, etc. Instead the term *Ausländerfeindlichkeit* (hostility to foreigners) was used as an ahistorical euphemism, which hindered international comparison. It is only recent events that have impelled some German social scientists to begin serious research on racism, and to link up with some of the debates in British and French sociology (see Kalpaka and Räthzel, 1990; Bielefeld, 1990; Butterwege and Jäger, 1992). Here I will summarise some recent approaches to explaining current racism (for more detail see Castles, 1993).

A common approach is to attribute racism to the socio-economic effects of reunification on the East German population. Reunification led to high hopes of prosperity, but, within months, these were dashed. The East German economy collapsed, West German firms were reluctant to invest, and many people found themselves unemployed. At the same time, social institutions that had given structure to life in East Germany disappeared. Children and young people had been members of state youth organisations. Many of them rejected the political indoctrination and regimentation, yet these organisations had provided low-cost meeting-places, as well as sporting and hobby activities. The Federal Government did little to provide youth clubs and job-creation schemes, believing that this should be left to the private sector. Churches and welfare organisations did their best, but it was the neo-Nazis who were quickest to start youth groups, providing meeting places, comradeship and an integrating ideology (Korfes, 1992).

A second approach emphasises psychological factors. The corrupt and inefficient system of the GDR had left a legacy of cynicism. After 1989, many people believed that values imported from the West would provide a new orientation. However, this belief disappeared as the economy collapsed and it became apparent that many West Germans saw the *Ossis* (East Germans) as comical and inferior. The situation was complicated by people's feelings about their own role in the GDR. Those who had believed the official ideology and worked hard to build 'socialism' were now told that their life's work had been misguided. Thousands had spied on their neighbours, friends and even families for the *Stasi* (secret police). Since 1989, the collective guilt and denial of the parent-generation has made it difficult for them to provide moral authority and guidance to youth. A best seller by an East German psychotherapist explained the growth of violence through the removal of repressive control which allows the blocked inner feelings (*Gefühlsstau)* to surface through aggression (Maaz, 1992).

But there are problems in explaining racism through the crisis in the ex-GDR. The frequency of racist attacks is somewhat higher in the East than in the West, but violence has escalated in the West as well. Racist violence is a problem affecting the whole of German society. Indeed one can observe an increased acceptance of violence in youth sub-cultures and in society as a whole – a phenomenon not unique to Germany. One sociological approach to explain this is the *Modernisierungsverlierer* (losers of modernisation) theory, put forward by Ulrich Beck (1986). The argument is that rapid changes in economic and social structures in the 1980s led to a social polarisation and the marginalisation of certain groups: displaced blue-collar workers, young people lacking qualifications, people in declining industrial or rural areas. Such people lack personal perspectives and economic opportunities, and compensate for their situation by aggressive behaviour and openness for extreme-right ideologies.

In this view, the reason why violence is mainly directed against foreigners is simply that they are visible, weak out-groups, against whom aggressions can be expressed almost without fear of punishment. Other out-groups, such as gays or handicapped people, also appear as suitable targets. East Germans are more likely to attack minorities, because more of them have become 'losers of modernisation'. But the *Modernisierungsverlierer* theory begs certain questions: why is racism and acceptance of violence so common among people who are not unemployed or socially disadvantaged? Why do the police often condone racist violence? Why do government policies often appear to encourage hostility towards immigrants?

An explanation for racism frequently put forward by politicians is that it is 'a legitimate reaction of the German people' to abuse of the right to asylum (Hoffmann, 1994: 36-48). The Government and the ruling parties claim that many of the recent asylum-seekers are not victims of persecution, but would-be economic migrants. The 1993 changes to Article 16 of the Basic Law were designed to restrict the right of political asylum. This is a 'blame-the-victim strategy' to stop racism by keeping out its objects. It merely encouraged the popular idea that it is the foreigners who are the problem, rather than German racism. In periods of economic growth, Germany has not found it difficult to incorporate millions of immigrants. Since the mid-1970s, economic growth has slowed while immigrant families have become highly visible in the cities, competing with Germans for housing and social services. But successive governments have told the people that 'the German Federal Republic is not a country of immigration'. Misleading people about the reality of settlement, and failure to grant citizenship and basic rights to a large section of the population are recipes for conflict and a divided society. Thus the real political explanation for racism lies in the unrealistic and discriminatory policies of the state.

Some of the best analyses of German racism are still to be found in the work of the Frankfurt School, which set out (in exile in the 1930s) to explain how such a civilised people could behave so barbarically. Adorno, Horkheimer, Marcuse and Fromm put forward a combination of economic, historical and psychological explanations. Germany was a 'late nation', which was unable to form a nation-state until 1871. Industrialisation was not preceded by a democratic revolution, so it took place under an absolutist state and a monopolistic bourgeoisie. Because Germany was late in the struggle for markets and colonies, its imperial expansion took on a specially aggressive form. Prussian traditions of discipline in family and school helped to form an 'authoritarian character', marked by obedience to the strong, aggression towards the weak and lack of critical abilities.

Some sociologists are now beginning to take up this theme of historical continuity. Farin and Seidel-Pielen (1992: 26-41) studied protestant enclaves in mainly-catholic Bavaria, showing how areas which in 1932 voted over 90 per cent for the Nazi Party today demonstrate high levels of support for the extreme-right *Republikaner*. Protestant racism can be traced back to Luther's antisemitic tirades, and to the blind support of the state churches for the Prussian monarchy.

There is also debate on the failure to combat the deep-seated effects of Nazi ideologies after 1945. 'De-Nazification' was a superficial process, in which members of the Nazi Party were temporarily removed from official positions. With the onset of the Cold War, many former Nazis were quickly rehabilitated. In the GDR the official line was that the ruling party was socialist and internationalist and had no links with Germany's past. Racism and fascism were seen as results of capitalism and imperialism, and therefore no longer an issue. Yet many of the old bureaucrats, teachers and officers could not be dispensed with in the new state, despite the ideology.

German identity was seriously weakened after 1945. The division into two Germanies seemed appropriate not only to the European neighbours, but to many Germans too. Few people expected reunification ever to come, and little thought had been given to the character of a new all-German nation-state. Racism is linked to insecure national identity. The debate often hinges on the meaning of the Auschwitz extermination-camp, as a symbol of the bankruptcy of nationalism. Adorno asked whether there could be German culture after Auschwitz, while Günter Grass said as late as 1989: 'The German people has lost its right to unity through Auschwitz' (quoted from Farin and Seidel-Pielen, 1992: 11).

Bodo Mörshäuser (1992) has shown how the meaning of 'being German' has shifted across the three post-war generations. The first generation were 'the survivors' – those who lived through the Nazi period by conforming. Afterwards they kept silent, to hide their complicity. The second generation were those who came of age in the 1960s, and asked what their parents had done in the Hitler-period. They broke the silence, expressed their shame at being German, and were against nationalism. The third generation are those who are in their twenties today. They question the orthodoxy of many of their parents and teachers, and want to reassert a German nationalism based on ideas of achievement and ability, even if this means a reinterpretation of the past.

The *first generation* wanted to be silent about Auschwitz, because Auschwitz had hurt their pride. The *second generation* wanted to talk about Auschwitz, because it explained their shame at being Germans. The *third generation* does not accept Auschwitz as the centre of a moral code, and insists that they are proud to be Germans. Each new generation has a clear instinct about the taboos of the preceding ones – and digs them out (Mörshäuser, 1992: 114).

It is above all young people who lack strong emotional ties or good economic chances who accept extreme-right ideologies. They cling to 'being German' because it is their only claim to identity. They find models among older leaders. Former Bavarian Prime Minister Strauss said in 1969: 'A people which has brought about such economic achievements has a right not to want to hear any more about Auschwitz'. Alfred Dregger, Chairman of the CDU parliamentary party declared in 1982: 'I call upon all Germans to step out of Hitler's shadow – we must become normal' (Mörshäuser, 1992: 129).

Herein lies the German dilemma: being 'normal' means either suppressing the past or reinterpreting is as something no longer shameful. Under Wilhelm II, the 'late nation' was told it had to fight for 'a place in the sun.' Between the Wars, the Germans were the losers who had to pay reparations to the victors. Reassertion of national pride took the extreme form of Nazism. After 1945, the mood was one of shame and self-denial. Today, economic achievements are seen as a source of pride, and reunification has reinforced the desire for national identity. Yet the only successful models for German nationhood – Bismarck's Second Reich and Hitler's Third Reich – are authoritarian, racist and chauvinistic. The problem is thus to find a new model for national identity which takes account of the reality that Germany has become a multi-ethnic society.

Germany is like most other highly-developed countries in that the current crisis of modernisation has brought about a deep malaise, which is partly expressed through racism and racist violence. But Germany also has unique features which have led to more extreme violence: the sudden and poorly-planned reunification has led to severe strains, particularly in the East; immigration policy has been unrealistic and deceptive, so that the population have not been prepared for the reality of a multi-ethnic society; and German history has left the country without an acceptable model for national identity.

V The Debate on Citizenship for Immigrants

The issue of incorporating minorities into German society as citizens is therefore crucial. The problem is that German citizenship is closely linked to an outmoded notion of ethnocultural identity. The very principle which has allowed the rapid integration of 'ethnic Germans' prevents the integration of foreign residents. What is needed is a civic identity which permits membership of a political nation irrespective of ethnic origins. This could take two possible forms: assimilation, which would turn immigrants into citizens as individuals and which would not permit recognition of cultural collectivities; or pluralism, which accepts political citizenship without denying the importance of cultural affiliations and preferences.

After four Turkish girls and women were burned to death in a neo-Nazi attack in the small industrial town of Solingen in May 1993, there were large anti-racist demonstrations all over Germany. One of the main slogans was the demand for dual citizenship. This is an important issue especially for Turks who cannot easily give up their previous citizenship. Current German law requires renunciation of any other citizenship as a precondition for naturalisation (although exceptions are made in some cases). The 'asylum compromise' of 1993, which changed Germany's Basic Law to restrict the right of political asylum, did at last create a legal right for third generation immigrants to choose German citizenship, although again the new rules stopped short of allowing dual citizenship. In fact, in Germany – as in all other immigration countries – there are growing numbers of people with dual or multiple citizenship, as a result of bi-cultural marriages. The official estimate for Germany is 1.2 million people (Beauftragte der Bundesregierung, 1993: 9).

The situation is in flux in Germany. There are widespread fears of further immigration. The constitutional change of 1993 was the culmination of a long series of measures designed to increase border control and reduce entries. The most important was the Schengen Agreement of 1985, which provided for close cooperation on border control by a number of Western European states. This was finally implemented in 1995. The Dublin Convention of 1990 laid down common rules for asylum procedures, so that refusal of refugee status in one country would preclude applications in others. There have also been agreements with Hungary, the Czech Republic and Poland to stop people using their countries for transit to the West. Germany has played a major part in erecting the walls of 'Fortress Europe'.

But, at the same time, the myth of not being 'a country of immigration' has become unsustainable (see Bade, 1994). Authorities at the Federal, *Länder* and municipal levels have had to adopt measures concerned with employment, education and social policy, which take account of the real issues arising from immigrant settlement. Welfare agencies and education authorities have set up special services and adopted policies to deal with a wide range of problems in neighbourhoods and cities with immigrant concentrations. Despite official ideologies, one can speak of 'de facto multiculturalism' in many places. Such policies are beginning to be institutionalised by offices of multicultural affairs, or commissioners for foreign citizens, at the various levels of government.

In the political arena, the Left – that is the Green Party, some sections of the Social Democratic Party (SPD) and the unions – has advocated anti-discrimination measures and stronger rights for immigrants for many years. A key demand was for local voting rights for resident non-citizens – a measure introduced in Schleswig Holstein but subsequently ruled invalid by the Federal Constitutional Court in 1990. This idea has now been replaced with the further-going demand for dual citizenship. However, the Left has an ambivalent attitude towards multiculturalism. It has often been seen as a model for cementing the identity of ethnic groups, and for maintaining cultures which are seen by some as anti-modern and repressive – especially towards women. Some immigrants fear that multiculturalism would commit them to a group identity which they do not want. Other people on the Left, however, see multiculturalism in terms of creative cultural interaction, and welcome the changes it brings for social and cultural life (see Leggewie, 1991; Cohn-Bendit and Schmid, 1993).

Until recently the parliamentary Right – the CDU-CSU – was strongly opposed to recognition of permanent settlement. Now the CDU is rethinking its position. From the mid-1980s, a group around then CDU General Secretary Heiner Geißler called for recognition of permanent settlement, and significant improvements in immigrant rights. The initiative was unpopular, and contributed to Geißler's dismissal from his influential post. More recently, some theorists of the Right have called for radical changes. An important contribution is the book *Der Wahn des Nationalen* (roughly: T*he Delusion of the National Idea)* by Dieter Oberndörfer, a prominent political scientist and adviser to the CDU. Oberndörfer calls for the replacement of the nation-state by an 'open European republic', based not on ethnic belonging but on liberal-democratic principles. The key principle would be '*Verfassungspatriotismus* [constitutional patriotism], the active identification of the citizens with the political order and values of the republic' (Oberndörfer, 1993: 14).

In this approach, which is very like the French Republican model, granting citizenship to immigrants would be no problem, because the idea of the nation as ethnic or cultural belonging is replaced by the idea of a purely political community. This would mean a radical change in the understanding of notions of citizenship, people and nation. However, citizenship is conceptualised in terms of individual political participation, and there is little room for ideas of social citizenship, nor for a form of multiculturalism based on the collective integration of groups with diverse cultures. Thus, Oberndörfer's model is essentially assimilationist, and it is questionable whether it would be adequate to overcome the exclusion and marginalisation of minorities. Experience in both France and Britain has shown that access to citizenship for ethnic minorities does not in itself avoid socio-economic disadvantage, nor prevent racism.

Oberndörfer's approach has some similarities with work by Jürgen Habermas (1993; 1994). Indeed the concept of *Verfassungspatriotismus* seems to have been coined by Habermas. However, Habermas' central idea is rather different to Oberndörfer's assimilationist view. Habermas argues that in a democratic state there can be no absolute opposition between individual rights and culturally-based collective differences: 'A correctly understood theory of rights requires a politics of recognition that protects the integrity of the individual in the life contexts in which his or her identity is formed' (1994: 113). In other words, a system of equal rights which abstract from actual differences in people's life experience and socialisation cannot in fact lead to equality. Thus Habermas implies the need for collective social and cultural rights – something very close to what we mean by multiculturalism in Australia.

Habermas goes on to argue that, in the long run, a democratic society has no alternative but to incorporate immigrants, even if this means fundamental changes in culture and politics. He describes 'two levels of assimilation':[2]

> 1. 'Assent to the principles of the constitution within the scope of interpretation determined by the ethical-political self-understanding of the citizens and the political culture of the country; in other words assimilation to the way in which the autonomy of the citizens is institutionalised in the recipient society and the way the 'public use of reason' is practised there'. (Habermas, 1994: 138)
> 2. 'The further level of a willingness to become acculturated, that is, not only to conform externally but to become habituated to the way of life, the practices, and customs of the local culture. This means an assimilation that penetrates to the level of ethical-cultural integration and thereby has a deeper impact on the collective identity of the immigrants' culture of origin than the political socialisation'. (Habermas, 1994: 138)

According to Habermas, a democratic constitutional state can demand the first type of assimilation: political socialisation and acceptance of basic constitutional principles. But it has no right to demand the second type, which would mean 'compulsory assimilation for the sake of the self-affirmation of the cultural form of life dominant in the country' (Habermas, 1994: 139). Habermas goes on to present us with: 'An important implication...namely, that the legitimately asserted identity of the political community will by no means be preserved from alterations in the long run in the wake of waves of immigration. Because immigrants cannot be compelled to surrender their own traditions, as other forms of life become established the horizon within which citizens henceforth interpret their common constitutional principles may also expand. Then the mechanism comes into play whereby a change in the composition of the active citizenry changes the context to which the ethical-political self-understanding of the nation as a whole refers'(Habermas: 1994: 139-40).

Thus Habermas argues for the imperative of incorporating immigrants as citizens in Germany (and in other countries), but states clearly that this will, in the long run, lead to institutional change in major sub-systems of society, such as political and economic structures. He also stresses that this means a shift away from the old ethno-cultural notion of the 'German nation'. The authoritarian and nationalistic form taken by German reunification threatened what Habermas calls 'the process of civilising politics that was underway until 1989'. He now calls for a resumption of this process to achieve a national self-understanding that 'is no longer based on ethnicity but founded on citizenship'.

VI Enzensberger's *Great Migration*

What does Enzensberger's *Great Migration* contribute to our understanding of these key issues arising from migration to Germany? Unfortunately, it appears, very little. Enzensberger seems to have retreated into a form of cultural pessimism which could paralyse all political action. The book presents a graphic description of the racism, group-egoism and the indifference to the rights of others which is indeed to be found in Germany – and elsewhere. The author is keenly conscious of the historical dimensions of the relationship between North and South, between core and periphery which leads to labour migration and refugee movements.

Yet Enzensberger does not analyse the causes for such phenomena. Moreover, his allegorical treatment – based on trivial anecdotes, like his description of people in a railway compartment – homogenises behaviour and attitudes, and ignores the important variations within each group that lead to political conflicts and change. His fatalistic approach ignores the fact there is a major anti-racist movement in Germany. Enzensberger makes much of categories like the 'territorial instinct' (*CW*, 105), which we usually associate with the highly suspect work of sociobiologists.

He states baldly that 'every migration leads to conflicts' and that 'sectional self-interest and xenophobia are anthropological constants' (*CW*, 106). He claims that 'the multicultural society remains a confused slogan as long as the difficulties it throws up...remain taboo' (*CW*, 134) without making the effort to examine actual multicultural societies or to compare them with Germany. Enzensberger repeats the tired slogans of the right on pluralism as tribalism (*CW*, 136), and makes sweeping statements on the attitudes of the 'European population' (*CW*, 105) with neither data nor analysis. Of course, this is a literary treatment rather than a social-scientific one, but even here one has a right to expect adequate substantiation of assertions and differentiation of judgements. In sum, I do not find that Enzensberger's *Great Migration* makes a useful contribution to a very important debate. On the contrary, it is open to misuse by those who want to polemicise against reform, on the basis of fatalistic and poorly-balanced arguments.

VII Conclusion

Citizenship has become one of the major issues in both political science and in practical politics in many countries – including Germany and Australia. A few years ago it was hardly a theme of discussion – now there is a plethora of books, conferences and debates on the theme. There are several reasons for this:

> With the end of the Cold War, the liberal-democratic model has become the only conceivable one for highly-developed countries.

This makes it necessary to reassess the model and to make sure it achieves its full democratic potential.
Economic rationalism and deregulation has made the question of social citizenship crucial.
The proliferation of new forms of identity (regional, local, sexual, cultural, etc) question the central role of national identity and hence of citizenship.
Globalisation is raising the question of the future salience of the nation-state as the pre-eminent political unit.
Growing international population mobility leads to questions about the exclusion of minorities as well as about naturalisation and multiple citizenship.

These issues are important in all democratic countries, but nowhere more so than in Germany. The emotional, irrational concept of the 'German nation' has contributed to authoritarian regimes, genocide and international conflict in the past. Yet, despite all the changes since 1945, it has not yet proved possible to move to an inclusive model for a political nation. Now the issue has become unavoidable. The question of citizenship for immigrants is emerging as a touchstone for achievement of a modern and democratic form of national identity in Germany. As discussed above, thinking especially on the Left but also on the moderate Right is moving towards reform. Yet change will not be easy, and the process of reunification has had a regressive effect in this context. The 'asylum compromise' and the continued failure to bring about fundamental change in rules on naturalisation and acquisition of citizenship by second generation immigrants shows the difficulties.

In my view, the ideas developed by Habermas and other democratic political theorists provide a political-philosophical basis for rethinking German national identity and citizenship. The work at the grassroots in creating an anti-racist movement and in introducing 'de facto multiculturalism' in many areas provides the material basis for change. But important questions have yet to be resolved:

How long will it take to achieve an inclusive civic identity based on territoriality, rather than an exclusionary ethnic identity for Germans?
Is there likely to be openness to fundamental change, or will there be attempts at further unworkable compromises (like the *Kinderstaatszugehörigkeit* mentioned at the beginning of this chapter)?
What will be the cost in racist violence and social division before real change comes about?

NOTES

1 It should be noted in passing that the French revolutionary model was of short duration. More restrictive notions of citizenship soon reappeared. Today, French political scientists like Dominique Schnapper (1994) and Patrick Weil (1991) still defend the Republican model, but in reality cultural definitions of belonging have long since re-asserted themselves. This issue cannot be pursued further here.

2 The following passage is quoted from Habermas' 1994 essay, but a similar formulation is also to be found in the 1993 article in *Die Zeit* : 'Die erste verlangt Zustimmung zu den Prinzipien der Verfassung – eine Assimilation also an die Art und Weise, wie in der aufnehmenden Gesellschaft die Autonomie der Bürger verstanden und wie der "öffentliche Gebrauch der Vernunft" (Rawls) praktiziert wird. Die zweite Stufe erfordert Bereitschaft zu einer weitgehenden Akkulturation, und zwar zur Einübung in die Lebensweise, in die Pratiken und Gewohnheiten der einheimischen Mehrheitskultur. Das bedeutet eine Assimilation, die auf die Ebene ethisch-kulturelle Integration durchschlägt'.

REFERENCES/BIBLIOGRAPHY

Anderson, B. (1983), *Imagined Communities*, London, Verso.

Bade, K.J. (ed.) (1994), *Das Manifest der 60: Deutschland und die Einwanderung*, Munich, Beck.

Beauftragte der Bundesregierung für die Belange der Ausländer (1993), *Das Einbürgerungs- und Staatsangehörigkeitsrecht der Bundesrepublik Deutschland*, Bonn, Beauftragte der Bundesregierung für die Belange der Ausländer.

Beck, U. (1986), *Risikogesellschaft*, Frankfurt am Main.

Bielefeld, U. (ed.) (1990), *Das Eigene und das Fremde*, Hamburg, Junius.

Björgo, T. and Witte, R. (1993), *Racist Violence in Europe*, London, Macmillan.

Butterwegge, C. and Jäger, S. (eds.) (1992), *Rassismus in Europa*, Cologne, Bund Verlag.

Castles, S. (1993), 'Explaining racism in the new Germany', *Social Alternatives* 12, 1, pp. 9-12.

Castles, S. and Miller, M.J. (1993), *The Age of Migration: International Population Movements in the Modern World*, London and Melbourne, Macmillan Education; New York, Guilford Books.

Castles, S., with Booth, H. and Wallace, T. (1984), *Here for Good: Western Europe's New Ethnic Minorities*, London, Pluto Press.

Castles, S., with Booth, H. and Wallace, T. (1987), *Migration und Rassismus in Westeuropa*, Berlin, Express Edition.

Cohn-Bendit, D. and Schmid, T. (1993), *Heimat Babylon. Das Wagnis der multikulturellen Demokratie*, Hamburg, Hoffmann und Campe.

Enzensberger, H. M. (1994), *Die Große Wanderung*, Frankfurt/Main, Suhrkamp.

Farin, K. and Seidel-Pielen, E. (1992), *Rechtsruck: Rassismus im neuen Deutschland*, Berlin, Rotbuch.

Gellner, E. (1983), *Nations and Nationalism*, Oxford, Blackwell.

Habermas, J. (1993), 'Die Festung Europa und das neue Deutschland', *Die Zeit*, 28 May.

Habermas, J. (1994), 'Struggles for recognition in the democratic constitutional state', in A. Gutmann (ed.) *Multiculturalism: Examining the Politics of Recognition*, Princeton, NJ, Princeton University Press, pp. 107-48.

Hoffmann, L. (1994), *Das deutsche Volk und seine Feinde*, Cologne, Pappyrossa Verlag.

Kalpaka, A. and Räthzel, N. (eds.) (1990), *Die Schwierigkeit, nicht rassistisch zu sein*, Leer, Mundo (2nd ed).
Korfes, G. (1992), 'Rechtsextreme Bewegungen und rechtslastige Jugendkulturen in Ostdeutschland', in Butterwegge, C. and Jäger, S. (eds.), *Rassismus in Europa*, Cologne, Bund Verlag.
Leggewie, C. (1990), *Multi Kulti: Spielregeln für die Vielvölkerrepublik*, Berlin, Rotbuch.
Maaz, H.J. (1992), *Der Gefühlsstau. Ein Psychogramm der DD*, Munich, Knaur.
Mörshäuser, B. (1992), *Hauptsache Deutsch*, Frankfurt/Main, Suhrkamp.
Oberndörfer, D. (1993), *Der Wahn des Nationalen*, Freiburg, Herder.
OECD (1994), *Trends in International Migration, Annual Report 1993*, Paris, OECD.
OECD (1995), *Trends in International Migration, Annual Report 1994*, Paris, OECD.
Schnapper, D. (1994), *La Communauté des Citoyens, Sur l'Idée Moderne de Nation*, Paris, Gallimard.
Weil, P. (1991), *La France et ses Étrangers* Paris, Calmann-Levy.

Chapter Fourteen

On the Train: Enzensberger, Kafka and the Dilemmas of Racism

Thomas Wägenbaur

I Enzensberger's *Great Migration*, September 1995

The German media have every reason to make migration a prime topic and they seldom lack the occasion. As Enzensberger notes, they do so to cash in on fascinating apocalyptic images of natural catastrophes as in the common German metaphor for what is perceived as a deluge of refugees: 'The boat is full' (*CW*, 114). But after the new legislation on seeking asylum in Germany, barely passed in 1993 with the help of the Social Democratic opposition, the 'flood' of immigrants has ebbed and the media concentrate more on stories of individual hardship. This is maybe welcome but adds another ironic twist as Enzensberger would have remarked. The pendulum of legislative activism has swung to the other side: with regulations like the 'third-country clause' (if you enter Germany from a safe country you cannot seek asylum, which means you have to enter by plane), 'safe country of origin' (which allows for no individual case) and 'fast airport trial' (which is not a fair trial, since evidence must be presented on arrival), the media lack sensational threats and turn towards the legislation that deprived them of their apocalyptic news-bit. Two years after its proclamation this legislation is up for review by the Federal Constitutional Court, preparing for another swing of the pendulum. The dilemma is that the legislation had the unspoken purpose of crushing the radical right-wing Republican party and rendering neo-fascist violence obsolete by reducing the object of attack: immigrants. But this purpose has been over-fulfilled almost to the extend that the law itself has come to exert the violence that it was supposed to suppress. This at least is what the German media are beginning to point out.

Two articles on the title page of the influential weekly *Die Zeit*, for instance, take two legal events as occasions to keep migration a prime topic. One addresses the judgment that bans the crucifix in schools as discriminating against non-Christians, the other addresses the refusal by the minister of the interior, Manfred Kanther, to halt the deportation of a group of seven Sudanese until at least an alternative refuge could be found perhaps in Eritrea. The latter article debates the individual hardship the law is willing to take into account which makes its own legal status inhuman. The first article was written by bishop Kamphaus who confronted the state authorities – since Bavaria would prefer the crucifix in schools – with a clear alternative: if you take it down you will project your illusions on an empty wall, but if you put it up you will have to change the legislation on asylum in order not to be discredited by your own children who will expect equal standards towards people familiar and strange alike. Both articles are somewhat moralistic. In the name of humanity and the individual, the one appeals to the democratic institutions and the parties, the other to one of its symbolic codes and the people. Neither has a criterion to solve certain discursive dilemmas in terms of legal action: how to distinguish between refugee and migrant, political persecution and economic need, safe country and persecuted individual, etc. In the title of his article bishop Kamphaus puts the ultimate dilemma in the question: 'Do we want to protect the refugees or do we want to protect ourselves?' which repeats the closing dilemma of Enzensberger's essay:

> The more fiercely civilization defends itself against an external threat and puts up barriers around it, the less, in the end, it has left to defend. But, as far as the barbarians are concerned, we need not expect them at the gates. They are always already with us. (*CW*, 138)

Kamphaus begins his article by citing the train compartment parable from the beginning of Enzensberger's *Great Migration* essay: two passengers enter a train compartment and make themselves comfortable, two newcomers arrive and are being rejected with a common hostility which is only overcome by a then joint hostility towards another two newcomers. Kamphaus alludes to the truism of this parable and states like Enzensberger that such territorial behavior cannot be rationally explained: that community can only be founded on the exclusion of a third and in a transitory space as the metaphor of the train compartment indicates.

The problem with this parable is of course its truism, since it loses its quasi-literary significance when taken from the realm of ethical theory into social and political practice. The real dilemma of racism is that it is yet another discursive construct, in real life we do indeed get answers to our problems if we deal with them on an individual basis. This is what both writers on the title page of *Die Zeit* demand but which seems impossible to demand from an institution like the state – or the church for that matter. And yet any institution is as virtual as the events on the train so that any discursive intervention will ensue social and political progress – in one way or another. Enzensberger as the narrator of the train compartment parable need not be subject to the behaviorist territorialism or differential communitarianism and that is maybe the only way out of the dilemma of racism. He is on a different train, the train of 'second order observation' (see part V of this essay).

The discursive status of Enzensberger's dilemma of racism is half-analytical and half-literary. It is literary in that it uses a metaphor to coin a paradox, it is analytical in that it interprets one action in terms of its counteraction and equates these terms as a zero-sum game. The metaphor and the equation are of a fictional and abstract nature, which is its cognitive value and socio-political risk at the same time. Enzensberger's art of the essay shares this ambivalence with all aphorisms or parables on dilemmas of all kinds. The problem with the above mentioned truism of these literary forms of discourse is that their analytically valuable abstraction can serve as an excuse for ontologizing the nature of racism, suggesting: 'This is how it always is'. The formula is not the event formalized. This, of course, is not Enzensberger's intention, but his essay lacks the literary narrator who always adds one more level of observation, leaving the reader as the ultimate author of any statement on matters of the text. This is the point of Kafka's parable 'Fellowship', which anticipates thematically and structurally Enzensberger's train parable and the closing dilemma. This text avoids the danger of replicating a certain kind of discursive violence in an ontological definition of racism, but, of course, erasing the author's intention from the text fails to make a socio-political statement. The following remarks on Kafka's literary analysis of racism will help to distinguish the different discursive status of strikingly similar texts on racism.[1] Enzensberger and Kafka may have had the same intention of fighting racism with words, but Kafka seems to do it more effectively.

II Kafka's 'Fellowship' and the Discourse of Racism

Kafka's 'Fellowship' represents a racist situation and performs its critique at the same time. Like all other texts by Kafka its concrete specificity seems to hide an abstract generality and it is this discrepancy which attracts the reader:

> Fellowship
>
> We are five friends, one day we came out of a house one after the other, first one came and placed himself beside the gate, then the second came, and placed himself near the first one, then came the third, then the fourth, then the fifth. Finally we all stood in a row. People began to notice us, they pointed at us and said: Those five just came out of that house. Since then we have been living together; it would be a peaceful life if it weren't for a sixth one continually trying to interfere. He doesn't do us any harm, but he annoys us, and that is harm enough; why does he intrude where he is not wanted? We don't know him and don't want him to join us. There was a time, of course, when the five of us did not know one another, either; and it could be said that we still don't know one another, but what is possible and can be tolerated by the five of us is not possible and cannot be tolerated with this sixth one. In any case, we are five and don't want to be six. And what is the point of this continual being together anyhow? It is also pointless for the five of us, but here we are together and will remain together; a new combination, however, we do not want, just because of our experiences. But how is one to make all this clear to the sixth one? Long explanations would also amount to accepting him in our circle, so we prefer not to explain and not to accept

> him. No matter how he pouts his lips we push him away with our elbows, but however much we push him away, back he comes.[2]

In order to see how Kafka falls short of and yet goes beyond a theoretical definition of racism, it is necessary to refer to one of the standard definitions of racism, for instance one by Albert Memmi:

> Racism is the generalized and absolutized evaluation of real or fictitious differences to the advantage of the accuser and the disadvantage of his victim, with which his privileges or aggressions shall be justified.[3]

The social sciences extend this definition with regard to circumstances:

> Racism is the sum of all forms of behavior, laws, regulations and perceptions that fail to accept people of different ethnic origin as equals but result in depreciating their ethnic origin and judge and treat them accordingly. Racism is based on an imbalance of economic, political and social power relations.[4]

While these two definitions characterize racism ideologically and sociologically, Kafka reduces a threefold psychic structure to a merely numeric relation. As a common discourse strategy, racism need not be defined in terms of race itself, it clearly can take up other pretexts or none at all as Kafka demonstrates.

The narrator gives a numerical 'ac-count' of the relation between we-group and stranger. We learn nothing about the psyche of the characters, he simply counts to five and the group is complete and closed to the sixth one. Enzensberger's 'train compartment' or the proverbial German 'boat' allows only for five passengers. The first element of the psychic or rather psychotic structure, since it is ruled by arbitrariness and compulsion, reveals itself when the narrator projects the shortcomings of his own group onto the stranger. He attests to the stranger's innocence and at the same time blames him for it: 'He doesn't do us any harm, but he annoys us, and that is harm enough'. His mere existence makes him responsible and a scapegoat for the group's shortcomings: 'one doesn't know one another', 'the continual being together is pointless', and one has had bad 'experiences'.

Another element of the psycho-social structure of the group's identity is its only positive definition, which is a definition by other people: 'People began to notice us, they pointed at us and said: Those five just came out of that house. Since then we have been living together'. But this is no positive self-determination of the group, since it is superfluous. These five simply were constituting a series when they all came out of the house one after the other and the public simply stated it. These people are as strange to the group as the stranger, it is only what *they* say that 'counts'.

The third element of this algebra of identity is the group's admission of its negative definition and its confession of racist self-appreciation – which should allow the stranger as number six into the group: 'Long explanations would also amount to accepting him in our circle, so we prefer not to explain and not to accept him'. If the group honestly admitted that its members are strange to themselves the stranger would become a member of this 'group of strangers'. This at least is the point of Kafka's social algebra. Either all are strange to one another, then there is no real stranger or – which is the same – all belong to each other, then there is no reason either to exclude a stranger.

The narrator's words doubly betray the narrator: in the indicative he speaks of a group that is hostile to the stranger, in the conditional he implies a more hospitable group. He shifts the truth of 'explanations' to the conditional in order to avert the danger that the group means to itself by projecting the danger that the stranger means to the group. This is a standard procedure of any racist ideology formation and, in reverse, of discourse analysis. The narrator allows for one social differentiation (exclusion of the stranger) in order to prevent another (the group falling apart). If, however, social integration (group formation) is always based on social disintegration (exclusion of strangers), racism and its threefold psychic structure seems to become a social necessity: the danger of a group to itself (ignorance, pointlessness, bad experiences: second element) can only be averted (third element) by projecting these dangers on a stranger (first element). So much for the narrator's discourse, disregarding the literary form of the parable that performs the critique of this representation of racism. Kafka's parable presents the dilemma of racism in as bleak and general a form as Enzensberger does. However, contrary to Enzensberger, he suggests an alternative that is implied in the narrator's conditional clause.

III Short History of the Definition of Racism

Kafka's simple parable is a subtle reconstruction and reduction of social history and a subversive deconstruction of social identity. It falls short of the standard definitions of racism, since neither the we-group nor the stranger need to be characterized in terms of race or any other stereotype and yet it goes beyond a theoretical definition of racism, since it implies that racism can be or is based on the very equality of people. A short introduction into the history of the definition of racism may help to solve this seeming contradiction that Kafka's parable constitutes.

In his essay *The Great Migration* Enzensberger refers back to the original biblical parable:

> The conflict between nomadic and settled tribes is made manifest in the myth of Cain and Abel: 'And Abel was a keper of sheep, but Cain was a tiller of the ground.' The territorial conflict ends in murder. The point of the story is that the farmer, after he has killed the nomad, is dispossessed in turn: 'A fugitive and a vagabond shalt thou be on earth'.
> The history of mankind can be read as the unfolding of this parable. Stationary populations form again and again over the millennia. On the whole, however, they remain the exception. The rule is: conquests and

> pillage, expulsion and exile, slavery and abduction, colonization and captivity. A considerable proportion of humanity has always been in motion, migrating or in flight for the most diverse reasons, in a violent or peaceful manner – a circulation which must lead to perpetual turbulence. It is a chaotic process which frustrates every attempt at planning, every long-term forecast. (*CW*, 104)

This parable explains the conflict between the order of 'having' and 'being',[5] the psychic and material bases of society, by mythologizing it. It is a parable on the original racist sin of mankind that denies others the right to live because their form of existence is supposedly less valuable. The Christian teaching of equality tries to correct this original sin; the hierarchical Christian churches, however, have always promoted it.[6] Any missionary work presupposes proto-racist education, legitimization and propaganda. The distinction between believers and non-believers was the basis of the European and any other myth of superiority and its bloody triumph.

After this indication of the history of racism *avant la lettre*, let us go back to the thesis from Kafka's 'Fellowship' which implies that it was the notion of equality that brought about the foundation of racism. Tzvetan Todorov has formulated it even more pointedly: 'Racism (like sexism) becomes an increasingly influential social phenomenon as societies approach the contemporary ideal of democracy'.[7] The notion of equality had been theorized in the Enlightenment and was codified finally during the political revolutions in those well-known phrases: 'All people are created equal' and 'Les hommes naissent libres et egaux en droit'. However, the philosophers of the Enlightenment took a peculiarly ambivalent stance toward equality. Buffon and Condorcet both belonged to the *encyclopédistes*, but one promoted slavery, the other was against it. Kant, in his 'Beobachtungen über das Gefühl des Schönen und Erhabenen', is racist and sexist; in his *Grundlegung zur Metaphysik der Sitten* he is egalitarian. These contradictions are no coincidence, as it is no coincidence that modern racism originates in the universalist and egalitarian Enlightenment.[8] In his *Geschichte des Rassismus in Europa*, George L. Mosse tries to solve this contradiction the following way: The contemporary view of nature and natural order was the *scala naturae*. It was the ruling paradigm of science which assigned all living beings from the most primitive to the most developed its hierarchical place. The latter, of course, was man, and among human beings the hierarchy had to be repeated with the blacks of Africa taking the lowest steps of the ladder – close to the apes – and the white Europeans – following the classical Greek ideal of beauty – the highest step.[9]

This Enlightenment paradigm of classification allowed for the scientific foundation of racism. Physiognomics and phrenology were disciplines that testify to its positivistic zeal, measuring the outside in order to grasp the inside of the human being. What Lamarck and Darwin applied to plants and animals was to be applied to human beings in the human sciences. The parameter of this pseudo-egalitarian hierarchical paradigm was survivability. History had obviously proven that whites were better at survival and the question was what should happen with the colonialized others.

The ridiculous absurdity of this positivism of races reveals itself as in Kafka's parable numerically. It is a scientific differentiation which takes away the racial criterion from scientific racism and leaves no common definition for race as such. In his *Geschichte des Rassismus*, Imanuel Geiss refers to Darwin, who himself emphasized that opinions differed widely whether humanity 'should be classified as a single species or race or as two (Virey), three (Jaquinot), four (Kant), five (Blumenbach), six (Buffon), seven (Hunter), eight (Agassiz), eleven (Pickering), fifteen (Bory St. Vincent), sixteen (Demoulins), twenty-two (Morton), sixty (Crawford) or, according to Burke, sixty-six'.[10] Scientific racism, like other sciences, fails to determine its distinctions by differentiation since one distinction is always based on another, leading to an infinite regress and rendering any position obsolete. The advocates of scientific racism, Gobineau, Taine, Le Bon or Galton, were less self-contradictory than Voltaire or Kant. They resisted the Enlightenment, revolution and democracy which certainly impede the selection of the best genetic material. This attitude follows a shift which was already in progress and which continues until today: from feudal to racial to cultural differentiation of society. Gobineau was the only one to believe that races could be distinguished by the composition of their blood. All other scientific racists knew that races had been mixing far too long to be still able to speak of a purity of blood. But this did not mean giving up on the term 'race'; they transformed instead the physical category into a cultural one. Joseph Renan for instance speaks of 'linguistic races', Taine of 'historic races', and Le Bon of 'psychological races'. Todorov again formulates this transition very pointedly: 'The word "race" thus became virtually synonymous with what we ourselves call "culture", and nineteenth-century racialism subsists today in the idea of cultural difference.'[11]

Scientific racists had of course the best altruistic intentions. Francis Galton for instance believed the problems of social politics could be solved by artificial breeding if crime, poverty, stupidity or intelligence are determined by genetic heritage. Since phrenology did not render satisfying results one had to probe into the brain and that is what one did and still does with intelligence tests in Western democracies. This is another indication for the obsoleteness of the category 'race' for racists and for the possibility of using culture as a racial category. Modern genetics has done its share in withdrawing this pseudo-scientific category from racism. In our behavior we are neither completely determined nor completely free from determination by our genetic code, it enables us to constantly adapt to a changing environment. Genetics in all its inherent dangers today has become democratic when it conceives of every cell of the body as being basically 'omnipotent'.

The historical shift from racial to cultural differentiation in the discourse of legitimizing scientific racism also constitutes a systematic problem: racism is neither universalistic nor relativistic and cannot be defeated easily since it is both. It is relativistic with regard to facts. It denies a common humanity and emphasizes the separation and distinction between the races. But it is also universalistic with regard to values which should be everywhere the same and should be determined according to the criteria which proved one race superior to another. The problem is, as Todorov points out, that the epistemological dilemma of racism is our own: 'The ideology of cultural difference, which in our day and age has replaced that of racialism, has inherited this ambiguity and finds itself similarly threatened by both excessive universalism and excessive relativism.'[12]

Excessive universalism refutes cultural difference in the name of a multiple but equal humanity. Our attempts to avoid stereotypes may result in denying others their individual characteristics. The 'orient' or the 'gypsies' are of course discriminating categories since they homogenize a heterogeneity. But does that mean that there is no Turkish or Romani culture and that one could not describe it? Could it be that we learn from an ethnographic study nothing but the prejudices of the ethnographer or do we still learn something about that culture in spite of theses prejudices?

Excessive relativism is the more pressing problem today. The pretentious universality of many cultural theorists is nothing but an unconscious ethnocentrism, the projection of their own values and properties onto the world. But this racism cannot hinder us from holding on to at least the idea of a common humanity. The ongoing debate on human rights shows that giving up on this idea would be more dangerous than any ethnocentric universalism. An unrestricted universalism should take account of the multiplicity of cultures and also of differences within a given culture.[13] This would comply with the 'account' Kafka indicates in his parable.

IV Kafka's 'Fellowship' and the Critique of Racism

Only if we know that racism is a necessary phenomenon can we avoid the trap of racism when applying the logic of identity to any group formation.[14] This knowledge is the reflection of a racist differentiation in yet another differentiation – or 'second order observation'. Kafka's parable not only represents an event of racism but performs its critique. In order to show this one has to turn from the difference between we-group and stranger drawn by the narrator in the text to the difference drawn by Kafka between the narrator and the text itself. The following scheme may indicate the kind of possible readings the text invites to undertake (slash: difference; arrow: perspective of observation):

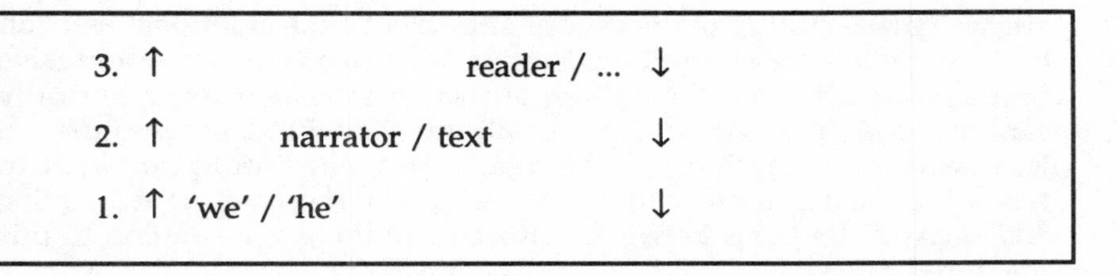

The suggested kind of reading foregrounds the narrator's form of expression vis-à-vis its content. At the beginning of his account the narrator chooses the peculiar image of a *Quecksilberkügelchen* ('then came or rather slid, as lightly as a *tiny pearl of mercury* glides, the second') to indicate the natural attraction of the five before the social confirmation of the group. This image, which Pasley has omitted in his otherwise literal translation, contradicts the narrator's question: 'Why does he intrude where he is not wanted?' The stranger 'intrudes' because he follows his 'natural attraction' to the group. According to this narrative contradiction the group has been alienated from its social nature while the stranger still follows it. At the end the narrator repeats this tendency of 'natural attraction': 'But however much we push him away, back he comes'. The narrator is obviously unaware of this contradiction since he does not discuss the nature/culture opposition which he has established himself in his discourse. Silently he has taken sides with the group's cultural definition without considering that it was its social nature which enabled it in the first place. The reader of the text, of course, observes more than the narrator: what the narrator says contradicts how he says it, his metaphorical expression betrays him and exposes his racism to the reader's critical perspective. Günther Anders was one of the first readers of Kafka to recognize his quasi-political narrative technique when he pointed out that 'Kafka dis-joints the seemingly normal appearance of our disjointed world in order to visualize its dis-jointedness' ('Kafka ver-rückt das scheinbar normale Aussehen unserer verrückten Welt, um ihre Verrücktheit sichtbar zu machen').[15] What appears to be absurd, the numerical social experiment of 'Fellowship', is actually realistic:

> Methodical distortion should be familiar to all of us. Modern science places its object in an *artificial*, an *experimental situation* in order to find out about its reality. It creates an arrangement in which it places its object by *displacing* it: but the result is its *placement*.[16]

The interpretive 'placement' of racism in Kafka's 'Fellowship' is therefore marked by a double alienation as an anti-racist narrative strategy. The narrator experiences the sixth one as a stranger, while the reader experiences the narrator as (self-e)strange(d). Because of the narrator's racist arbitrariness the reader may take sides spontaneously with the stranger and decide for universal human nature and not for the always partial culture of the group. This may be the emotional reaction to the parable effected by Kafka's narrative strategy, but the discursive problem remains that the natural attraction indicated metaphorically cannot be simply repeated in a cultural context. This would be a Rousseauistic deception. On the other hand, one would not want to remain restricted to one culture, bound to a nature/culture distinction and racist distinctions between cultures. But there is a solution to this dilemma of racism.

Kafka conceived of this problem in the form of a parable not in order to grant the reader the pleasure of unmasking a racist narrator, but in order to turn the question of (anti-)racism back to the reader. Contrary to Enzensberger's formula for the dilemma of racism, it is the reader who constructs this dilemma in the first place. As mentioned above, the real dilemma of racism is that it is yet another discursive construct. Pasley unknowingly avoided this meta-dilemma when omitting an important metaphor in his translation. Kafka leaves the reader alone with his own reading. Whatever we decide, taking sides with or against the stranger or the group, we depend on another distinction, immediately followed by another hierarchization of the different elements, perpetuating the racist structure as soon as we apply it to the identification of individuals. It is not the narrator who is contradictory – he is decidedly racist – it is the text. Narrator and stranger could be exchanged since they are variables in the game of socialization. If the group would admit that it is strange to itself, the stranger would have to be admitted into the group. Kafka's algebra of identity implies that nobody can identify him- or herself, that instead one is always identified by others, that the individuals of the group can be identified with the stranger and vice versa. In that sense Kafka's parable represents the dilemma of racism, performs its critique and implies a solution to it.

This quasi-therapeutic notion of the identity of things own and strange has become popular through Julia Kristeva's *Étrangers à nous mêmes*.[17] Edmond Jabés recently wrote: 'The stranger allows you to be yourself by turning you into a stranger'.[18] This is a formula that he and many other intercultural writers of the new 'world literature' have recently turned into a very rich literary production. Its diagnostic value, however, had been theorized earlier by Georg Simmel in his 'Excursion on the Stranger' ('Exkurs über den Fremden') of 1908.[19] Simmel is the founder of a sociology of the stranger based on the ambivalence of fear and fascination of the stranger. The stranger is free from social relations, but in exchange for his independence he is made the projective aim of the surrounding society's compensatory attacks. The genuine object of sociology is therefore the interactive and feedback nature of social action. Kafka's parables can be read very well in terms of such a systemic sociology (see below). In Simmel there is no trace of the optimistic trust in collective progress shared by other nineteenth century sociologists; on the contrary, he attests to the hostility of modernism.[20] The basic symptom for this diagnosis is the loss of the right to hospitality that becomes the touchstone of western democracies and their Enlightenment ideal of equality. In her commentary on Simmel's writings, Almut Loycke has pointed out:

> One glance on the right to hospitality verifies one decisive theorem of the theory of modernity – the denial of the belief in progress. In its relation to the stranger, most Western societies demonstrate no moral or legal superiority over the societies of antiquity, the Eskimos, the Tallensi, Ashanti or Tswana. What paragraph of the German legislation on foreigners would express the respect for human dignity as well as it is expressed in the myth of the Tallensi where the founder of the Golib-feast recognizes the humanity of the leprous stranger.[21]

Loycke also refers to Hermann Cohen and his *Charity in the Talmud* (*Die Nächstenliebe im Talmud*, 1888). Charity has of course its foundation in the Talmud, but the Hebrew word 'Rea' indicates a complex that requires three meanings in German: *der Nächste* (the neighbor), *der Andere* (the other), *der Fremdling* (the stranger). The biblical love for one's neighbor thus always includes the stranger. The legal notion of equality developed from the Talmudic 'Rea', but in the course of its secularization this unity of meaning seems to have become lost. Kafka's performance of the racist experiment instead makes sense: according to the Talmud, we-group and stranger would belong together not only naturally but also culturally. A reading of Kafka's parable in terms of an unrestricted universalism may be able to halt constant differentiation whereas Enzensberger's formula for the dilemma of racism instead seems to perpetuate it.

It might be useful to consult an earlier text by Kafka, 'An old manuscript' ('Ein altes Blatt', 1917[22]) which lends itself to support this analysis. This parable is even more interesting than 'Fellowship' as it adds a meta-communicative reading to the interpretive scheme suggested above. It clearly represents an earlier stage of Kafka's reflection on the dilemma of racism, more colorful and less reduced to a threefold psychological structure and a numerical relation.

V Postcolonialism and Systems Theory

In conclusion, I should like to point out some theoretical implications of the analysis suggested above. The literary discourse analysis that Kafka stages in 'Fellowship' shares its basic structure with recent post-colonial theory. Here performative contradiction becomes programmatic in order to allow marginal or otherwise discriminated identities to resist a dominant and dominating culture. Gayatri Spivak for instance defines her position as one 'in which one offers an impossible "no" to a structure which one critiques, yet inhabits intimately'.[23] Linda Hutcheon suggests the migrant should subversively inscribe herself into the dominant culture: 'Inside yet outside, inscribing yet contesting, complicitous yet critical'.[24] This is also what Homi K. Bhabha advocates:

'Insinuating itself into the terms of reference of the dominant discourse, the supplementary antagonizes the implicit power to generalize, to produce the sociological solidity'.[25] However, the problem of subversion remains the dilemma that first I have to speak the language of the other in order to present my own, which then might have become superfluous. This problem can only be solved if we start to think about a we-group/stranger encounter in systemic terms and not in dialectical terms, if we enter into feedback loops of interaction with strangeness instead of appropriating it into our own.[26] Instead of notions of cultural identity and synthesis Bhabha conceives of a cognitive space where we are able to affirm differences: 'Hybridity to me is the "third space" which enables other positions to emerge.'[27] If this third space is the conditional of the narrator in Kafka's 'Fellowship' it presupposes self-reflection or 'second order observation'. This notion marks nothing less than an epistemological turn which von Foerster has described in his *CybernEthics* which is systemically analogous to our reading of Kafka's parable: a primary difference (or primary observation) is being traced back to a secondary difference (or secondary observation). He describes this operation by proposing the following choice:

> That on the one hand one sees oneself as an independent observer who watches the world passing in front of him; or, on the other hand, that one sees oneself as a participant actor who himself plays a role in the drama of human relationships, the drama of give and take, in its circularity.
> In the first case, because of my independence, I can tell the others what to think and do: 'You should...', 'You should not...' This is the origin of moral principles.
> In the second case, because of mutual dependence, I can only determine for myself what to think and do: 'I should...', 'I shouldn't...' This is the origin of ethics.[28]

From this distinction it is clear that the racist narrator is moralistic and that the parable calls for an ethical reader. Von Foerster makes his point with Wittgenstein's sentence 6.421 from his *Tractatus logico-philosophicus* that an ethics presupposing self-observation will result in an implicit and performative ethics.[29] The foundation of ethics lies in ethical behavior and nowhere else, not in any metaphysical, universalist, or ontological foundation. This is exactly what Kafka demonstrates through his literary text, but which is so very hard to do assuming the perspective of a reader who is not supposed to perform his reading in another literary text. The reader will always find himself in the place of the blind narrator in Kafka's text – 'observing' the text, making a distinction between himself and the text – never able to know that he has become (like) Kafka's narrator.[30]

In order to maintain feedback loops of interaction with strangeness or a dynamic balance between one's own system and one's strange environment,[31] both marginal identity and dominant culture need the irritation and impulse of the strange. Subversion might result in subjection but an effect that destabilizes a given system can be vital to both in order to maintain its dynamic balance. This may sound paradoxical, but until Western societies have not reached a critical state[32] they will only survive in their existing dynamic state as long as there is enough irritation: flow of goods, capital and migrants. This at least would follow from a thermodynamic understanding of social systems. It is precisely what Enzensberger suggests when he speaks of 'a circulation which must lead to perpetual turbulence' in his re-telling of the parable of Cain and Abel. With Enzensberger one can say that Western societies in the post-modern age are reaching their critical state not by being overrun with refugees but by losing their dynamic momentum. A 'fortress Europe' will hardly be a safe or livable place. If the historic knowledge of Western hybridity is being suppressed one should at least become aware of its blatant eclecticism and obvious desire for transcultural hybridization expressed in almost all trends of its popular culture, from pop-music to ethnic food. We are all of us always 'on the train' – thus, we should not be surprised to encounter strangers.

NOTES

1 For standard discourse analyses of racism see Teun A. van Dijk, *Elite Discourse and Racism*, Newbury Park, 1993; Margaret Wetherell and Jonathan Potter, *Mapping the Language of Racism. Discourse and the Legitimation of Exploitation*, New York, 1992; on German conditions in the crucial year of 1989 see *Notwendige Maßnahmen gegen Fremde? Genese und Formen von rassistischen Diskursen der Differenz*, eds. Bernd Matouschek, Ruth Wodak, Franz Januschek, Wien, 1995.

2 Franz Kafka, *The Great Wall of China and Other Short Works*, ed. and trans. Malcolm Pasley, Harmondsworth, 1991, p. 118. The text in the German original reads as follows:
Gemeinschaft (1920)
Wir sind fünf Freunde, wir sind einmal hintereinander aus einem Haus gekommen, zuerst kam der eine und stellte sich neben das Tor, dann kam oder vielmehr glitt, so leicht wie ein Quecksilberkügelchen gleitet, der zweite aus dem Tor und stellte sich unweit vom ersten auf, dann der dritte, dann der vierte, dann der fünfte. Schließlich standen wir alle in einer Reihe. Die Leute wurden auf uns aufmerksam, zeigten auf uns und sagten: 'Die fünf sind jetzt aus diesem Haus gekommen.' Seitdem leben wir zusammen, es wäre ein friedliches Leben, wenn sich nicht immerfort ein sechster einmischen würde. Er tut uns nichts, aber er ist uns lästig, das ist genug getan; warum drängt er sich ein, wo man ihn nicht haben will? Wir kennen ihn nicht und wollen ihn nicht bei uns aufnehmen. Wir fünf haben früher einander auch nicht gekannt, und wenn man will, kennen wir einander auch jetzt nicht, aber was bei uns fünf möglich ist und geduldet wird, ist bei jenem sechsten nicht möglich und wird nicht geduldet. Außerdem sind wir fünf und wir wollen nicht sechs sein. Und was soll überhaupt dieses fortwährende Beisammensein für einen Sinn haben, auch bei uns fünf hat es keinen Sinn, aber nun sind wir schon beisammen und bleiben es, aber eine neue Vereinigung wollen wir nicht, eben auf Grund unserer Erfahrungen. Wie soll man aber das alles dem sechsten beibringen, lange Erklärungen würden schon fast eine Aufnahme in unseren Kreis bedeuten, wir erklären lieber nichts und nehmen ihn nicht auf. Mag er noch so sehr die Lippen aufwerfen, wir

stoßen ihn mit dem Ellbogen weg, aber mögen wir ihn noch so sehr wegstoßen, er kommt wieder.
Cf. Franz Kafka, *Gesammelte Werke, Beschreibung eines Kampfes* , ed. Max Brod, Frankfurt/Main, 1992, p. 108.

3 Albert Memmi, *Rassismus*, trans. U. Rennert, Frankfurt/Main, 1992, p. 103.

4 Linda van den Broeks, *Am Ende der Weißheit. Vorurteile überwinden*, Berlin, 1988, p. 32. Instead of 'people of different ethnic origin' van den Broeks writes 'blacks'.

5 Cf. Erich Fromm, *Haben oder Sein? Die seelischen Grundlagen einer neuen Gesellschaft*, Stuttgart, 1976.

6 Cf. J.P. Reemtsma, 'Die Falle des Antirassismus' in *Das Eigene und das Fremde. Neuer Rassismus in der alten Welt?*, Hamburg, 1991, pp. 269 –282.

7 Tzvetan Todorov, '"Race", Writing, and Culture', in *'Race', Writing, and Difference*, ed. Henry Louis Gates, Chicago, 1986, pp. 370-380.

8 See also David Theo Goldberg, *Racist Culture. Philosophy and the Politics of Meaning*, Oxford and Cambridge, Mass., 1993.

9 George L. Mosse, *Die Geschichte des Rassismus in Europa*, Frankfurt/Main, 1990, pp. 40-41. See also Lothar Baier, 'Die Sache mit der Gleichheit. Zur widersprüchlichen Geschichte einer Anstrengung', in *Freibeuter. Vierteljahresschrift für Kultur und Politik 10* (1981), pp. 39-48.

10 Imanuel Geiss, *Die Geschichte des Rassimus*, Frankfurt/Main, 1988, pp. 38-39.

11 Tzvetan Todorov, '"Race", Writing, and Culture', p. 373. See also Thomas Sowell, *Race and Culture. A World View*, New York, 1994.

12 Tzvetan Todorov, '"Race", Writing, and Culture', p. 373.

13 This kind of unrestricted universalism has been theorized by Derrida who opposes the dialectical identity between difference and identity and emphasizes the 'différance' between difference and identity. Even though Derrida nowhere speaks of racism he always tries to undercut its logics of identity prevalent in western metaphysics. See Jacques Derrida, 'From Restricted to General Economy: A Hegelianism without Reserve', in *Writing and Difference*, trans. Alan Bass, Chicago, 1978, pp. 251-277.

14 Cf. Stefan Majetschak, 'Der Fremde, der Andere und der Nächste. Zur Logik des Affekts gegen das Fremde', in *Universitas* (1/1995), pp. 11-24.

15 The commonly used figurative meaning of the German *verrückt* is 'crazy', its literal connotations can be translated as 'displaced', 'disjointed' or 'distorted'. Günther Anders plays on all these meanings.

16 Günther Anders, 'Kafka, pro und contra' (1934/1946), in *Mensch ohne Welt. Schriften zur Kunst und Literatur*, München, 1984, p. 47. The passage reads in the original: 'Entstellung als Methode sollte uns allen vertraut sein: Die moderne Naturwissenschaft bringt, um der Wirklichkeit auf den Zahn zu fühlen, ihren Gegenstand in eine *künstliche*, die *Experimentalsituation*. Sie stellt eine Anordnung her, in die sie den Gegenstand hineinstellt und *entstellt* dadurch ihr Objekt: aber das Resultat ist *Feststellung*'.

17 Julia Kristeva, *Etrangers à nous-mêmes*, Paris, 1988.

18 Edmond Jabés, *Ein Fremder mit einem kleinen Buch unterm Arm*, trans. Jürgen Ritte, München, 1993, p. 7.

19 Georg Simmel, 'Exkurs über den Fremden', in *Der Gast, der bleibt. Dimensionen von Georg Simmels Analyse des Fremdseins*, ed. Almut Loycke, Frankfurt/Main, 1992.

20 See also *Georg Simmel und die Moderne*, eds. H.-J. Dahme und O. Rammstedt, Frankfurt/Main, 1984.

21 Almut Loycke, *Der Gast, der bleibt*, p. 108. The passage reads in the original: 'Ein Blick auf das Gastrecht anderer Kulturen verifiziert ein entscheidendes Theorem der Theorie der Moderne – die Verneinung des Fortschrittglaubens. In ihrem Verhältnis zum Fremden läßt sich in den

meisten westlichen Gesellschaften keine sittliche oder rechtliche Überlegenheit gegenüber den Gesellschaften der Antike, der Eskimo, der Tallensi, Ashanti oder Tswana feststellen. In welchem Pragraphen des deutschen Ausländerrechts käme die Achtung der Würde des Menschen ebenso zum Ausdruck, wie sie im Mythos der Tallensi der Begründer des Golib-Festes dem aussätzigen Fremden zollt?'.

22 Franz Kafka, *Gesammelte Werke, Erzählungen ('Ein Landarzt')*, ed. Max Brod, Frankfurt/Main, 1992, pp. 118-119.

23 Gayatri Chakravorty Spivak, 'The Making of Americans: The Teaching of English and the Future of Culture Studies', *New Literary History* 21 (1990), pp. 781-98, here p. 794.

24 Linda Hutcheon, 'The Post-modern Excentric: The Center That Will Not Hold', in *Feminism and Institutions: Dialogues on Feminist Theory*, ed. Linda S. Kauffman, Cambridge, 1989, pp. 141-65, here p.158.

25 Homi K. Bhabha, 'DissemiNation: time, narrative, and the margins of the modern nation', in *Nation and Narration, ed.* Homi K. Bhabha, New York, 1990, pp. 291-322, here p. 306.

26 See the two volumes of *Cultural Critique* (Spring 1995, Fall 1995), 'The Politics of Systems and Environments, Part I and II'.

27 'The Third Space Interview with Homi Bhabha', in *Identity, Community, Culture, Difference*, ed. Jonathan Rutherford, London, 1990, pp. 207-221, here p. 211.

28 Heinz von Foerster, 'Ethik und Kybernetik zweiter Ordnung', in *KybernEthik*, Berlin, 1993, pp. 60-83, here pp. 65-66.

29 Heinz von Foerster, 'Ethik und Kybernetik zweiter Ordnung', p. 67.

30 Compare Kafka's parable 'Before the Law' which thematizes the reader always getting in his own way to gain access to the law.

31 Dynamic balance is an expression from thermodynamics which has been introduced to systems theory and the respective literary theory. A simplified idea gives the state of a tent supported by pressured air sometimes used for tennis courts. These fragile tents can be maintained only if as much warm air gets pumped into it as gets lost – otherwise it would be an ordinary tent that maintains itself statically. Dynamic balances can take the shape of stable structures as for instance the light of a candle. Also living beings exist through dynamic balances. If the flow of nutrition is cut off, a 'true' balance is reached which is death.

32 For a discussion of the question whether Germany has or has not reached this 'critical state' in economic terms see Walter Gorenflos, *Keine Angst vor der Völkerwanderung*, Hamburg, 1995.

All translations are my own except where otherwise noted.

Chapter Fifteen

On Enzensberger and Postwar Migration, or: Transcending Nativism – Reflections of a Notorious Expatriate

Andrzej Wirth

Enzensberger's diagnostic essay on postwar migrations concentrates on migration as a sociological mass phenomenon. Understood in this dimension, migrations are explainable as an instinctive desperate flight from oppression, deprivation and poverty. But for some individuals who don't count in the statistics, migration may be a conscious choice, prompted by different motives. I happen to be one of them.

The main motive for individuals in this group is an attraction of living in a culture or in cultures of their own choice, and this choosing transcends determinants of nativity as something accidental. A belief in the very possibility of such a project became part of the post-modernist utopia and an as yet unverified part of multicultural politics. The multicultural project as practiced in the last two decades in the United States seems to encourage an opposite tendency: the strengthening of nativism and a defensive, if not aggressive, reaction to everything outside of indigenous cultural discourse.

I will present my own biography not for any narcissistic pleasure or in any belief in its special importance. I am tempted to do it, because it contains personal experiences of civil wars in what is now called 'Central Eastern Europe', and because it contains as well personal experiences of migration in two different countries. In this sense I will try to use my biography as my own personal response to Enzensberger's theses on civil war and migration.

Far from being unusual for a Polish-born person, my biography and my family's history show a geographical mobility which resembles 'patterns of migration' but actually cannot be defined as such. My mother's family was deported from Eastern Poland as part of a punitive action for supporting the uprising of 1863 against the Tsarist Russian occupation. She was born in Voronezh, educated in Russian schools, but returned with her parents to the recently recreated Poland in 1918. This was a voluntary repatriation following the compulsory displacement a generation earlier. She had survived under both the Soviet and the German occupation regimes, protecting her family's children, and she died in the early 1980s in Poland.

My father was born at the turn of the century in Eastern Galicia which was at that time part of Austria; he died ninety years later in Chislehurst, Kent. He was buried in the cemetery of Polish political emigrants in London. He would have been offended if he had been called a 'migrant'. He thought of himself as living in the tradition of the so-called 'Great Polish Romantic Emigration'. He joined the political emigration protesting from London against the Soviet domination of Poland. He didn't petition for a British passport as a matter of principle, and he died as a stateless person. My father was the last classical *émigré* in the style of the 'Great Polish Romantic Emigration', living by choice outside of his native country but gesturing towards it. His departure from Poland in 1939 was not an act of liberation from nativism, but a manifestation on behalf of it.

My parents belonged to a generation which was formed by the idea of an independent Polish state which did not exist at the time they were born, and which became a short-lived reality when they were in their early twenties. Their migratory movements toward the East were not voluntary (deportation, political repression, and my father's captivity as a prisoner-of-war). Their repatriation, however, was voluntary; it was not organized by any state, oppressive or supportive; and it involved considerable personal risk, the loss of property and status. In 1939 my father who fought as a Polish officer against the Nazi German invasion, became for the second time in his life a prisoner-of war. But he escaped the P.O.W. camp, crossing illegally many borders to join the Polish army being formed in France in 1940. This was the beginning of his war time odyssey which led him through England, Egypt and Italy (where he fought in the battle of Monte Cassino); it concluded after the war with his voluntary chosen *émigré* life in England. The biography of my father is, thus, paradigmatic for the distinction between a *migrant* and an *émigré*; the first, a *migrant*, meaning simply a person translocating from one to another country, the second, an *émigré* person forced to emigrate for particular reasons.

The term *émigré* designated primarily – at least since 1792 – a Royalist who fled at the time of the French Revolution: the name was used in the plural since 1863. In Polish the term *Pilgrimage* (*Wychodztwo*) was used earlier in the nineteenth century (cf. Mickiewicz's *Books of the Polish Nation and its Pilgrimage*, 1832). The so-called 'Great Emigration' (Mickiewicz, Stowacki, Krasinski, Norwid, Chopin) considered itself to be the 'spiritual' government of Poland abroad. My father was in his early forties as he joined first a combat unit, then a political movement supportive of the Polish government-in-exile, which was protesting for decades against the injustices of the Jalta settlement and the Soviet domination of Poland.

It occurred to me later that I was just about the same age as my father when I made my decision no longer to live in Poland. Confronted with the descent of my native country into nationalist and racist demagoguery, and under the shock of the Kremlin's invasion of Tschechoslovakia in 1968, I decided not to return from a visiting professorship in the U.S.A. I didn't think of myself, however, as an *émigré*. I didn't ask for political asylum, although I was attacked and ostracized in the Polish government-controlled press, my books were blacklisted, and my family had to face travel restrictions for many years.

Seeking the right of residence in the United States, I incriminated myself answering with a double 'no' the standard questions from the McCarthy era: 'Are you, or have you ever been a communist?' It was, I think now, an unnecessary cavalier's bravado for which I had to pay with three years of delay in my application for naturalization, and a long discomfort of being a stateless person whose 'pending' status was always under the shadow of the immigration extradition law. I have always associated emigration with a romantic addiction to lost causes, and I thought of myself as a free agent who decided to live in a culture of his own choice. It became obvious: as a self-appointed expatriate I was *persona non grata* in Poland as well as in the U.S.A.

Nevertheless I was tempted to transcend the determinism of nativity. I understand nativism in reference to a culture one was born into, as opposed to a culture acquired through study and acculturation. Acculturation is more than assimilation, which is a condition of mutual acceptance (e.g., Turks in Germany are accepted but not acculturated).

I suppose my case could be described as a double attempt of acculturation. When I left Poland, I had already 'expressed myself' in my native literary culture by having published three books of criticism, some poetry, and a number of translations from Latin (Lucretius, Horace) and German (Brecht, Kafka, Dürrenmatt, Weiss). I was an academic in Poland and became a university professor at Stanford and New York. I was accepted into the American PEN-Club, but I couldn't call myself a 'Polish-born American'. This would be in analogy to Henry Kissinger's self-definition: 'German-born American'. Kissinger was fourteen years of age when he emigrated with his parents to the U.S.A., while I was almost forty and already accomplished in my own culture. At American universities I was lecturing in my slavonically inflected English, and publishing on Brecht in my germanically contorted syntax. As a matter of fact, my first pedagogical success in American academia was due to miscommunication. I was lecturing on Brecht's *model*, but my students understood *mother*, and liked it much more than my theory.

Transcending nativism as an adult in a diaspora is a risky and frivolous undertaking. I was teaching Brecht because my PhD thesis was published in German. This was a happy circumstance: I would never have attracted the interest of great universities if I had published only in my native language. By my own choice I lived and made a living in a *diaspora* which was not an *exile*, nor emigration (although the Polish government, when it withdrew my passport, defined it so). I had to give up so much – my own apartment, library, paintings, etc., and other niceties which went along with the special status of belonging to the so-called *priviledgentsia* in a developing country – that my departure couldn't be interpreted as a quest for materialist gains. I became at once accepted by the Palo Alto community where I lived (which in any case was composed of international scholars); but my acculturation was a difficult solitary act, not free of self doubt and cultural shock. It was clear that while I was living in America I could draw only in a very limited way from my own culture. Sobering was also the discovery that once I had been a big fish only because my pond was so small, and things were different in gigantic America. May acculturation was possible only through an estrangement from my indigenous culture; and in turn, the gradual acquisition of a new culture made it even more strange through the contrast with my initial cultural conditioning.

Was I really succeeding in transcending the determination of the culture I was born into? Not quite. If I was appreciated in the diaspora by locals it was because I was seen as 'exotic', not so much 'a Pole' but generally as an unspecified kind of 'European'. My colleagues were often not aware whether I came from Poland or Germany or some other far away country of which they knew little. What made me different in the eyes of others were traces of my origins, of my historical experience, of my idiosyncratic professional training; these all provided some elements of an exoticism (including my accent) for my academic audiences. Surely enough my process of acculturation took place in a privileged environment, under the protective umbrella of an international university, where even a failure could be defended as being of didactic value. As a matter of fact, acculturation in this context meant primarily learning how to be 'an American professor', something drastically different from its European equivalent. It included learning about the university's 'red tape' but also the unwritten rules of socializing with colleagues and students, including a custom of keeping all office doors open. It included also the mystery of capitalist economics for somebody who did not grow up with it, and who was in the past irreparably demoralized by the unstable and unpredictable currency values in the Iron Curtain Empire. Earning as much as my American colleagues, I couldn't quite understand why as a new arrival I felt less economically secure than they were. In this area early conditioning makes the acquisition of unwritten rules of economic behaviour almost impossible. On a larger social scale this can be studied now in the painful transitions from a socialist to a capitalist economy in the countries of Eastern Europe. Living in a diaspora of one's choosing one cannot, however, afford to be dysfunctional.

The experience of 'American ways' made me aware how much I was a European. This resulted not so much in nostalgia for Europe, as in frustration that the world, the drama, the theatre, which remained through all these years the center of my interest and expertise, remained in America a relatively unimportant cultural phenomenon for the society at large. And this in spite of an impressive contribution to theatre arts which I witnessed in New York in the sixties and seventies, an experience which in fact had a formative impact on my own concepts of the theatre. Indeed, I would have remained in New York where I felt 'assimilated' and less uncomfortable than elsewhere, if it were not for a frustrating instability of academic institutions, as exemplified through the short blossoming of the City University of New York and its sad decline in the financial crisis of New York in the mid-1970s. Having had the experience of many visiting appointments in England and Germany, I decided finally, in 1982, to terminate my American acculturation, and I accepted a call from the Justus-Liebig-University in Gießen to create an Institute of Theatre Studies, according to my own ideas and experiences. Deriving from my American experience, I called it 'applied theatre studies', or 'theatre praxeology', *Angewandte Theaterwissenschaft*, an attempt to combine Theatre Studies American-style with the German tradition of *Theaterwissenschaft*, the lessons of the *Bauhaus* and the 'praxeology' which I had learned in Warsaw as a young adept of the Polish analytical school of philosophy.

After 15 years of 'acculturation' outside of Europe I was leaving America as a 'naturalized' American citizen to become a German professor. At this time I had already comprehended a critical experience that acculturation is a dialectical process. Transcending nativism and one's indigenous culture was already out of fashion in America. A quite opposite tendency was gradually making its way in the advent of politics of multiculturalism, which I found being expressed at the universities in their reaction against canonic academic curricula. The notion of 'mainstream' was no longer normative and under violent attack by 'minorities' of one kind or another. In effect, nobody wanted to be a 'majority'. This was certainly not the case in (West) Germany as German culture is in its essence an 'exclusive' one: *nur für Deutsche*. It led to an outlandish argument voiced not so long ago by politicians that Germany is not a country for immigrants (*kein Einwanderungsland*).

I came to Germany not as an immigrant but as a foreigner, already naturalized in a third country. This triangular situation was difficult to explain in my new host country: 'Have you been born in Poland? What passport do you have?' – 'I have a U.S. passport'. – 'So you are an American'. – 'Not quite, I just said I have an American passport.' I was more entertained than irritated on the occasion of such exchanges, and began to enjoy my life with this built-in distancing device. (As a student of Bertolt Brecht, I never had enough of *Verfremdung*.)

Professors in Germany are civil servants who take a loyalty oath to the state. To make me professor in Germany required a special governmental decree which would waive this requirement. At any rate, with my Polish past of national persecution, and as a survivor of Hitler's and Stalin's proscription lists which had left my family decimated, I found it morally not quite feasible to petition for German citizenship. Having a German family name, I could have obtained it easily. In fact adaption to Germany was paradoxically easier than in the United States. Not only because German was my first and best foreign language, but also because of my apprenticeship at Brecht's *Berliner Ensemble*, and membership in the influential literary Writers Club *Gruppe 47*, prior to my departure from Poland. Helpful was also the cultural memory in my new adopted country – beneficial for the theatre (which is the most perishable of arts) and for all those who contribute to its understanding. I was astonished at being still remembered in professional circles because of my publications on Brecht and the Polish theatre. In my new role as a German professor and as founding director of a University Institute, I found myself promoting careers of young German scholars and importing visiting experts from around the globe to comfortable teaching appointments. This resulted in contradictory political sentiments. As reaction to some of my propositions concerning guest faculty, I came to know Germany's subliminal anti-Americanism, and I found it to be as suspect as the newly acquired enlightened philo-slavonic and philo-semitic sentiments.

The institute I have founded in Germany as an invited alien altered the theory about teaching theatre at university in a country which had invented *Theaterwissenschaft*. The newly postulated discipline of *Angewandte Theaterwissenschaft* was a synthesis of new 'theatre studies' American-style and the old German *Theaterwissenschaft* together with a 'praxeology' which I had learned in Warsaw as a young adept of the Polish analytical school of philosophy.

My cultural adaption in Germany was paradoxically a syncretist enterprise. From a life project which started as an attempt to 'transcend nativism', something unexpected emerged which makes of acculturation not so much an act of renunciation of one's indigenous culture as an attempt to integrate diverse cultural experiences, and make them useful in a new context.

Having the experience of living and working in three different cultures is not only an exercise in distancing which provides some satisfactory feeling of liberation. This sense of freedom has also its prize. My three cultural biographies are convergent but not cumulative, and somebody who has taken the risk for such a life, has to learn modesty – his life's effort would be no doubt much more notable left in the realm of his original culture.

We don't have any kind of theory of cultural transgression – although in the past we were confronted with many prominent cases of literary transgressors, e.g., Joseph Conrad, Eugène Ionesco, Paul Celan, et al. After the Second World War, the phenomenon was prompted by mass migrations; however, the mass translocation of the poor and uneducated led at least in the first generation to a measure of assimilation without perceptible cultural adaption. One of the possible criteria of cultural adaption is the command of a required language. In a classical country of immigrants, however, the U.S.A., there is no agreement even on that minimum of cultural coexistence (I refer to the case of California). Although this was never stated unequivocally, the U.S.A. seems to be ready to accept on the wave of the new 'political correctness' an assimilation without cultural adaption. The propaganda of multiculturalism is accompanied by a strengthening of group particularism, and a growing and approved reluctance to accept in the process of acculturation a notion of what is 'mainstream'. An individual with an ambition of making a contribution to the acquired culture is far from being typical for the process at large, provides however some examples which can be analyzed.

I have some friends who gained such status. In Germany, after his immigration to West Germany at the age of 36, Marcel Reich-Ranicki, born in Poland, and for a while a Polish writer, became the leading literary critic of unprecedented influence. As the *Wall Street Journal* wrote: 'He is the pope of critics in this country of readers'. Now Poles who managed in the past to make his life very uncomfortable in Poland, refer to him proudly as 'our Ranicki', while the Germans refer to him as 'our Reich' which means in this case: somebody sharing all our virtues and vices. Reich-Ranicki's credo that his real native land, his *Heimat*, was in fact German literature, or all literature in the German language, is studiously overheard. A successfully acculturated prominent individual is a controversial figure. He has to defend his right to refuse to be defined neither from the perspective of his 'exit', nor from the perspective of his 'entry' culture.

Another example is the controversy centering on the Polish writer Jerzy Kosinski. His bravado literary career in America included an acquisition of the foreign language at the age of 25, publication of at least two American bestsellers, and two terms as a President of the American PEN-club. Kosinski was accused by his colleagues in America of having ghost-writers (no proof provided), and in Poland of misrepresenting tendentiously his actual experience of the Holocaust in order to receive acclaim in America. This may have been very well the case, as Kosinski was more aware of the mechanisms of popularity in America than many a local writer. A creative person who succeeded to make a contribution to an adopted culture may paradoxically encounter difficulties with acceptance at home and in an adopted country as well. In Poland there was a witty saying: 'He speaks too well Polish to be a Pole' – this usually meant that he was probably an acculturated Jew.

'Transcending nativism' is a tricky venture. If you don't succeed, you are at the mercy of a community which accepts you as a 'foreigner' and tolerates your *différance*. If you are a success, however, you emerge as not a 'native-born', or a native-born-but-ethnically-different individual (e.g. French-born Moroccan in France) – in other words, a person who will always be slightly suspect. You unwittingly elicit resentment if you speak better (or worse), as the case may be, than indigenous local inhabitants. Some successfully acculturated persons claim that it is advisable to retain some accent in order not to irritate the natives who may sometimes speak their own native language not very correctly.

Acculturation is an act of mental migration, usually as a consequence of physical displacement. Enzensberger's well known analysis concentrates more on the latter, stressing the destabilizing effects on culture of the receiving country. Acculturation in Europe, to be sure, is visibly determined by post-colonial developments. This is particularly the case in France and Great Britain where mass arrivals are from the former colonies and Commonwealth countries.

The situation in Germany could be interpreted in a different sense as post-colonial. Germans were divided for almost half a century into a two-state nation. After unification they have to deal with the consequences of colonialism which was not of their own making; it was made in the Soviet Empire, although it was brought to central Europe through Hitler's imperialist adventures. The process of adaption now on the way in Germany is a kind of reluctant mental migration of the 'East' into a foreign political and economical discourse. The 'West' in turn, confronted with traces of the 'Homo Sovieticus' in the minds and hearts of their compatriots became helpless, disorientated and ready for a revision of its own premises.

I see here an instance of two nativisms, a 'native Westerner' facing a 'native Easterner' in an attempt to transcend, through a nonpartisan adaption effort, the gap which unification had opened. Unification in terms of a mutually reluctant acceptance has already taken place. The East pleaded to join the West, and the West was not in a position to say 'no' to unification under the constitution of the *Bundesrepublik*. Thus we have 'Native Germans' of the once divided country trying to erase differences, not through desperate migration and escape (although such movements continue after unification) but through mental adjustments. One could see it as a peculiar process of cultural adaption within one culture, a kind of immanent process which requires transgressions of habits.

I have been concerned in this essay with some aspects of contemporary migration which are not in the focus of Hans Magnus Enzensberger's sociological analysis. They belong to a realm of individual psychology and resist statistical quantifying methods. An old fashioned word, 'expatriation' (1768, *OED*) refers to the act of banishing a person from his own country, and in another meaning to renunciation of one's allegiance (1825, *OED*). The great migrations which Enzensberger describes are not caused by individual banishment. In the case of Islamic migration to Europe they are not accompanied by the withdrawal of allegiance to the country of origin. I would like to reserve this old fashioned term 'expatriate' to cases of a conscious and voluntary individual decision to live in another culture of one's own preference.

Most great migratory movements lack this element. They occur on the level of a kind of Pavlovian physiology which puts millions on the road leading away from domestic misery towards an unknown land of phantasized prosperity. The expatriate is a migrant who takes pride in living in a diaspora as a challenge to the conditioning of his nativity. He chooses his own diaspora as an exercise in the way of a transgressor. I would reserve this term only to persons motivated by such transgression. Gertrude Stein, James Joyce, Samuel Beckett, and Slawomir Mrozek are not by this definition expatriates – but Vladimir Nabokov, I. B. Singer, and Josef Brodsky are. An expatriate performing his solitary act of transgression can live with the alienation he experiences on his way. Anyway, his alienation is of his own choosing. (You cannot escape alienation, but it can be freely chosen.) It could be that living with a sense of distance amounts to the delusion of a jester. But a perspective of living without identifying oneself with everything could for him be worthy of some sacrifice, something he would never be permitted to achieve at home. Expatriates are the unrecognized aristocracy of migrants. It is a group too insignificant to make a difference in statistics; nevertheless they are the only professional actors in what Enzensberger describes as a drama of our century.

A Personal Footnote

My family's history, and my own life experience as a person with three distinct biographies – a Polish, an American, and a German one – modifies my understanding of the words: migration, emigration, expatriation, repatriation and exile, adding a region and period specific connotation. The migrations of my mother's family after the anti-tsarist uprisings of 1831 and of 1863 were not quite voluntary, and took a form of political banishment. Nevertheless, on the new location in Russia, my mother's family did not consider itself *émigré*. Poland did not exist at that time as a nation state, and such migrations far from a homeland were technically movements within the one country. Returning to their home (near the so called Lord Curzon line) which after 1918 became a territory within the independent Polish state, they were repatriates in a more complex sense. My grandfather was returning to the place of his birth (he and his family belonged to the rural gentry), his daughters were returning to the country of their allegiance, and none of them was returning to the country of their citizenship (as they were all technically Russian subjects).

During World War II, at the age of thirteen, I was repatriated with my mother, avoiding luckily a deportation order to Russia from the Soviet occupied part of Poland into the German occupied part. This move also had the special connotation of not being a return to a country of birth, as both parts of occupied Poland were legally a country of my birth; but neither was it a return to a country of our citizenship (as in both parts the population was stripped of their citizenship). It was also not a return to a place of our allegiance, because both Soviets and Nazi Germans were violators of our elementary human rights. This repatriation was rather a kind of banishment from one penal colony to another.

After the war, ethnic Poles from eastern territories annexed by the Soviets, were forced to move to the former Eastern German territories (Silesia, Pomerania, and Eastern Prussia) from which the German population was banished westward under Stalin's order. Ethnic Poles who were moved from Lvov to Breslau were called *répatriés* in official parlance, although the term *déportés* would have been more appropriate. After the uprising of 1944 I was myself deported by Nazi Germans, and I succeeded in escaping a transport which was heading in the direction of Auschwitz. The official name for this action was 'evacuation'.

The socialist states of Stalinist breed considered their citizens serfs of the state. It was virtually impossible to leave one's homeland with official permission. A personal decision to stay abroad was automatically interpreted as a hostile action against the state and as the withdrawal of allegiance, and was followed by the withdrawal of the passport (meant as a punishment).

This was what had happened to me in 1968 as I decided to stay in the United States and to continue my academic career there. I was immediately ostracized by being expelled from the Writers' Union; my books were blacklisted and withdrawn from circulation; state censorship received an instruction not to allow for my name to be mentioned in any favorable context (sic!); my name was removed from a book I had translated and it disappeared from theatre posters. I was denounced in a party newspaper as a revisionist who had supposedly settled in Germany (sic!), supporting its political claim to former Eastern territories. In a meantime I was in living in America where I avoided making any public political statements.

All of this was for me an important lesson. Totalitarian states take from their former subjects along with other liberties also the liberty to be an expatriate. They don't leave to anyone an option to decide if he intends, while abroad, to withdraw his allegiance to his country of origin. This created a paradoxical situation of banished writers who claim their unshaken allegiance to their homeland, as the illustrious cases of Aleksandr Solzhenitsyn and Wolf Biermann demonstrate.

My older daughter, now 36, has been living in the U.S.A. since 1980 (imposition of martial law in Poland) and has now become a naturalized citizen. She considers herself neither an *émigré* nor an expatriate. She was able to keep a double citizenship, visits Poland occasionally, and sees herself simply as a person residing in America.

For all its risks and discomforts, my own triadic biography – now a little antiquated – offers to a double expatriate a unique escape from total identification. He may consider himself an American while in Europe, and a European while in America, and he has two countries in Europe to be happy or unhappy about. One could consider such a stand frivolous; it is difficult, however, to ignore its therapeutic value.

Chapter Sixteen

Debating Ethnicity and History: From Enzensberger to Darville/Demidenko

John Docker

> It is impossible to have a linear discussion on this theme. Merely stating your own position fans the flames of conflict.[1]

> I had an appointment with an editor in a West Berlin publishing house...I gave her a brief sketch of *The Hand that Signed the Paper*. She shook her head. A book like that couldn't have been published in Germany, she said, even if its author had been Ukrainian. The subject's too dan-gerous.[2]

I Enzensberger, Darville/Demidenko

In this chapter the focus is on three texts, Hans Magnus Enzensberger's essays *Great Migration* (1992) and *Civil War* (1993), and, in their apocalyptic shadow, Helen Darville/Demidenko's novel *The Hand that Signed the Paper* (1994), a book that has launched controversy and combat in this the middle passage of the *fin de siècle*. In these debates, Darville/Demidenko's novel is perceived as raising questions of ethnicity and cultural identity, as well as of historical responsibility, and the author has spectacularly drawn attention to herself as problematic creator of her text. Helen Demidenko, a young author, in her early twenties, won three prestigious Australian literary prizes, including the Miles Franklin award, for this her first novel, and effected many public appearances where, tall, with striking blonde hair, and wearing ethnic blouses, she spoke of her Ukrainian ancestry on her father's side, and of Irish descent on her mother's. During subsequent controversies, in print and on television, over whether *The Hand that Signed the Paper* might or might not be anti-semitic, it was publicly revealed that Demidenko was actually the daughter of north-country English immigrants, Harry and Grace Darville, living quiet surburban lives in Brisbane.[3] She has also been accused of plagiarising sentences and passages – seven at last count – from various other authors and texts.[4] In this essay I will argue that *The Hand that Signed the Paper* invokes questions of ethnicity and identity in ways that can be discussed in terms of Enzensberger's arguments, tropes and parables about citizenship and culture. In general, I will be defending Darville/Demidenko's novel, and trying to understand Darville's public dramatisation of herself as non-Anglo-Australian.

II *Great Migration* and *Civil War*

As genre, the essays collected in Enzensberger's *Civil War* mine a millennial mode that mixes (much) nightmare with (little) hope, consternation with panic. In Enzensberger's nervous narrative, his originary psychology and anthropology, civil war is the primary form of all collective conflict, the venting of hatred on the enemy you know, one's immediate neighbour. People destroy what they most dislike, and that is usually the rival they perceive to their space, their territory. With the formation of larger communities, the neighbour on the other side of the border is declared an object of hate. In many ancient societies, as in Greek and Jewish, strangers were welcomed as guests, as deserving hospitality and perhaps asylum, but always on the understanding that they would move on or did not truly belong.[5] With the ending of the Cold War, the new world order is sliding into the human condition Hobbes described, the war of everyone against everyone else. As it lumbers towards the millennium, with conflicts like that occurring in Bosnia, or the events in Somalia, or the resurgence of neo-Nazi attacks on Turkish people in Germany, humanity is returning with frightening despatch to its primordial origins in unreason and particular, warring, identities. As in Yeats' *The Second Coming*, the beast of barbarism will grasp our future. As in science fiction dystopias like the Mad Max movies, we may already be in a post-catastrophic world, where survivors pick amongst the ruins, trying to rebuild before the next devastation. The essays in *Civil War* turn on trope after trope of history, with its 'epidemic of wars', as diseased, humanity experiencing a terrifying 'retrovirus', one's brain 'infected' with 'chemical messengers' that threaten complete loss of control. In this whirlpool, those who wreak destruction are in a state of 'autism', for community and society and *polis* as cooperation and sharing and recognition of difference and debate and discussion are now fatally receding. And such autism, such pathological absence of self (Enzensberger here calling on a phrase of Hannah Arendt's), is intensified by the ever lurking presence of mass culture, particularly American mass culture, in rock music like that of Guns N' Roses.[6]

Enzensberger's readers may not find it easy to resist being drawn to his metaphysics of history, his ur-myth that the story of humanity is conquest and pillage, expulsion and exile, slavery and abduction, colonisation and captivity, and that while stationary populations are always forming, much of humanity is continually in motion and commotion across the globe. I admire his desire not to be Eurocentric. Yet, contradictorily, his own voice as narrator appears very much a universal voice of reason, assuming a magisterial knowledge of the consciousness of diverse peoples as well as, anywhere and everywhere, of facts, reality, and truth. When, recalling the dreary modernist tropes of Adorno and Horkheimer's Culture Industries essay demonising and unifying the media, Enzensberger writes that some people are unable to distinguish 'between reality and film', or that the media magnifies the person who has become 'unreal' and gives him a kind of proof of existence, we might ask: on what grounds of absolute knowledge, of assured possession of reason, does Enzensberger know that some people can't distinguish between reality and film, and how does he so assuredly know what reality is, and by what loftiness does he presume to judge that a fellow human being is in a state of unreality?[7] When Enzensberger writes that in the Second and Third Worlds advertising is believed to be a 'reliable description of a possible way of life', we might ask: isn't the narrator here the familiar figure of the all-knowing European sighing sadly over the simplicity and gullibility of the non-European? These essays still present the gaze of Europe as commanding and central. Further, in its mode of address, *Civil War* assumes a male audience, its players and actors always 'he' and 'him' (I particularly liked the 'men of Asia' in *Great Migration*). The language of the essays is masculinist in its assertiveness and aggression, and the author's judgements are blanketly political, the politics and happenings of the public world. On a rare occasion when women are mentioned, we learn that it is absurd for the evening news to presume that 'every supermarket checkout girl' can distinguish between various warring ethnicities.[8]

I also didn't like the way Enzensberger dismissed with so little interest multiculturality in Australia, in one derisory quickly totalising reference. Enzensberger argues (quite rightly) that in most states the leading national group finds it difficult to reconcile itself to the existence of minorities. The most important exceptions to this pattern are, he adds, countries like the United States, Canada, and Australia that owe their existence, after an attempted extermination of the indigenous peoples, to large scale migration. When Enzensberger writes his anger at the treatment of Turkish people in Germany, he uses the term 'foreigners' for them: he deploys this conventional term with irony and distress, but he suggests no alternative terminology. In contemporary Australia, they would be referred to as Turkish-Australians, as migrants who have been granted naturalisation and full legal rights as citizens in a liberal democracy, as part of a mosaic of different peoples who constitute the society. Enzensberger does not discuss the lack of citizenship and naturalisation rights of the 'guest workers' in Germany (an issue interestingly analysed elsewhere by Andreas Huyssen),[9] and his own sense of multiculturality strikes me as disturbingly impoverished. He notes how difficult it is in Germany for the notion to be accepted that migration might be beneficial, and then concludes that the 'multicultural society', with its 'readiness and capacity for integration', can no longer be assumed 'in any country or group'.[10] Whatever is bad in Europe, it appears, will be bad in the rest of the world.

As *fin de siècle* genre, *Civil War* and *Great Migration* are impelled by a Gothic logic, conceding little to hope and possibility, hysterically humourless. There is little sense conveyed of the interest and excitement, the challenge and surprises, the cosmopolitanism and internationality, of an ethnically diverse society: a multiculturality that is, I think, despite a continuing history of racism and ethnocentrism, being explored and negotiated in Australia. In these terms, cultural and legal, Germany, and indeed much of Europe, seems very much behind, still drawing, as Enzensberger agrees, not only on an ever-protean Eurocentrism, but on a Central European notion of ethnic nationalism, of blood and belonging, as against an inclusive Enlightenment notion of citizenship.[11] The essays in *Civil War* are at their most interesting not when they so confidently and insistently universalise about the state of the world, but when they regionalise knowledge, in their specific passages on Germany and Europe.

III *The Hand that Signed the Paper*

The controversy surrounding the story of Helen Darville/Demidenko and her novel offers a different literary paradigm for a debate on history, ethnicity and identity. Yet – also in a spirit of regionalising knowledge – it is clear that multiculturality in contemporary Australia does not mean the end of racism or of imaginaries of ethnicity: multiculturalism is an impossible ideal, a utopia that can never be. Further, the fantastical jumbling of different peoples with different languages and origins has led to an intensification of both racism and anti-racism, and of awareness of inherited ethnic identities and diaspora histories, including histories of bitter conflicts and anguished memory.

In Enzensberger's framing story, history has failed Hegel's desire for a narrative of progress. Enzensberger refers to Hegel's fable that the original condition of human society is war, not only over resources, but for peer-group recognition. Those who lose a war become the humiliated servants of the winners. But, given the logic of the dialectic, it is the servant who will change history, as the master becomes dependent on his labour. At this point, the servant forces his own recognition. For Hegel, this historical stage was reached with the French Revolution, where every citizen was guaranteed the recognition of his fellows, and freedom, equality, and emancipation were achieved, or achievable, for all. In Enzensberger's view, the ending of the Cold War has not delivered hope of the spread of Enlightenment ideals of reason, for in the new world order humiliation and resentment try to force recognition through violence that is endlessly destructive and self-destructive. Enzensberger sees this history of regression, of negative dialectic, as the unfolding of the myth of Cain and Abel, signifying territorial conflict between nomadic and settled peoples, where the farmer, after he has killed the nomad, is dispossessed in turn, is condemned to be a fugitive and a vagabond.[12]

Enzensberger's mythos of history as cycles of conquest, suffering, humiliation, hatred, quest for recognition, lust for revenge, destruction and self-destruction, has clear relevance for Helen Darville/Demidenko's controversial novel. The most frequent charge is that *The Hand that Signed the Paper* is anti-semitic in that, in seeking to explain why Ukrainians assisted the Nazis in the Holocaust, it condones or humanises those who committed brutality and atrocity. Others, mainly literary critics, have gestured that *The Hand that Signed the Paper* is a novel that represents many attitudes and points of view, and that it is a simple error to identify the author's attitudes with either that of the narrator or those of any of the characters.[13] My contribution to the debate will immediately declare its hand here: *The Hand that Signed the Paper* has no single point of view that can be abstracted and identified as the novel's opinion or message or argument.[14] In Bakhtin's by now familiar terms, we can say that *The Hand that Signed the Paper* is polyphonic, presenting many voices that clash and contradict each other in ways that are challenging, disturbing, and enigmatic.

I do not approach *The Hand that Signed the Paper* lightly. I was raised in a Communist and Jewish family, and my Jewish relations, through my mother and her brothers, are both English and Russian. At one point in the novel a character mentions that Australian trade unionists visited the Soviet Union in the 1930s, but never noticed or made mention of the famine in Ukraine.[15] One such was my father, a founding member of the Communist Party of Australia, who went as a delegate to Moscow in the mid-thirties, and who, like many of his radical generation, returned with no criticisms of the Soviet Union at all; he had been, and continued to be, a fervent supporter of a system he thought history, almost miraculously, had delivered as the ideal alternative to a capitalism he saw as endlessly destroying working people's lives. Utopianism is not easily affected by perception. The history of communism and socialism of this century may indeed have been different if Communists from outside the Soviet Union had noticed its disasters of enforced collectivisation and state authoritarianism.[16]

The narrator of *The Hand that Signed the Paper* is a young student, Fiona, whose mother is Irish (Protestant and fiercely pro-British) and father Ukrainian. When she is thirteen, Fiona accidentally comes across some photographs in her parents' bedroom, showing her father Evheny and her uncle Vitaly in Nazi, indeed SS, uniforms, and her aunt Kateryna in the company of a German officer. She realizes that there is an air of furtiveness around these photos and what they might represent, that there is a secret family history she is prevented from knowing. There is a kind of split narration in *The Hand that Signed the Paper*, two Fionas. There is the Fiona who introduces herself at the beginning of the novel as having just learned that her uncle Vitaly, now an old man, living near Brisbane, is to be charged with war crimes; she has heard that he immediately dived under the table, saying the Israelis are coming to get me. This Fiona belongs to contemporary Australia, is interested in Greenpeace, supports the Labor Party, lives in a student household, is part of a successful migrant family whose children, including herself, are excelling in school and university, had a best friend at school whose grandmother died in the Holocaust, and now, with this bombshell, suddenly feels like the daughter of Eichmann. This Fiona is a seeker, uncertain, not knowing what to think or how to explain her shameful family history.

But there is another Fiona, one who in her later teens had already, to the discomfort of her family, probed that history, including receiving tapes of interviews with her aunt, and visiting Poland to meet and talk to Magda, the first wife of her uncle Vitaly whom he'd married when he was a Ukrainian guard at the Treblinka death camp, doing the hands-on killing of Jews that the Nazi officers thought was appropriate for what they considered the Ukrainians to be, *askeri*, savages, natives, cattle, peasants to be derided to their faces as stupid, even though they had been told they were to be accepted as honorary Aryans, because so tall, with hair strawberry blonde or white and eyes green or blue. Throughout the novel there are long passages of narration by this Fiona, told in an impersonal omniscient way, imaginatively reconstructing what it was like for her father, but especially for her uncle and aunt, to grow up in the 1930s in a Ukraine dominated by the Soviet system. They were faced with Russians colonising their land, and, as later, were openly derided to their faces as animals, cattle, dumb worthless peasants, by the local Communist Party officials. The Ukrainians, in this powerful evocation, were, like colonised peoples everywhere, punished for speaking their own language. They were brutally beaten and selectively deported (like Fiona's paternal grandfather) or assassinated by Stalin's security forces the NKVD, and, in the enforced collectivisation of the early 1930s, suffered starvation in a famine that killed some five million, including Vitaly's baby brother.

In the view of this narrator, this Fiona, the suffering and oppression and humiliation and insult the Ukrainians experienced led to the hatred and desire for revenge that Enzensberger writes of as recurring in history. As farmers, they murder, including with pitchforks and scythes, the nomads in their midst, the Jews whom they saw as being more kindly treated by the regime and as being prominent as Bolshevik officials, including Judit, the doctor wife of the local drunken kommisar, the doctor who had been merciless towards them and would not assist the starving child their baby brother. When the German army arrives, Vitaly and Evheny participate in the mass rape and bashing and killing of Jews at Babii-yar – a detailed evocation I found very hard to read. They then choose to join the SS as part of a Ukrainian division; the Nazi officers tell the Ukrainians that they need them as part of a vast admirably anti-semitic community east of Germany.

Much of this narration concerns consequent scenes at the village near Treblinka, of the joy of the local Polish village which profits from the death-camp, growing prosperous from the high pay the Ukrainians receive from the Germans, and the valuables looted from the Jews they've killed, many by strangling. These scenes in Poland reprise Hieronymous Bosch, the Ukrainian killer-workers and Polish villagers together in public exhibitions of dancing, drunkenness, gluttony, and fornication, followed by lamentation when Treblinka is closed down after an uprising. The story of aunt Kateryna is also imagined, a young woman who when she was thirteen had been beaten by a female Jewish cadre at a komsomol school, and who immediately takes up with Wilhelm Hasse, the young German officer who manages the massacre at Babii-yar, marries her, and takes her to be with him when he is a high official at Treblinka: the same blonde-haired German officer Fiona had noticed in the photo when she was thirteen.

It is these passages of narration, told in a language of undoubted historical truth, always concerned to identify the Russians who oppressed the Ukrainians as both Communist and Jewish, that have in particular caused consternation with the hostile commentators the novel has attracted. I share this dismay and anger. I too want to ask of this narration, why did it matter if some Soviet officials were Jewish, since enforced collectivisation, or the Soviet state use of Marxism as an ideology of technological reason and progress, are hardly part of Jewish religion. Why the insistent hatred, shared by this narrator, this Fiona, with her uncle and aunt in their own stories and self-representations, against female Jewish bolsheviks? Why is the school cadre leader always referred to as the Jewess from Leningrad, or the hated kommisar's wife called Judit – what a remarkable choice of name, suggesting both Jew and the mythological Judith, too powerful in the local community, who is raped and left for dead when the frenzy of mass revenge killings is launched.

Such narration fully deserves Bakhtin's term of opprobrium as monologic, as confident of delivering final and finalized judgements on any character that comes before it, recalling the magisterial claims to knowledge of every inner state of the narrator of Patrick White's *Riders in the Chariot*, also a novel with Holocaust and deathcamp scenes.[17] Unlike in *Riders in the Chariot*, however, this kind of all-knowing all-seeing narration is met in *The Hand that Signed the Paper* by other narrative modes, including the photos as well as the stories of the aunt and uncle, which are presented as stories, not as truth, as memories shaping the past for the present, for Fiona, the other Fiona, the young uncertain questioning Australian niece. Their stories can be read against the grain, and be seen to contradict other accounts and happenings. For example, Vitaly now old tells this Fiona that the Ukrainians had no choice, they were forced to go along with the Germans. But the photos Fiona has witnessed suggest Vitaly worked a machine gun at Babii-yar with insolent pleasure. And in one of her stories aunt Kateryna tells of a conversation she had near Babii-yar with a local Ukrainian from their village, Barsek Ohlobla, who is trying to save Jews from the massacre. He upbraids her for sleeping with Hasse the Babii-yar overseer, asks her if Jewish children are communists, and points out that the Germans also intend to colonise Ukraine. Barsek is caught, shot at Babii-yar, but escapes to join the partisans fighting against the Nazis. Aunt Kateryna herself mentions the anti-semitism of Tsarist times, when the Black Hundreds led mobs of sabre-wielding Cossacks into the shtetl, especially at Easter, blaming the Jews for the death of Christ, indicating that Ukrainian anti-semitism long predated the famine and Soviet oppression of the 1930s. Kateryna, Vitaly, and Evheny also learn their anti-semitism from their mother.[18]

Further, their equation of Jew and Communist is not borne out by observations and events. When Evheny as a young boy escapes from the komsomol school to return to his village, he passes through a town where an elderly Jewish man gives him food, some bread and cheese and butter (though the moment is ambiguous, since the Jewish man thinks the boy is a komsomol student). Evheny 'sat on the curb, eating guiltily. His mother said that Jews polluted everything they touched, but he was hungry'. Evheny notices that the town's orthodox Jews are prevented by NKVD troops from entering their synagogue, which has been turned into a revolutionary museum. The Jews, however, are given food parcels, while Ukrainians are shot for asking. It is one of these food parcels that the elderly Jew gives to the Ukrainian boy. In another incident, in Poland, when Magda doesn't report an escaping Jew during the Treblinka uprising, he says to her that he doesn't want to join the Polish partisans in the woods, as she suggests, but simply wants to be what he is, a doctor.[19]

While the long history of anti-semitism in Ukraine *and* Russia *and* Poland and Central and Eastern Europe generally is sketched in, it is not explored in the novel, as is the immediate context of the 1930s and subsequent events of the 1940s. At one point Vitaly as old man says defiantly that ethnic hatreds are in his soul.[20] The narratives of *The Hand that Signed the Paper* create an historical Ukraine and Central and Eastern Europe of mutual ethnic suspicion, of daily racialised perception, where Ukrainians would define Jews, Poles, Hungarians, Germans, Russians, Byelo-russians, Estonians, Latvians, Tartars, Volksdeutsche, not in terms of religion or nationality, but as other and distinct races.[21] In Enzensberger's terms, the Ukrainian characters of the novel believe in an ethnic nationalism that is as far away as can be on the continuum from a French Enlightenment ideal of citizens being those who reside in a particular nation, irrespective of ethnicity, religion, region, class.

Yet Vitaly all his life in Australia had worn spectacles that he had looted from a Jewish man he had killed at Treblinka, and had been told, when he visited Warsaw on a day off from his gruesome work, made him look like a scholar.[22] In terms of Enzensberger's metaphysics of history as the unfolding of the Cain and Abel story, the farmer kills the nomad he hates. But he also desires what the nomad has, here, for the illiterate Vitaly, knowledge. He wants to *be* the nomad and, in Australia after the war, at a migrant camp, he learns to read and write. But, in killing the nomad, Vitaly the farmer condemns himself to being a fugitive and vagabond. In Australia after the war, alive, unlike his victims, Vitaly the mass murderer can only lead a shadowy half-life, afraid of the next generation, unable to acknowledge his past. He condemns himself to being a person without a history, and so is much less than a person. *The Hand that Signed the Paper* does not claim that all Ukrainians thought and acted in the same manner. For Fiona's father, uncle and aunt, Jews were part of colonial oppression, or favoured by it. For them, such involvement justified their hunger to participate in the Holocaust. They did not see Jews as victims, including victims of their own anti-semitism. Other Ukrainians in the novel angrily repudiate these connections and justifications, and certainly see Jews as victims of massacre and slaughter.

The Hand that Signed the Paper has its clumsinesses, not least the mechanical writing in which the Jewish character Judit presents herself as technological rationalist.[23] Yet it is a remarkably courageous novel, calling attention in multicultural contemporary Australia to the history of not only Ukrainian but also Polish and Latvian active participation in the horrors of the Holocaust. It puts this century's Ukrainian history openly on the intellectual map, for all to consider and ponder and judge, not as claimed truth, but as controversy, as provocation.[24]

IV Conclusion

Darville/Demidenko has, with flair and theatricality, called attention to the general aesthetic issue of the Death of the Author. As much as any Russian Formalist or New Critic or post-structuralist might like, her impersonating and publicly performing an Ukrainian heritage (including doing an Ukrainian dance at an Australian literature conference) has underlined the point that a text is not an expression of its author's presumed personality or sensibility or identity. Texts are made out of other texts, out of contradictory flows and eddies of textuality; in these terms, the charges of plagiarism are trivial, since they constitute what we expect, a novel appropriating and doubling other fiction in ways that create new meanings.

In effect, Helen Darville has created two texts to interest, entrance, and irritate the Australian public, the novel and a persona, Helen Demidenko, who claimed that she came from a poor Ukrainian family, that her father was a taxi-driver called Markov Demidenko who met her Irish-born mother on a refugee ship to Australia, that many of her Ukrainian ancestors had been killed by Jewish Communists in the 1930s, that she herself had visited Ukraine when she was twelve years old, her uncle sleeping on the dirt floor of his hut, and that since the publication of her novel she had been spat on in the street and threatened with rape and death.[25] According to reports and what she has written herself, Darville has also claimed to be of Norman ancestry, as well as variously French, Belgian, and Czech.[26] She declared she was a fully trained lawyer, and fabricated part of her schooling.[27] Debate and jokes rollicked on the Internet.

> Question: How many Helen Demidenkos does it take to change a lightbulb?
> Answer: How many are there?[28]

Some have felt her impersonations to be a symptom of psychosis, perhaps of Münchausen syndrome, or *pseudologia fantastica*.[29] Maybe so. I prefer to relate her playing with ethnicity to uncertainties of identity in Australian cultural history. Think of J. F. Archibald, the famous editor of the Sydney *Bulletin*, who changed his given names to Jules François, and went about in the 1880s and 1890s claiming French and Jewish ancestry. Francophilia, Judeophilia, Italophilia, Germanophilia, were features of pre-WWI cultural history, suggesting a dissatisfaction with inherited English identifications, and a desire for the other or others. More recently, Patrick White, of English descent, was both Judeophile and Grecophile.[30] Yet the news that Darville's parents were English was greeted almost with hilarity, as if being of English heritage in an Australia approaching the millenium was not to be ethnic at all, that it had no diasporic interest, no cachet, no pathos.[31] Can we see, then, Darville's restless desire for other identities as a symptom of crisis for English heritage and ancestry in Australia? More generally, it may be possible to see her desire as part of the fragmentation, uncertainty, contradictoriness, multiplicity, anguish and fear that are perhaps becoming characteristic of identities in postmodernity.

NOTES

1 Hans Magnus Enzensberger, *Civil War*, trans. Piers Spence and Martin Chalmers, London, 1994, p. 49.
2 Andrew Riemer, *The Demidenko Debate* , Sydney, 1996, pp. 9-10.
3 'Prize winning writer exposed', *The Sun-Herald*, 20 August 1995; *Canberra Times*, 26 August 1995; *Sydney Morning Herald*, 31 August and 6 September 1995.
4 Similarities have been found to work by Patrick White, Grahame Greene, Robin Morgan, Alexander Donat, Thomas Keneally, the 1953 work, *The Black Deeds of the Kremlin*, Toni Morrison. See Gerard Henderson, 'Literary judges who don't want to be judged', letter by John Peel, *Sydney*

Morning Herald, 12 September 1995, and also protest by Brian Matthews, *Sydney Morning Herald*, 3 October 1995.

5 *Civil War*, p. 124. Jonathan Boyarin, 'Reading Exodus into History', *New Literary History*, 23, 3 (1992), refers to the 'Biblical command not to oppress the "stranger"' (pp. 530, 539).

6 *Civil War*, pp. 11-13, 30-31, 47, 49, 54, 58, 124.

7 Cf. John Docker, *Postmodernism and Popular Culture: A Cultural History*, Melbourne, 1994, ch.4, 'The Frankfurt School versus Walter Benjamin'.

8 *Civil War*, pp. 53-5, 58, 60, 67, 99, 104, 111-12, 121.

9 Andreas Huyssen, 'Nation, Race, and Immigration: German Identities After Unification', *Discourse*, 16, 3 (1994), pp. 12-13, 18-20. See in particular Huyssen's statement (p. 19): 'Maybe the 1913 law that still defines German citizenship via blood lineage should be repealed or modified to permit at least second and third generation foreigners to claim German citizenship if they so desire...By defining citizenship via blood lineage and descent, this law not only gives credence to the phantasm of uncontaminated Germanness, but worse, it constructs this phantasm in the first place'.

10 *Civil War*, p. 134.

11 *Civil War*, pp. 99, 108, 129, 134. Cf. Michael Ignatieff, *Blood and Belonging: Journeys into the New Nationalism*, London, 1994.

12 *Civil War*, pp. 37-8, 104.

13 See in particular Andrew Riemer, *The Demidenko Debate*, passim. See also Kate Legge, 'The Demidenko Affair', *Weekend Australian*, 15-16 July 1995, and David Marr, 'Australia's Satanic Verses', *Sydney Morning Herald*, 26 August 1995. Not all literary critics of course supported Darville/Demidenko in the controversy: see Ivor Indyk, *Weekend Australian*, 26-7 August 1995, and letter to *Sydney Morning Herald*, 26 August 1995 by Michael Sharkey and P.K Elkin; see also essays by Bill Schaffer and Serge Liberman in *Southerly*, Spring 1995. Critics Frances de Groen, Peter Kirkpatrick, and Ken Stewart, *The Australian*, Higher Education Section, 26 July 1995, defended their award of the Australian Literature Society Gold Medal to the novel.

14 A point well made by Andrew Riemer in *The Demidenko Debate*, pp. 26-7, 80. Robert Manne, in his critique, *Australian Book Review*, August 1995, p.15, refers to what he calls 'the argument' and 'thesis of the book'. For a consideration of Manne's historical argument in *Quadrant*, September 1995, see Riemer, *The Demidenko Debate*, ch. 4.

15 Helen Demidenko, *The Hand that Signed the Paper*, Sydney, 1994, pp. 8-9. The book was later re-printed with the author's name given as Helen Darville.

16 See John Docker, 'Growing up a Communist-Irish-Anglophilic-Jew in Bondi', *Independent Monthly*, December 1992/January 1993, 'From Old Left to New', *Island Magazine* 18/19, 1984, and '"Those Halcyon Days": The Moment of the New Left', in *Intellectual Movements and Australian Society*, eds. Brian Head and James Walter, Melbourne, 1988.

17 Cf. 'White Mythologies: Ethnicity and Identity in *Riders in the Chariot*' in my *Citizenship and Culture* (forthcoming).

18 *The Hand that Signed the Paper*, pp. 16, 21, 29, 68-70.

19 *The Hand that Signed the Paper*, pp. 21, 144.

20 *The Hand that Signed the Paper*, p. 83.

21 *The Hand that Signed the Paper*, pp. 31, 82, 98, 114.

22 *The Hand that Signed the Paper*, pp. 42, 140.

23 *The Hand that Signed the Paper*, pp. 22-5.

24 See, for example, Diane Armstrong, 'Into the Shadows', *Weekend Australian*, 9-10 September, 1995, an account, mentioning Darville's *The Hand that Signed the Paper*, of Armstrong's journey to contemporary Ukraine where she had lost most of her relatives in the Holocaust. For a

reply to Armstrong, see Marko Pavlyshyn, 'Ukrainians reject stereotype image', *Weekend Australian*, September 16-17, 1995.

25 *Sydney Morning Herald*, 22 and 26 August 1995. For a taste of the Demidenko Controversy, see letters page, *Sydney Morning Herald*, 24 August 1995. For her claims to Irish as well as Ukrainian ancestry, see Helen Demidenko, 'Alcohol and I', *Independent Monthly*, September 1995.

26 *Weekend Australian*, 26-7 August 1995. In the same issue Darville gave a public apology for her literary hoax.

27 *Sydney Morning Herald*, 26 August 1995

28 There was also an hilarious letter by my favourite Australian comedian Austen Tayshus (Sandy Gutman), *Sydney Morning Herald*, 7 October 1995.

29 Dr Robert Kaplan, letter to *Sydney Morning Herald*, 24 August 1995, and columnist Paddy McGuinness, *Sydney Morning Herald*, 29 August 1995.

30 Cf. John Docker, 'Romanticism, Modernism, Exoticism: Patrick White in Biography and Autobiography', *Southern Review* , 26, 3 (1993).

31 Cf. Natalie Jane Prior, *The Demidenko Diary*, Melbourne, 1996, p. 61.

Notes on Contributors

Klaus J. Bade is Professor and Chair of Modern History and Director of the Institute for Migration Research and Intercultural Studies (IMIS) at the University of Osnabrück. He was a Fellow at the Center for European Studies, Harvard University (1976/77) and at St. Antony's College, Oxford (1985); during 1996/97 he will be a Fellow at the Netherlands Institute for Advanced Study, Wassenaar. Author of many books on nineteenth century colonial history, on social history as well as on the history of population and migration past and present.

Stephen Castles is Professor of Sociology and Director of the Centre for Multicultural Studies at the University of Wollongong. He has been studying migration, ethnicity and racism for many years and has worked in Australia, Germany, Britain and Southern Africa. Books include *Immigrant Workers and Class Structure in Western Europe* (with Godula Cosack, 1973) and *The Age of Migration: International Population Movements in the Modern World* (with Mark J. Miller, 1993).

John Docker is an Australian Research Council Research Fellow attached to the Department of English and the Humanities Research Centre at the Australian National University (Canberra, ACT). His most recent work is *Postmodernism and Popular Culture* (Cambridge, 1994).

Horst Domdey, born 1933, is Professor of Modern German Literature at the Free University of Berlin. His major interests in teaching and research are in contemporary German literature and, in particular, the literature of the GDR.

Bernd Fischer, born 1953, is Professor of German at Ohio State University (Columbus, Ohio). Books on Achim von Arnim (1983 and 1990), Friedrich Schiller (1987), Heinrich von Kleist (1988), Christoph Hein (1990), and on constructions of national intentionalities in German literature (1995). Articles on Felix Mitterer, Christoph Hein, Martin Walser, Peter Turrini, B. Traven, Charles Sealsfield, Kleist, Goethe, Schiller, Fichte, and Herder.

Gerhard Fischer teaches German Studies at UNSW in Sydney. Research interests and publications in modern drama/theatre, social history of World War I, migration history and multiculturalism. Books include *The Paris Commune on the Stage* and a study of Australia during World War I (*Enemy Aliens*, 1989); edited volumes on Heiner Müller (1995), Walter Benjamin (1996) and *The Mudrooroo/Müller Project* (1993). He is currently working on a history of the Grips Theatre Berlin.

Richard Herzinger, born 1955, teaches modern German literature at the Free University of Berlin. Numerous publications, particularly on the literature of the GDR, on the tradition of conservative cultural criticism in Germany, and on the New Right. Most important publications: *Masken der Lebensrevolution. Vitalistische Zivilisations- und Humanismuskritik in Texten Heiner Müllers* (1992) and *Endzeit-Propheten, oder Die Offensive der Antiwestler* (with Hannes Stein, 1995).

Markus Joch, born 1966, is a graduate of the Humboldt University of Berlin where he is currently conducting research for his doctorate in German literature.

Gert Mattenklott is Professor and Chair of Comparative Literature and Director of the Institute for General and Comparative Literature at the Free University, Berlin. Numerous publications on German literature (eighteenth century, *Goethezeit*), on the history of the novel, and on literary and cultural history and aesthetic theory.

Peter Morgan has worked in the area of ethnic community relations and now teaches German and European Studies at the University of Western Australia. Publications include *The Critical Idyll: Traditional Values and the French Revolution in Goethe's 'Hermann und Dorothea'*, and articles on classical and contemporary German literature.

Tom Morton studied at the universities of Adelaide and Erlangen-Nürnberg. His doctoral thesis undertook a re-interpretation of the political and historical theories of Novalis and Schlegel, in the light of their use of metaphor. He now works as a journalist and documentary maker with the Australian Broadcasting Corporation and has reported on contemporary European politics from Germany, Spain, the former Soviet Union and Bosnia.

David Roberts is Professor of German Studies at Monash University, Melbourne. Numerous publications in the field of modern German literature and aesthetics. Recent publications include *Art and Enlightenment. Aesthetic Theory after Adorno* (1995) and as editor, *The Modern German Historical Novel* (1991) and *German Social Theory Today* (1995).

Pam Stavropoulos teaches courses on nationalism and gender in the School of History, Philosophy and Politics at Macquarie University, Sydney. She is interested in the problematics of interdisciplinary analysis, and is currently researching the potential of psychoanalytic theory to enhance the understanding of nationalism.

Reiner Stollmann teaches in the Department of Cultural Studies at the University of Bremen and is Assistant Professor of German at Dickinson College (Carlisle, Pennsylvania). Research interests in theories of culture and cultural history. Publications include *Ästhetisierung der Politik* (1977), *Weltuntergänge* (with G. Vinnai and H. Boehncke, 1984), and articles on literature and National Socialism, exile, Alexander Kluge, and on laughter and *Lachkultur*. He is currently working on a study of *Enlightenment and the Grotesque*.

Thomas Wägenbaur, born 1958 in Tübingen; 1982 M.A. in Comparative Literature at UC Berkeley, 1990 Ph.D. in Comparative Literature at University of Washington, Seattle. Currently Assistant Professor in the Department of German Literature, University of Tübingen. Publications on Ecological Literature, Intercultural Literature, Literary Theory.

Andrzej Wirth has retired from his last position as Professor and Foundation Director of the Institute for Applied Theatre Studies at the University of Gießen. He now lives in Berlin.